REMINISCENCES

OF

MILITARY SERVICE.

REMINISCENCES OF
MILITARY SERVICE
WITH THE
93RD SUTHERLAND HIGHLANDERS

SURGEON-GENERAL MUNRO, M.D., C.B.
FORMERLY SURGEON OF THE REGIMENT

The Naval & Military Press Ltd

published in association with

**FIREPOWER
The Royal Artillery Museum**
Woolwich

Published by
The Naval & Military Press Ltd
Unit 10 Ridgewood Industrial Park,
Uckfield, East Sussex,
TN22 5QE England
Tel: +44 (0) 1825 749494
Fax: +44 (0) 1825 765701
www.naval-military-press.com

in association with

FIREPOWER
The Royal Artillery Museum, Woolwich
www.firepower.org.uk

In reprinting in facsimile from the original, any imperfections are inevitably reproduced and the quality may fall short of modern type and cartographic standards.

TO

MY OLD COMRADES

OF

THE 93RD SUTHERLAND HIGHLANDERS,

WITH WHOM AND IN WHOSE SERVICE THIRTEEN
BUSY AND HAPPY YEARS WERE SPENT;

AND

To the Memory

OF

THOSE WHO HAVE PASSED AWAY;

THESE REMINISCENCES ARE DEDICATED

BY THEIR OLD SURGEON AND FRIEND.

CONTENTS.

CHAPTER I.

War declared with Russia, 1854—Volunteered for Active Service—Ordered to Halifax, N. S.—Appointed Surgeon 93rd Highlanders—Sail for Turkey—Sir George Cathcart and Staff of Fourth Division—Malta—Grecian Archipelago—Dardanelles—Golden Horn—The Grand Fleet—Landing in Crimea—Storm—Night Alarm—Bought a 'Tartar' Pony—Appearance and Physique of the Army—Medical Arrangements   1

CHAPTER II.

Advance of Allied Armies—The Bulganak—Before a Battle—Battle of the Alma—After a Battle—Colonel Seymour, A.A.G. Fourth Division—Messages for Home—Abercrombie Killed—Housing the Wounded—Further Advance of Army—Cholera—Meeting an old Friend—Attachment of Men to Officers—The Belbec—Dr. Mackenzie—Balaklava—93rd left Behind—Major Banner, 93rd 14

CHAPTER III.

Kadikoi—Turkish Redoubts—Preparations for Bombardment—Battle of Balaklava—Advance of Russian Cavalry—Flight of Turks—Sir Colin's few Words to the Regiment—Reply of the Men—Their Affection for Sir Colin—Cavalry Charge against 93rd—'The Thin Red Line'—Wounded men able to Ride—Kokana Smith—Old Dobrez—Quarter-master Sinclair —Heavy Cavalry Charge—Cheering the Greys . . 29

CHAPTER IV.

First Winter in the Crimea—Sufferings—Scurvy—A Bitter cold Night—Carrying off a Log of Wood—Sir Colin's Servant— The Scotch Peer—Increase of Sickness in the Army—Appearance and Bearing of British Soldier—Our Countrymen at Home—Private Supplies of Food and Clothing—What was required of Medical Officers in Olden Times . 46

CHAPTER V.

Duties—Road from Balaklava to the Front—Carrying Shot and Shell—Housing the Regiment Underground—Cossacks dressed in Red—Drafts from England—Young Kirby—Sir Colin's Visit—Constantinople—St. Sophia—The Sultan Abdul Medjid—Turkish Ladies—Return to Crimea—Sir Colin resigns his Command 60

CHAPTER VI.

Spring of 1855—Fall of Sebastopol—Preparations for Second Winter—Highland Camp—Valley of Vanutka—Spring of 1856—Tartar Villages—Baidar Valley—Baghcheserai— Palace of the Khans—Gipsy Village—Russian Monastery— Jewish town of Tchoufut Kaleh—Simpheropol—Hospitals— Sisters of Charity—Evening with Russian Officers . 76

CHAPTER VII.

Ride to Yalta—Early Start—Tartar Villages and Vineyards— Ruined Villas—Alupka—Prince Woronsoff's Palace—Oreander, the Summer Palace of the Empress—The Emperor's Room—Yalta—Rides without Passports—Cossacks—Pass of Coralie—Jewish town of Mungoup Kaleh—Valley of the Tchernaya—Sebastopol in Ruins 91

CONTENTS. ix

CHAPTER VIII.

Tartar arabah Driver—Assault by a Man of 93rd—Threats—
Warnings—Sixteen Months Afterwards—A Struggle—
Sudden Death—Court-Martial—Charge of Murder—Medical Evidence—Guilty of Homicide—Penal Servitude—
Communication from Prison Official Sixteen Years Afterwards 102

CHAPTER IX.

Embark for England, June, 1856—Land in Portsmouth, July, 1856—Aldershot—Her Majesty's Inspection—Dover—Prepare for India—Sudden Orders for China—Presentation of new Colours—Head-quarters, under Leith Hay, sail for China—Arrive at the Cape—Ordered to Calcutta—Calcutta—Sir Colin's Visit—Chinsurah—Cawnpore . . 110

CHAPTER X.

Cases of Presentiment—The little Army for the Relief of Lucknow—Parade for Sir Colin—His Address to the 93rd—Lord Sandhurst—Sir Hope Grant—9th Lancers—The Advance—Death of Lumsden and Dalzell—Funeral Services at Midnight—Recognising an old Brother-Officer by his Wounds—Meeting a Relative of Lumsden, and Describing his Death and Burial 122

CHAPTER XI.

Another case of Presentiment—A man Reports himself Sick to avoid Battle—Refuse to Excuse Him—Behaves Bravely during two Days—Killed on the third Day—His last Words—Malingering—Frequent in Olden Times—Causes—The common Soldier—The Soldier's last Gift for his Mother 134

CHAPTER XII.

Adrian Hope—March to Rohilcund—Attack on Fort Rohea—Hope Killed—My Belief that he Laboured under a Presentiment of approaching Death—The great Love the Men had for Him—His Burial—Window in Westminster Abbey—Recklessness of Young Officers—A Wounded Brother 144

CHAPTER XIII.

Home-sickness—Old Reserve Battalions—Transfers—Case of Home-sickness and Court-Martial—Home-sickness in an Officer—Strange Delusions 157

CHAPTER XIV.

The Residency Relieved—March to Cawnpore—Cross Ganges under Heavy Fire—Enemy try to break Down the Bridge of Boats—Removal of Wounded to Allahabad—Battle with Gwalior Contingent—Pursuit to Serai Ghât—Nana Sahib's Palace—Ride to Cawnpore—Battle on the Kaleh Nuddee—Return to Lucknow—Reception of the 93rd by Peel's sailors 167

CHAPTER XV.

Fort Rohea—Enemy retired during the Night—Intense Heat—Skirmish at Allygunge—A Rebel Prisoner blown from a Gun—Joined by another Brigade—The Commander-in-Chief assumes Command of the whole Force—Battle of Bareilly—Charge of Ghazies—Enemy's Cavalry attack the Baggage—Narrow Escapes 185

CHAPTER XVI.

Our Army—Old Memories—The old Regimental Numbers—Long Service—Esprit-de-Corps—The Reserve—The Old and New Schools—The Regimental Surgeon of Old Times—A Sentimental Institution—The old Surgeon re-visiting his former Regiment—His own Arrangements still in Force 194

CHAPTER XVII.

I re-visit my old Regiment—Find few old Friends and Com-

CONTENTS. xi

rades—Kindly Greeting from the Few—The Sergeant-major—Drum-major—My old Batman—My Faithful old Orderly—His care of Me—The old Pipe-major—His Affection for 'the Doctor'—Some of his Sayings and Doings 203

CHAPTER XVIII.

John McL.—His Amiability—Isaac T.—His Love of Fun—McL——'s Illness, and Extraordinary Delusions on Recovering Consciousness—His gallant Behaviour at Lucknow—His last Illness, and last Message—The Regiment before the Assault—Young MacDonald—His Death—Surgeon on the Day of Battle . . . , ... 213

CHAPTER XIX.

Penalty attaching to the writing of Reminiscences—The Memory of old Friends—Brave Acts—Surrounded by the Enemy—MacBean—His Receiving the Victoria Cross—Private George McK.—Refuses to be Attended to by Anyone but his 'ain Doctor'—Burroughs Wounded—Two Distressing Scenes 220

CHAPTER XX.

Encamped at Bareilly—Narrow Escape—General Troup—Nainé Tal—The Terai—Beauty of Hill Scenery—Cheenie—Almorah—View of Snowy Range—We enter Oude—Engagements of Posgaou and Russelpore—Rebel Cavalry attack Baggage Column—Noorunghabad—Attack on Mithoulie—Nepaul Frontier 233

CHAPTER XXI.

Ordered to Subathoo—Bareilly—42nd Highlanders—Nawab of Rampore—Natch—Water Supply—Simla—Umballa—Ordered to Rawul Pindi—Lahore—79th Highlanders—Goldie-Scot—Intense Heat and Famine—Ordered to Peshawur—Climate and Scenery—Sir Sidney Cotton—Sir Hugh Rose—The Soldier's Soup—Attack on a Lady . . . 250

CONTENTS.

CHAPTER XXII.

A Sad Chapter—Earthquakes—Cholera—Archie White's kind Assistance—Increase of the Pestilence—Middleton—MacDonald—Hope and Drysdale—Flying before the Pestilence—A Surgeon's Responsibility—Our Chaplain—General O'Grady Haly—Leave the Peshawur Valley—Encamp at Campbellpore—March for Sealkote—Thanksgiving . 266

CHAPTER XXIII.

The Punjaub—Aspect of the Country—Settling down in Quarters—Hunting the Jackal—George Greig—Rajah of Jummoo—Ordered back to Peshawur—The Umbeylah Campaign—Baggage Attacked in the Pass—Colonel Hope, 71st—The Travelling Artist—Old Peter—The Hill-men—Labroo—Derbund—Return to Sealkote 285

CHAPTER XXIV.

Back at Sealkote—Dalhousie—Difficult of Access—Travelling by Dhoolie Dâk—Scenery—The Snowy Range—The Ravee—View from Buckrota—Climate—Trees—Flowering Shrubs—Population—Meeting the Leopard—Ten Thousand Feet above the Sea—Broad Valley—The Golden-headed Eagle—Fitzroy Macpherson 302

CHAPTER XXV.

I Re-join my Regiment—Changes in my Absence—Charming Cold Season—General Haly—Dr. Beatson—Amusements—Hospital—Regimental Arrangements—The Apothecary—Ordered to Jhansi—Our Route—Delhi—Agra—Gwalior—Putteala's Piper—Arrival at Jhansi—Scenery—Ruined Castles—Lakes—Deserted City—Unexpected Promotion—Take Leave of my old Regiment 311

REMINISCENCES

OF

MILITARY SERVICE.

CHAPTER I.

War declared with Russia, 1854—Volunteered for Active Service—Ordered to Halifax, N. S.—Appointed Surgeon 93rd Highlanders—Sailed for Turkey—Sir George Cathcart and Staff of Fourth Division—Malta—Grecian Archipelago—Dardanelles—Golden Horn—The Grand Fleet—Landing in Crimea—Storm—Night Alarm—Bought a 'Tartar' Pony—Appearance and Physique of the Army—Medical Arrangements.

IN 1854, when war was declared by England against Russia, many officers both old and young in the army, and in the different departments of the army, volunteered for active service, being desirous of sharing in the duties and glories of the expected campaign.

I was myself one of these volunteers, and at the time of the declaration of war was serving in Bermuda, whither I had gone, also as a volunteer, from Halifax, Nova Scotia, during an outbreak of yellow fever in the islands.

I was ambitious of advancement in my department, and perhaps a little anxious to get away from Bermuda, not a very lively place at any time, and especially just then, having accomplished the duty on which I went thither. I had not gained anything by volunteering on that occasion, but, being young, was not disheartened by failure, nor deterred from offering my services again. I had already seen something of war with the 91st Regiment during a Caffre war, and was, therefore, sanguine that my offer would be accepted. It was accepted, for very shortly afterwards I was ordered back to Halifax, and from thence to England; and on arrival in London, I found myself appointed surgeon to the 93rd Highlanders, then with the army in Bulgaria. This was an agreeable surprise, for, being a Highlander, I was anxious to belong to 'a national regiment.

Within a few days my preparations were completed, and I sailed for Turkey in the *Harbinger*, on board of which were the generals and staff of a division which was to be added to the strength of the army already in Turkey.

It was a privilege as well as a pleasure to me to make the voyage with a party so distinguished as to include Sir George Cathcart, General Arthur Torrens, (afterwards Sir A. Torrens), Colonel Wyndham, (afterwards Sir Charles Wyndham), Colonel Charles Maitland, Lieutenant-Colonel Seymour, Major Greville, the Honourable Captain Elliott, and several others. As far as I am aware only one of these, General Maitland, survives, but their names live in the history of their country.

Sir George Cathcart was very courteous to us all, but there was a condescension and dignity in his manner that reminded one of the 'Grand Seigneur.' Of all on board, the one who impressed me most by his courtesy and affability was General Torrens. He was accessible at all times, was always the same, kind and gentle in his manner, and his conversation was so refined and so free from constraint that one always felt not only its charm at the moment, but that some personal improvement had been gained from it.

I believe that he had made a laborious study of his profession, and that he was an accomplished classical scholar. I discovered his classical attainments accidentally. One day during the voyage I observed him engaged reading on deck; and as he got up to walk about, leaving his book open on the seat, I ventured to look at it, and found that it was a Greek copy of Homer's 'Iliad.' On resuming his seat and book, he asked me if I 'could still read Greek,' and, on my replying in the affirmative, we went over several passages of Book II. together, and afterwards conversed about several Greek and Latin authors with whom he was more familiar than I was. I never saw him after landing in the Crimea. He was killed early in the war; I think at Inkerman.

At Varna, the Honourable A. Cathcart, captain

93rd Highlanders, and Lieutenant Torrens of the 23rd, (now General Torrens), joined our party; the former as A.D.C. to *his* uncle, Sir George, and the latter as A.D.C. to *his* uncle, General Torrens.

From the date of leaving England I commenced a journal, and kept it up with creditable regularity during the Crimean War, and afterwards during the mutiny in India, and for some years succeeding.

On referring to this now, and also to a number of private letters written by me to friends at home, but which have been returned to me, I find records of various matters of interest, which I propose to bind together as a 'Bundle of Fagots,' which I will offer for the acceptance of my old brother officers, and, I hope, of the general public also.

The greater part of what is written in the following pages is transcribed from my journal and letters; but occasionally I have written from memory.

From my journal I copy as follows:—Arrived at Constantinople. Our voyage has not been altogether a pleasant one, and it has been longer than usual. Not pleasant because the conversation has been invariably too warlike, and everyone has been in a constant state of anxiety, as evidenced by word and manner, to reach the army before the commencement of hostilities. Longer than usual because our ship was only an 'auxiliary screw,' as the sailors called her, and depended on her sails as well as steam. But calms and head winds prevailed, rendering sails useless; and just as we headed eastwards to enter the Straits of Gibraltar, a Levanter met us in the teeth, blew so furiously, and raised such a heavy sea that we made no headway for three days and nights. This caused us to run short of coal, so that for twenty-four hours before arrival at Malta we were obliged to steam at half-speed. On arrival in Valetta Harbour we found that we should be detained two days, and as this further delay made all on board, to say the least of it, a little irritable, I got on shore, and spent the time in what was to me, who had never seen anything of eastern life or ways before, a new world.

After leaving Malta* we had fine weather, and the run amidst the picturesque islands of the Grecian Archipelago, which, clad in russet garb and under the influence of the autumnal sunset, shone like masses of burnished gold, and rendered even more conspicuous and beautiful by contrast with the deep blue waters of the Ægean Sea, made this part of our voyage not only pleasant, but interesting, for it revived our memories of classic lore. As we passed close to Tenedos, *notissima famâ insula,* I could not help feeling and expressing surprise that so insignificant a spot should have afforded shelter and concealment to the mighty Grecian fleet, and that the Trojan Intelli-

* At Malta an admiral and his secretary joined our ship. I forget the admiral's name, but think it was Dundas. He had been appointed Admiral of the Fleet, an appointment, I think, analagous to our Chief of the Staff.

gence Department (doubtless, like our own, efficient) should not have discovered that their enemies were hidden there.

As we steamed through the Dardanelles, I looked in vain for the site of ancient Troy, and sought to trace the

'Mighty Simois rolling its waves into the sea,'

as described by the immortal poet, but could perceive no traces of a ruined city, and only a shallow streamlet trickling slowly over a bed of rocks. I have, however, been since informed by Sir John Kirke, who has travelled over great part of Asia Minor, that, after a heavy fall of rain, the Simois becomes a roaring torrent, and when in this state fully agrees with the poet's description. There was only one object to break the monotony of the plains of Troy, viz. : a huge mound close by the sea-shore, supposed by some to be the tomb of Patroclus, a Grecian warrior and the friend of Achilles, killed by mighty Hector, the prop of Troy; and by others to be the tomb of Ajax, the son of Telamon. From the deck of our ship, for we were not allowed to land, we gazed entranced on the distant beauties of Constantinople, on mosques with lofty dome and graceful minaret, on castellated palaces and cypress groves, and deemed ourselves in fairyland, and retained these pleasant memories until a future visit, when they were unpleasantly dispelled.

We remained at anchor in the Golden Horn but a few hours, and then steamed quickly through the Bosphorus, and on to Varna, and from thence to Baltsick Bay, where we arrived just in time to take a place in the grand fleet composed of the navies of England and France and some two hundred transports, on board of which the allied armies were embarked.

It was a wonderful sight that mighty fleet, even while lying at anchor; but when it got under weigh and steamed out into the open sea, spreading out in long, parallel lines, and covering the face of the waters as far as the eye could see, it appeared to be magnified one hundredfold. The light-armed war-ships led the van, and on either flank hovered the mighty leviathans, which, with their huge hulls, immense spread of canvas, and tiers of heavy guns, inspired us with confidence in their power to protect, and at the same time reminded us of the old homely simile of hens gathering their chickens under their wings.

On the evening of September 13, 1854, this great fleet came to anchor off the shores of the Crimea; and on the following morning, which was fair and calm, the allied armies commenced to land on a long stretch of sandy beach in Eupatoria Bay. On the evening of that day I landed with the generals and staff. We took nothing with us but the clothes we stood in, and three days' cooked provisions in our haversacks. In addition to these, I carried in my hand a large case of surgical instruments.

Shortly after we had landed, a strong west wind began to blow, raising a heavy sea that rolled in great waves upon the beach, and bringing up with it dark, ominous-looking clouds. By sunset a storm of wind and rain burst upon us. There was no shelter of any kind upon the open, sandy beach; so each man wrapped his greatcoat round him, and sat or lay down upon the sand exposed to the full fury of the storm. Wearying, after a time, of my bed, and feeling that my greatcoat was a poor protection against wind and rain, I rose and walked along the beach in search of some spot where I might find even temporary shelter. As I wandered on, several dark objects on the sand attracted my attention. On reaching them I found that under each was snugly stretched a human form. Thinking that all had a right to share on such a night, I laid my hand on one, and, feeling that it was a waterproof, I gently raised a corner. Creeping underneath, I was welcomed by the friendly voice of Colonel Charles Maitland. It was an awful night of wind and rain and growling thunder, which often woke us from our sleep; and though I had passed many a night before upon the ground, *sub cœlo*, never a more uncomfortable one than that. Next morning, however, dawned fine and bright, though the wind was still blowing half a gale; and we arose refreshed by sleep, and were soon dry, and hungry too, and therefore none the worse of wetting and discomfort. After all, to make one's bed upon the sand is no great punishment when one is young and in good health.

That day I joined my regiment, which was bivouacked with the other regiments of the First Division upon the heights above the landing-place, but did not meet with a very demonstrative reception. I was prepared for this, however, knowing that Scotchmen, including Highlanders, are chary of giving confidence at first, but felt confident that time would help us all to know one another better. And so it did. Before many days I was at home with my brother officers, and they with me; and thereafter during many years, and until the day we parted, I felt a pride in being the devoted servant of a regiment which was never weary of showing gratitude to me, and kindly appreciation of my services.*

Here I met Sir Colin Campbell for the first time, and, on being introduced to him, he shook me kindly by the hand, and bade me to 'look well after my regiment as it would soon need all my care and attention.' He was the picture of a soldier; strong and active, though weather-beaten. Ever after my first introduction to him, in the Crimea and in India, Sir Colin was kind and friendly to me.

During the night of September 16, we had an alarm, the cause of which I never heard satisfactorily explained. Suddenly we were startled from our sleep by a rushing sound, as of many horses galloping through or past our bivouac.

* The first to receive me kindly were Captain Lockhart Ross and Lieutenant Dawson, both afterwards lieutenant-colonels of the regiment. Both long since dead.

We all heard the noise, and sprang to our feet, but, after the first rush, the trampling sound grew fainter, until it died away in the distance on our left flank. It was thought probable that this alarm was caused by a body of Cossacks which, sent out to pick up information, and learn our whereabouts and our doings, had lost their way, and, finding themselves suddenly within our pickets, had made a dash across our front or along our flank.

On the following day I made a fortunate purchase. I had been so hurried during my short stay in England that I had not been able to suit myself with a horse; and, as it was necessary that I should be mounted, I walked down to the landing-place to see if I could pick up any sort of animal. Just as I was about to give up the search, I saw a drove of animals in charge of several men, who, I supposed, were Crimean Tartars that had brought in their ponies for sale. Walking up to one of them, I pointed with one hand to the ponies, while in the other I displayed four sovereigns. At sight of the gold, the man went in amongst the drove and caught a shaggy little beast, which he handed over to me, receiving and pocketing the money; more probably than he had ever owned before. This proved a very useful purchase. In spite of a deformed foot, the little beast did my work until I became the possessor of a wounded Russian charger, taken at the battle of Balaklava, and which, on recovering from his wound, turned out a very handsome animal.

I still kept the pony, but as spring came on, and he began to cast his hair, a very distinct 'broad arrow' became visible upon his flank. Then it dawned upon me that he was commissariat property. On inquiry I found that such was the case, and that the men, whom I had taken for Crimean Tartars, were Bulgarian peasants in charge of public baggage-animals. Of course I would have restored the pony to the public, but he died suddenly, and I was thus deprived of that pleasure.

No army ever took the field, or landed in a hostile country, with the prospect—nay, the certainty—of immediate battle, so unprepared and so imperfectly supplied with medical and surgical equipment as did our small but splendid Crimean army. The men that filled its ranks were the finest soldiers that I ever saw in stature, physique, and appearance. We have not had anything like them since, and never shall, I fear; and it is mournful even now to remember how rapidly those fine fellows disappeared, in a great measure because we did not understand how to take care of them, or, to speak more plainly, because we failed to take care of them. We had a large number of regimental medical officers, but no regimental hospitals, and there were no field hospitals, with proper staff of attendants. We had no ambulance with trained bearers to remove the wounded from the battle-field, and no supplies of nourishment for sick or wounded.

On landing in the Crimea, the regimental hospital was represented by one bell tent, and the medical and surgical equipment by a pair of panniers containing a few medicines, a small supply of dressings, a tin or two of beef-tea, and a little brandy, and these panniers were carried by a wretched pony woefully out of condition.

The instruments were the private property of the surgeon, paid for out of his own pocket, as one of the conditions attached to promotion. The only means of carrying sick or wounded men consisted of ten hand-stretchers, entrusted to the band.

In the event of battle, the transports were at hand, but these were not prepared for the reception of wounded, and we had no such thing as a hospital ship.

With such very limited preparations for the medical requirements of our army, we had entered on a campaign, landed in an enemy's country, and were about to fight our first battle. Taught a lesson by our shortcomings then, and watching and copying the improvements made by other nations since that time, we have completely changed our army medical organization, and adopted a system which we hope and expect will meet the requirements of any future great war.

It would appear that our new hospital system has not given satisfaction during the late Egyptian campaign. I am quite aware of the weak points in the system, but it seems hard that the officer who was selected to carry out the details and who, after great labour, successfully com-

pleted the duty, was suddenly removed from
his appointment, and, instead of meeting with
reward or even approval, incurred the displeasure
of the authorities, and at last was driven out of
the service by what he himself and many others
consider an act of injustice.

CHAPTER II.

Advance of Allied Armies—The Bulganak—Before a Battle—Battle of the Alma—After a Battle—Colonel Seymour, A.A.G. 4th Division—Messages for Home—Abercrombie Killed—Housing the Wounded—Further Advance of Army—Cholera—Meeting an Old Friend—Attachment of Men to Officers—The Belbec—Dr. Mackenzie—Balaklava—93rd left Behind—Major Banner, 93rd.

ON September 19, the allied armies moved southwards, over an undulating plain covered with long dry grass, and towards sunset our horse artillery and cavalry had a slight brush with the enemy, who had advanced into the plain to reconnoitre. There the first blood of the campaign was shed.

We bivouacked during that night on the banks of the little river Bulganak. Fortunately for us, who had to make our couch upon the ground, the night was beautiful and warm; not a breath of air was stirring, and though no moon shone out to enliven our bivouac, the vast canopy of heaven above was brilliant with innumerable stars, whose lustre was not dimmed by even a passing cloud. All Nature appeared to be peacefully at rest, and even men who in a few short hours would be engaged in mortal strife had not, at the time, a single angry feeling in their hearts.

As I lay upon the ground rolled up in my great-coat, I could trace the position of the whole force by the flicker of the thousand little fires, round which the soldiers sat and talked, or cooked their ration. Gradually these fires burned low and disappeared, and a deep silence fell over the mighty sleeping host, unbroken save by the occasional low challenge of the sentry, or the neighing and stamping of the war-horse at his picket. How many weary with the day's work only—how many weary, perhaps, with the work of life—how many thinking little of the past, and heedless of the future, were there sleeping their last sleep on earth!

Next day, September 20, the whole host was stirring early, without bugle call or beat of drum, and soon was moving forward in battle order, and in the same direction as on the previous day. Our progress at first was slow, and several movements, effected by the divisions with precision and exactness, tried the patience of the men, for we did not understand (few probably did, except the head-quarter staff) the necessity for our deliberate and careful advance.

Mr. Kinglake explains it in his second volume.

About eight a.m. we came in sight of a long, low range of hills, or rather heights, which mark the course of the river Alma, and on these heights could see, though not distinctly, on account of the distance, the Russian army in position. We were then halted on the crest of a long, sloping descent, at the bottom of which flowed the river in a deep, rocky bed, the right bank of which was covered by a belt of trees and vineyards, within which nestled several comfortable-looking farmhouses and the pretty village of Bourliouk. While we were halted, the allied generals rode forward to examine the ground, and make their final arrangements for the attack of the enemy's position, which was on the heights above the southern bank of the river.

During this halt, there was opportunity to observe how the prospect of battle affected different individuals. There was a general expression of satisfaction that at last, after long months of weary waiting, the anxiously looked-for day was at hand on which we were to meet and measure our strength with the enemy. Even those who were ill and dispirited (and there were many such who had contracted disease in Bulgaria) brightened up apparently to health and strength for the occasion. On every face there was visible an anxious look, betokening the consciousness that some event of great moment was impending, to meet which and attain success would test the courage and require the strength of every man. Those who had seen war before, and they were very few, were perfectly calm, and made their preparations in a quiet, methodical manner; of those who had no previous knowledge or experience of war, and they were the great majority of the army, some were restless and hurried in their words and movements, others silent, or calm in speech and manner. Some lay upon the ground examining the distant Russian position through their field-glasses; others stood in little groups, conversing in low voices, about the expected battle, and how it would be fought.

Not a few were giving verbal messages to be sent to friends at home in case of accident. A good old paymaster, Captain Whateley of the 42nd Highlanders, was the kind recipient of many a message; but when his regiment, in which he had served for forty years and upwards, moved into action, my old friend could not remain behind, but, hurrying forward, said to me, as he passed on, 'I must go and see how the boys behave.' He went into the thick of the battle, quite forgetful of all the messages he was freighted with, and of his own safety too, so anxious was he to see how his regiment would maintain its great and glorious character. When I met him afterwards, he remarked to me that he was 'satisfied.' The rank and file were silent, and employed themselves in carefully examining their rifles, and in arranging their dress and accoutrements, so as to give freedom to their movements. Very few of them, if any, had ever seen a battle, though one or two of the regiments had just returned from the Cape, where they had served through a Caffre war.

Just at this time, one of the officers with whom I had made the voyage from England, Colonel

c

Seymour of the Scots' Guards (so called now) and Assistant Adjutant-General of the Fourth Division, was taken ill, and sent for me to go and see him. He was a noble fellow, but suffering from painful illness, which, as he said to me, 'made life such a burden to him that he thought death would be the only release from his suffering.' I found him lying on the ground in great pain of body and distress of mind, and he begged me to give him something that would keep life in his body and enable him to do his duty, if only for that one day. Not that he feared to die, but he was unwilling to lose an opportunity of distinguishing himself, and wished to choose the manner of his death. He did live through that day, and was enabled to do his duty gallantly, for his courage mastered the sufferings of his body, and helped him to drag on, though wearily, during nearly three months longer, and *then* he died a soldier's death at Inkerman. There was another officer with the army, whose name I have forgotten, who also longed for death because he also suffered from a disease which in all probability would kill him suddenly, and who sought death at the Alma and at Inkerman, and often in the trenches before Sebastopol, but passed scathless through every danger, death coming to him suddenly at last, but by a lone wayside, and when not a single friend was near him.

I will not attempt any description of the battle, indeed it is beyond my power to do so; for I could only write of what occurred in that part of the field where my own regiment was engaged, and where I was employed myself. Besides, it is difficult to describe quite accurately even the little of a battle that comes within the sphere of vision of one actively busy under fire, and who has only time occasionally to cast a hurried glance at what is going on around and near him.

At the close of the day, we all knew that we had fought and won a great battle, and that we were standing as conquerors on the very ground which the enemy had selected and prepared to meet the invader, and to dispute his passage to Sebastopol, but from which we had driven him in confused flight.

In the first flush of victory, the thought in every mind and the words on every lip were, 'What will they say at home?' and, 'Will they think that we have done our duty?' And, in the temporary excitement, friends shook each other by the hand as if they had just met after long years of separation; and others who had never before met shook hands as if they were old friends, and congratulated each other on our great success. There was no thought, in the first moment of triumph, of the great cost of victory. *That* was an after consideration, which arose to weigh heavily on our hearts, and greatly to mar the glory of the day.

It is impossible to imagine a greater pleasure than that of meeting your old friend safe and sound from some great danger which you have shared together; but, on the other hand, there is nothing so sad and painful as the waiting in expectation of the appearance of a brother, or of a friend with whom you have lived in brotherhood for years, but to wait in vain, and at last to hear that he has fallen, killed perhaps in the very moment of victory.

Terrible are the experiences of war, wild is the excitement during the tumult and crash of battle, but intense are the pain and sorrow after; and who that has passed through battle safely himself, but has lost friends or perhaps a brother, has not felt, after the first flush of triumph, that victory for himself at least has been dearly bought?

In the 93rd there was only one officer killed, young Abercrombie, grandson of Sir Ralph Abercrombie. He was shot through the heart as the regiment was advancing in line up the heights occupied by the enemy.

We took possession of one of the farm-houses on the north bank of the river, and had the wounded of the regiment carried thither, and comfortably placed on beds of clean straw, of which there was a plentiful supply in the farmyard. The 42nd and 93rd were the only regiments that were fortunate enough to secure the shelter of a roof for their wounded.

I must not omit to mention a little incident which occurred during the battle, but before my own regiment was engaged. I was standing, watching the struggle, near the great redoubt, when, to my surprise, a gentleman in plain clothes

approached me. He was a stout and rather
heavy man, with prominent features; his face,
bronzed by exposure, was well-covered by a dark
brown beard and whiskers. He was on foot, and
appeared to suffer much from the heat and from
exhaustion, but was very observant of what was
taking place, and carried a note-book in his hand.
He addressed me in the following words: 'This
is a splendid sight! One that I have been looking forward to very wearily for months; and
now I am satisfied, and pleased to see it.' He
did not tell me who he was, and I never saw
him again; but he was so observant that I concluded he was some enthusiastic Briton, who for
his amusement was taking notes. It was not
Dr. Russell, whom I often saw afterwards in the
Crimea and in India.

We remained at the Alma during two days
after the battle, embarking our sick and wounded;
and, to effect this, were indebted to our allies, the
French, who placed mules, with litters and caco-
lets, at our service. During the removal of the
wounded, I saw for the first time H.R.H. the
Duke of Cambridge, and was introduced to him
by the late Sir J. Gibson, (then Dr. Gibson),
principal medical officer of the Highland Brigade. His Royal Highness appeared to be anxious
to see in person to the careful removal of the
wounded, and was very energetic on the occasion.

Having accomplished this duty, the army
moved on to the river Katska on September
23, and from thence to the Belbec on the 24th.

During these two marches cholera, which had scourged our army severely in Bulgaria, and during our short voyage across the Black Sea, but had disappeared under the excitement of landing in the Crimea and the prospect of battle, appeared among us again; and as we moved slowly along, men smitten suddenly by the disease would drop down in the ranks and die by the roadside, with scarce a moan or struggle, so weary and exhausted were they by previous illness, brought on by poor and insufficient food, by the poisonous malaria of Bulgaria, and by the depression which often follows great mental or bodily excitement.*

On the 23rd, as I walked wearily in rear of my regiment, I observed four soldiers carrying a stretcher on their shoulders, on which a sick man lay. They were moving slowly and carefully, so as to disturb the sufferer as little as possible; but when they saw me approaching they gently laid their burden on the ground, and asked me to do something for their officer. On stooping down I saw that the poor fellow was in the last stage of cholera, beyond help or even hope. He was so emaciated and so changed that I did not recognise an old friend; but he knew me, and, addressing me by name, implored me in a feeble whisper to do something to alleviate his sufferings.

Poor fellow, when we last met, in a gay ball-

* When I joined the regiment I was alarmed to find that the majority of the men were suffering from bowel complaint, many of them from dysentery.

room in England, he was a powerful, handsome man, a picture of health and strength, but before me lay a shrunken, helpless form, still alive and breathing, but his breath was icy cold, too certain sign that the end was near. There was nothing in my power to do for him; I had not even a drop of cold water to moisten his parched lips. So the soldiers raised their dying captain on their shoulders again and moved slowly on, while I walked beside them, as even my presence appeared to afford comfort to my poor friend. He died within half an hour after I saw him, by the road-side, and the only friends near him were the four soldiers of his own company and myself.

It was evident that the men were much attached to their officer. They were stalwart, rough-looking fellows, but walked so carefully, handled him so gently, spoke so tenderly, and, when all was over, covered the dead face so respectfully that I could not help expressing my thanks. But they said, 'Oh! no, sir, we do not deserve any thanks. We would have done anything for him, for we have served in his company for years, and he was always good and kind to us, and there was no braver man.' Who could think or speak lightly of a soldier after hearing this little tale? I have witnessed many such or similar scenes, and know of many acts of kindness and affection performed by soldiers to their sick or wounded officers and comrades. Indeed, I do not know any class of men amongst whom there is less selfishness and more brotherly kindness than amongst the soldiers of the British Army.

On September 24, at sundown, we entered the valley of the Belbec, and found ourselves in the midst of orchards and vineyards. The vines were laden with heavy bunches of grapes, ripe and ripening; and we ate eagerly of the tempting fruit, not overcareful to select the ripest bunches, for we were nearly choked by the dust, and were suffering from the great heat, and from an intolerable thirst. But we paid a heavy penalty for our imprudence, for during the night many cases of cholera occurred. Perhaps it was fortunate that these cases ended quickly and fatally in our bivouac, before we commenced our march on the following morning. Fortunate for the poor fellows themselves that their sufferings were soon over, for we had not the means of transporting sick with the army, except, as mentioned in the preceding chapter, a few hand-stretchers, intended only for the removal of wounded from the battle-field. To carry men in the agonies of cholera on these for hours was an awful labour and a heart-rending duty to comrades who were scarcely able to drag themselves along, and an almost unbearable misery to the sick. To be carried in this way, and terribly but unavoidably jolted, only added tenfold to the sick man's sufferings; and long exposure to the sun increased a hundredfold his burning, unquenchable thirst, which, on a march, we could neither carry nor find water to alleviate.

Soon after sundown, exhausted by the duties and fatigue of the day, I crawled under a bush, and, stretching myself on the bare ground, was soon asleep, but could not have slept long, when I was startled into sudden wakefulness by a piteous groan. I jumped up at once and groped about in the dark, but could not find the sufferer, and returned to my shelter under the bush, and was quickly asleep again. On awakening in the early morning, I heard that Mr. Mackenzie, a young civil surgeon belonging to Edinburgh, had died of cholera during the night. This gentleman had joined the army by permission, for the purpose of studying military surgery, so as to be able to teach this special branch of the profession, and was attached to the 79th Highlanders, of which regiment my dear old friend, T. Goldie Scot, was surgeon. It must have been poor Mackenzie's last groan that woke me from sleep, for he died within a very short distance of where I lay. He had been apparently in perfect health the evening before, for he and I had met in one of the vineyards, and plucked and eaten grapes from the same vine.

What uncertainty attends poor human life at all times, but how much greater is that uncertainty during war. Then we live and move from day to day, yea, from hour to hour, with our lives in our hands, or hanging by the most slender thread. This man was young, strong, and robust, and his appearance, even a few hours before his death, gave promise of long life.

On September 25, we had a long and weary march uphill and through dense wood during the first part of the day, and until we reached the Mackenzie heights, from whence we descended by a good road to the plains of Balaklava, and bivouacked for the night around and upon the Feducane heights. This was the celebrated flank march, during which, just as we reached the Mackenzie heights, our advance guard came into contact with the rear guard of the Russian army retiring hurriedly from Sebastopol, the same army which we had defeated on the 20th at the Alma.

On September 26, we took possession of the town of Balaklava, after a show of resistance from a small garrison which occupied an old Genoese fort that overlooked the town and harbour; and almost immediately after our having taken possession of the town, a number of our ships entered the harbour.

On the following day the armies moved onward to Sebastopol, distant about seven miles, and one British regiment, the 93rd Highlanders, and several battalions of Turks, were left behind as a protection to Balaklava and the shipping. This was a cause of great annoyance to both the officers and men of the regiment, who thought that they should thus be deprived of the honour of being present at the capture of the great city.

But things often turn out better than we expect. By being left behind on that occasion, the regiment earned the distinctive title of 'The thin Red Line,' and the privilege of being the only infantry regiment which bears upon its colours the word Balaklava.

We had no tents at this time, but lived in the open air, suffering much from the intense heat of the sun during the day, and more from the cold at night. Consequently there was an increase of sickness amongst us, and several cases of cholera occurred. One death from this disease was a peculiarly sad one. The senior major of the regiment, Major Robert Banner, had been long ailing, almost from the date of his arrival in Bulgaria, and should not have been allowed to accompany the regiment to the Crimea. But his zeal overcame his prudence, and he concealed his illness, or rather the extent of his illness, from the medical officer in charge at the time of embarkation. A few days after our arrival at Balaklava, as I was standing beside and conversing with him, he was seized with cholera, and fell to the ground. With the assistance of several men, I raised him and carried him to an empty tent close by, and laid him just as he was, dressed in uniform, on a couch of clean straw. There he lingered for several hours, but not in great suffering. I sat by and nursed him, moistening his parched lips with water, wiping the cold sweat from his brow, and chafing his cramped limbs. We were almost strangers, but at the time he clung to me as if I had been his oldest friend, accepted my attendance gratefully, and with his last breath whispered a prayer that God would bless me.

I have never forgotten that scene or that whispered prayer, and think that the recollection of them often influenced me in the performance of my duty in after-years. This, as I have said, was a distressing case; for I believe that, after a long attachment, he had been married only a few days before embarkation for the East.

CHAPTER III.

Kadikoi—Turkish Redoubts—Preparations for Bombardment—Battle of Balaklava—Advance of Russian Cavalry—Flight of Turks—Sir Colin's few Words to the Regiment—Reply of the Men—Their Affection for Sir Colin—Cavalry Charge against 93rd—'Thin Red Line'—Wounded men able to Ride—Kokana Smith—Old Dobrez—Quarter-master Sinclair—Heavy Cavalry Charge—Cheering the Greys.

AFTER the departure of the army for Sebastopol, the 93rd took up a position at Kadikoi (a village on the south side of the plain, and at the entrance of the gorge leading to the harbour and town of Balaklava), upon a knoll afterwards known by the several names of Highlander's, Dunrobin, and Sutherland Hill. On the southern slope of this hill our tents were eventually pitched, and on its crest defensive works thrown up, protected in front by strong abattis and tros-de-loups, within which several guns were mounted to command the plain both in front and to the right. Two companies of the regiment, under the command of Brevet-Major (now General) C. Gordon, C.B., were detached to a position higher up and to the right rear of the regiment, and a body of marines was stationed on the heights above them. Our cavalry were encamped on the plain, at some distance to our left front.

We were a good deal out of humour at being left behind, and this state of feeling was not much improved by our having nothing to do but watch the progress of entrenchments which the Turks were throwing up on a chain of heights at some distance in our front, and also by the constant passing of heavy guns, ammunition, and supplies in the direction of Sebastopol. Some of the guns were dragged up by horses, and some were hauled along by sailors of the fleet.

These seamen worked with so much energy and will, and with so much more noise, attended with mirth and laughter and 'frequent imprecation,' than the soldiers were accustomed to, that we thought them more like boys at play than men intent on serious work; but, observing the cheerful example they set us, we were gradually brought back to a more contented and happier frame of mind.

During our first weeks of idleness, we frequently visited Balaklava, and went on board the ships in search of food with which to supplement our rations of salt meat and biscuits, and occasionally rode up to the front to see what was doing there, and what preparations were in progress for the assault, but always returned not much enlightened on the subject.

Thus passed nearly three weeks, during which the allies were making their preparations for attack, and the Russians their counter preparations for defence. At last the rumour reached us that the allied batteries would open fire on the morning of October 17. So it happened, for in the early morning of that day the roar of heavy guns announced the commencement of the first bombardment, which all expected to be both first and last. Those of us who could be spared, and who possessed horses, rode up to see the fight, and to look on from a distance, as we could not share in it. About three p.m. I placed myself upon a height behind one of our batteries, from whence there was a good view of the artillery battle beneath, and of the line-of-battle ships in action with the forts at the entrance of the harbour. At the time I mention the fight was raging fiercely between the English and the Russian batteries, but languidly between those of the latter and the French, whose guns were nearly silent, and the frequent broadsides from the ships and the heavy firing from the forts told that there was fierce fighting there also.

As I sat and watched this storm of battle, a great explosion occurred within the Russian works opposite to our men, followed by loud cheering from our gunners, and by almost a cessation of fire from the enemy's battery. In my ignorance I concluded that all was over, and either that the assault would take place at once, or that Sebastopol would surrender.

It was a wonderful, an awfully grand sight to me, who for the first time was only a spectator of such a scene, and it seemed to me hardly possible that any place, so beset by enemies and so encircled by fire, could escape destruction. Great, therefore, was my surprise at the close of the day to see our ships haul out of action, our batteries on shore cease firing, while no white flag was displayed in token of surrender, and no divisions advanced to take possession of the city. In a state of bewilderment and mortification, I turned away, and retraced my steps to Kadikoi.

On the following and every succeeding day our batteries opened fire, and were replied to by the Russians with even greater energy than on the 17th, and we began unwillingly to understand that the capture of Sebastopol was not to be effected at once, though it did not occur to us then that our attack would end in a regular siege, and that we should have to winter in the Crimea.

After the first week of October, we occasionally saw single horsemen, and several times small groups of horsemen make their appearance on the distant heights towards the north-east of our position at Kadikoi, who, after hovering about for a short time, disappeared again. We therefore concluded that the Russians were collecting in our neighbourhood, but until the morning of October 25 the regimental officers did not know what was gathering round us, and were not aware of the proximity of a large force of the enemy, composed of all arms of the service.

At an early hour that morning, however, just after we had stood to our arms, as was customary, we were startled by the boom of a gun away in the distance on our right, followed almost immediately by the nearer report of answering guns, and by wreaths of white smoke curling upwards from our No. 1 redoubt. I was standing with the regiment at the time, and remained with it to witness the battle of Balaklava, from the firing of the first gun to the charge of the heavy cavalry brigade.

After the first exchange of shots, the firing became more rapid, and from a number of guns. Under cover of these, masses of Russian infantry advanced from the east in the direction of the redoubt, throwing forward clouds of skirmishers as they approached. The guns in the redoubt, meanwhile, kept up a constant fire. This, however, failed to arrest the advance of the Russians, who swarmed round the base of the hill, ascended its sloping side, and threw themselves over the breastwork. In a few minutes afterwards, the Turks retired from the redoubt in confusion, the crescent flag was hauled down, and almost immediately hoisted again, but with another flag, a yellow one, it appeared to me, flying above it.

When the Turks vacated, or rather were driven out of No. 1 redoubt, those in Nos. 2, 3, and 4 retired also, and all came streaming across the plain, pursued by cavalry, in the direction of the 93rd, which was drawn up in line on the crest of Highlanders' Hill, with a small body of the Rifle Brigade (invalids, who had been sent up from Balaklava), under Captain Inglis of that regiment, and with a Turkish battalion on either flank. Mr. Kinglake states that a few of the Guards also were present in line with the 93rd. Of course, he must be right, but I did not see any of the Guards. I speak confidently of the presence of a small party of the Rifle Brigade, for I saw them, and exchanged greeting with Captain Inglis, whom I knew intimately.

As soon as the Turks had retired from Nos. 2, 3, and 4 redoubts, a large body of Russian infantry appeared between Nos. 2 and 3, accompanied by artillery, which opened fire at once on the 93rd and Turks, causing a few casualties. Two men of the 93rd were wounded; one of them losing his leg, and the other being severely bruised by a splinter of shell. Sir Colin, observing these casualties, ordered us to retire, and to shelter ourselves by lying down behind the crest of the hill. This movement was executed quickly, and it appeared to me that this startled and shook the Turkish battalions a little.

While we were lying under the crest of the hill, a battery of our own (Captain Barker's, I think), and two of our guns on the high ground above and behind us, under the command of Wolf (an old Canadian friend of mine), kept up a fire upon the Russians; and I saw two shells fired from these guns (Wolf's) burst close over the very centre of the Russian column, which immediately retired to the north side of the captured redoubts.

Just at this time a great mass of Russian

cavalry came into view, and rode slowly down towards the plain; and, as this great body of horse moved westwards, a considerable body detached itself, and, wheeling south, advanced in our direction at a brisk pace, which gradually increased to a gallop. While they were approaching, Sir Colin ordered the 93rd and Turks to re-form line on the crest of the hill; and, as we were doing so, the two companies of the regiment, which had been detached, under the command of Major Gordon, arrived, and took up their position in the line. Thus we stood for a few seconds, while the cavalry was rapidly nearing us; but the Turkish battalions on our flanks began to get unsteady, and at last fairly turned, broke, and bolted. It was at this moment that Sir Colin rode along the front of the 93rd, telling the regiment to be 'steady;' for, if necessary, every man should have 'to die where he stood.' He was answered by the universal and cheery response, 'Ay, ay, Sir Colin; we'll do that.'

I write exactly what I saw and heard. The men of the 93rd were in excellent spirits, burning to fight; and I do not think there was a single soldier standing in the line who had an anxious thought as to our isolated and critical position, or who for a moment felt the least inclination to flinch before the charge of the advancing cavalry. On the contrary, they appeared to have settled themselves firmly where they stood to receive the expected shock, and to be pleased that everything depended on themselves in what they expected was to be a regular hand-to-hand struggle.

When Sir Colin thought that our Minie rifles might reach the enemy, he ordered the line to fire a volley; but, when the smoke from this had blown aside, we saw that the cavalry was still advancing straight for the line. A second volley rang forth, and then we observed that there was a little confusion in the enemy's ranks, and that they were swerving to our right.

The men of the 93rd at that moment became a little, just a little, restive, and brought their rifles to the charge, manifesting an inclination to advance, and meet the cavalry half-way with the bayonet. But old Sir Colin brought them sharply back to discipline. He could be angry, could Sir Colin, and when in an angry mood spoke sharp and quick, and, when very angry, was given to use *emphatic* language; and such he made use of on that occasion. The men were quiet and steady in a moment; and then the grenadiers, under my old friend Ross, were ordered to change front, and fire a volley. This third volley was at much nearer range than the previous ones, and caught the cavalry in flank as they were approaching, apparently with the intention of passing by our right. It shook them visibly, and caused them to bend away to their own left until they had completely wheeled, when they rode back to their own army, followed by a burst of wild cheering from the ranks of the 93rd, which from that day has been spoken of as the 'Thin red line,' and, as I have already said, is the only infantry regiment which bears upon its colours the word 'Balaklava.'

The Highlanders were a good deal elated and proud to think that under their old chief and in sight of three armies they had stood in line only two deep to receive the charge of European cavalry.

The men were very proud of Sir Colin as a leader, and were much attached to him also, and for the following reason. He was of their own warlike race, of their own kith and kin, understood their character and feelings, and could rouse or quiet them at will with a few words, sometimes spoken kindly, but at other times sharply and emphatically. He lived amongst them, and they never knew the moment when, in his watchfulness, he might appear to help and cheer or to chide them. He spoke at times not only kindly, but familiarly to them, and often addressed individuals by their names, for long use and constant intercourse with soldiers had made his memory good in this respect. He was a frequent visitor at hospital, and took an interest in their ailments, and in all that concerned their comfort when they were ill. Such confidence in and affection for him had the men of his old Highland brigade, that they would have stood by or followed him through any danger. Yet there never was a commanding officer or general more exacting on all points of discipline than he.

Though we had successfully checked the advance of the enemy, it was a matter of no little surprise and disappointment to us that the three volleys from our Minie rifles had done so little apparent execution amongst the charging cavalry, for scarce a dozen saddles were emptied. But afterwards, when peace had been declared, and we had permission to visit the different places of interest in the Crimea, we learned that we were mistaken as to the effect of our fire, and obtained our information on the subject from a Russian officer who had himself been present in the charge.

During a visit which several of us paid to Simpheropol, and while we were listening to the music of a military band on the public promenade, a Russian officer, dressed in hussar uniform, approached us, and introduced himself as a chéf d'escadron. He was very lame, and walked as if one leg were shorter than the other. Addressing us in French, and pointing to our uniform, he asked 'to what branch of the service that peculiar dress belonged.' On being told 'to a Highland regiment,' he asked again, 'if the regiment wore lofty plumes in its head-dress,' and on being informed that such was the fact, he further asked 'if it was a regiment of that description which had received the charge of cavalry in line.' On hearing that it was, and that we belonged to the very regiment, he told us 'that he was an officer of the regiment of hussars which had charged.' In turn we asked him 'why the cavalry had not ridden right down upon the line.' 'Impossible,' he answered. 'In the first place, we did not know that you were lying down behind the hill close to the guns which were keeping up a galling fire on our columns, and which it was our object to capture, until, when we were at the gallop, you started from the ground and fired a volley at us. In the next place, we were unable to rein up, or slacken speed, or swerve to our left before we received your second volley, by which almost every man and horse in our ranks was wounded. Again, when we were inclining to our left to wheel, as we thought, a wing of your regiment changed front, and fired a volley into our flank, which also took effect amongst us, one of your bullets breaking my thigh and making me the cripple that you see. But you know, of course, that a mounted man, though severely, or even mortally wounded, can retain his seat in the saddle long enough to ride out of danger.'

Here, then, was an explanation of the fact, which I have alluded to, of so few Russian saddles having been emptied as the cavalry charged down upon our line. It was a great satisfaction to us to learn from such reliable authority that, although so few had fallen on the field, all or nearly all who had ridden in the charge had been wounded by our fire.

We expressed regret at his crippled condition, but, as he said, 'it was only the fortune of war;' and we also thanked him for his information, which he appeared as pleased to give as we were to receive. I now mention the subject of this conversation, as I do not think the facts as I relate them have ever been stated in such detail, and especially by one who heard them from so good a source.

I may mention here that I have often seen wounded men ride out of action, and on that 25th of October I saw many who did so; but remember two who rode a considerable distance after having been wounded. These were two troopers of one of our own heavy cavalry regiments (the Scots Greys), who, after having been struck by rifle-bullets before the charge, rode, and, as they said, without difficulty or inconvenience, across the plain, a distance of nearly a couple of miles, and, on reaching the ground where the 93rd were standing, were able to dismount without assistance, but fell fainting the moment that they attempted to stand. The one was mortally wounded through the stomach, and died in a few hours, the other was dangerously wounded through the throat, but survived. I have no doubt that these men could have ridden farther than they did had it been necessary to do so in order to escape capture or death; but that, when they found themselves in safety, the excitement which had sustained them up to that moment ceased suddenly, and caused them to feel the effects of their wounds.

Mr. Kinglake in his fourth volume tells how, as the Turks rushed pell-mell down the hill, and swept through the Highland camp, shouting,

'Ship Johnie!' a stalwart Scotch wife confronted, attacked, and beat them with a stick. This is quite true, for I saw her in the act. She was employed at the time washing some articles of clothing beside a little stream that flowed through a vineyard at the base of the hill, on the crest of which the 93rd stood in line, apparently, and really, I believe, quite unconcerned about the battle, and unmoved by the sound of round shot which passed over her head. When she saw the Turks rushing down the hill and amongst the tents, she thought that they were bent on plunder, and watched them for a minute with suspicious eye; but when they swept past her, and trampled on the things which, being washed, she had spread out to dry, she broke out into a towering rage, and, seizing a large stick that lay on the ground near her, laid about her right and left in protection of her property. When she understood that the Turks were bolting from the battle, and had deserted her own regiment, which she saw standing firm upon the hill above, she laughed in scorn, and again plied her stick, striking heavily, at the same time using her tongue, a sharp weapon at times, she abused the flying 'Johnies' roundly in braid Scotch, to the great amusement of the men of her own regiment, who encouraged by applauding her.

She was a stalwart wife, large and massive, with brawny arms, and hands as hard as horn. Her face, though bronzed and weather-beaten and deeply freckled, was comely, and lighted up by a pair of kindly hazel eyes. Her voice was soft and low when she 'wasna angered,' and within her capacious bosom beat a tender, honest heart. I knew her well, and knew that she was always ready to do a kindness to anyone in need. She remained in the Crimea during the first part of the winter, till the bad weather came on, and was then sent to Scutari, from whence, at the conclusion of the war, she returned to England, and taking her old husband, who was discharged and pensioned, under her own care again (for she was the better man of the two), settled somewhere in the old countrie.

After her exploits at Balaklava, she was invariably spoken of as Kokana Smith (I give her name), and this title was first given to her, I believe, by old Dobrez, a poor friendless Tartar, who attached himself to the 93rd, and remained with it during the war, fully believing that he was a part of the regiment, and would accompany it to England. Great was the poor old fellow's disappointment when the time of our departure from the Crimea came, and he found that we could not take him with us. Old Dobrez was not without a knowledge of self-interest, for he attached himself specially to the establishment of the quarter-master, whom he always spoke of as the 'Rum Pasha.'

There was another member of the regiment who was roused to a condition of great wrath and indignation by the flight of the Turks, and who, drawing his claymore, rushed into the midst of the flying mass, trying to arrest their flight, and calling on them to rally round himself; but the Moslems were deaf to his entreaties, and ran all the faster, as if to get beyond the reach of his importunity. This little incident has never been chronicled, but my old friend, Mr. Sinclair, then quarter-master of the 93rd (now Captain Sinclair), will not, I am certain, feel any annoyance at my including his brave and well-intentioned act, of which I was an eye-witness, amongst my reminiscences and stories of old comrades.

While the squadrons were executing their charge against the 93rd, the main body of the Russian cavalry was riding westward, in the direction of our heavy cavalry, and, as we had repelled the attack against our own position, we had leisure to observe what was being done in other parts of the field.

To us, who were looking upwards from below, it appeared that our heavy brigade was advancing to meet the great mass of Russian cavalry in two lines. We could recognise our countrymen, the Greys, on their white horses, in the first line, with another regiment, but I did not know till afterwards that this other regiment was the famous Inniskilling Dragoons, with whom the Greys had been so gloriously associated at Waterloo. We were more interested, however, in the line of white horses, and observed their movements with feelings of national pride, free from anxiety, believing that whatever was to be done by them would be done gallantly and well. We followed with our eyes and with our hearts as the Greys began to advance slowly, then to quicken their pace, until at the gallop the whole line rolled along like a great crested wave, and dashed against the solid mass of the enemy, disappearing from our sight entirely. For a moment—just for a moment—we thought that they were lost, but, as we strained our eyes, we could perceive that the great dark mass into which they had disappeared was greatly agitated, and deep within it we got a glimpse every now and then of the bright red moving to and fro, and of flashing swords, and heard, high above the other sounds of battle, the wild cheering of our gallant fellows, and knew from these sights and sounds that they were not overwhelmed, but fighting hard and holding their own, although so outnumbered.

Some seconds, as it appeared to us, after the charge of the first line, the second line of the heavy brigade came charging along from different quarters, and making for different points of the dense dark body, within which our Greys and Inniskillings were enclosed. The shocks of their attack on different sides appeared to break and loosen the mass; and almost immediately after, or in fact at the moment, as we thought, that the second line came into collision with the enemy, the Greys and other red-coats emerging from the front of the column where they had entered, and fighting fiercely, led us to conclude that they had penetrated right through the column, and had charged back again. Then the great dense body appeared to shake and loosen and open wide, and to move backwards, slowly at first, then at a quicker pace, with many red-coats clinging to and riding close behind and round it. We understood what this meant—that the Russians were defeated, and that our gallant heavies were riding after and round them as conquerors.

We sent a cheer across the plain in greeting to the Greys, to let them and their comrade regiments know that their countrymen, who had just previously done their duty in the battle, and checked a charge of cavalry against themselves, had been witnesses of their success.

I have described the heavy cavalry charge and combat as it appeared to myself, looking upwards and from a distance; but, having read Mr. Kinglake's minute details, I perceive how imperfectly I understood the movements of the different regiments and separate squadrons before and in the charge.

The impressions conveyed to my mind, even through mine eyes, it would appear, were not minutely accurate; and yet I thought they were so at the time, and their inaccuracy only proves that even a looker-on may know little of what occurs in a battle, and that the same incidents seen by several at the same time may be differently described by all, and yet each individual speak with the confidence of being exact, and further proves that, to attain perfect accuracy of detail, it is necessary to hear the testimony of many witnesses.

CHAPTER IV.

First Winter in the Crimea—Sufferings—Scurvy—A Bitter cold Night—Carrying off a Log of Wood—Sir Colin's Servant—The Scotch Peer—Increase of Sickness in the Army—Appearance and Bearing of British Soldier—Our Countrymen at Home—Private Supplies of Food and Clothing—What was required of Medical Officers in Olden Times.

THE history of our army in the Crimea has been often written, but no description, written or verbal, can convey a true impression of the miseries we endured during the first winter. Only those who lived through those dreary days know the full extent thereof, and what it was to be without proper shelter and clothing and sufficient food and fuel, while cold, keen winds blew, and rain and snow beat down upon the earth, converting it into a sea of mud, through which we had to wade with half-shod feet. Even the ground within our tents was trodden into mud, and there we sat and slept, and fortunate was he who could secure a bundle of damp straw of which to make a bed. The tents afforded poor protection against the piercing cold, the boisterous winds, and driving rain; and our clothes, of which at one time we had not even a change, became so worn and filthy that we had to search and shake them carefully, that we might wear them in even a little comfort. We came to loathe our daily dole of salt beef or pork, and as we moved through our camp, and looked into the soldiers' tents, their ration meat might be seen piled up in heaps within, untouched for days, because they would not or could not eat, or had no fuel, or even did not know how to cook, so as to make it palatable. Indeed this necessary article (fuel) was so scarce at times that we had barely sufficient to boil the water for our tea, in which we soaked the hard, dry biscuit, the only process by which many who were not blessed with good teeth could make it eatable, and which, often for days together, was the only nourishment that many of us had. The consequence was that numbers of the men became scorbutic, and many of them died of scorbutic dysentery.

One night when it was bitter cold, and I was starving, but waiting patiently for my servant to bring the usual morsel, he appeared looking pinched and hungry as myself, and informed me that there was no food that night for either of us, as the fuel was all burned out, and he 'couldna lay his han's anyhow upon anither stick.' I therefore made up my mind to fast; but just at that moment a messenger arrived with a request that I would visit one of Sir Colin's staff who was ill, Captain (now Colonel) Charles Mansfield. I started off at once, and, in passing through the cottage in which Sir Colin and his staff lived to my patient's room, I saw up in the far corner a pile of logs, and immediately made up my mind to secure one of them. It may have occurred to me that Sir Colin would not object to spare me one, as he probably had dined, while I was fasting; or perhaps, which is most likely, I did not give a thought to anything but my necessity, and, seeing plenty within my reach, determined to have a share.

Having prescribed for my patient, I went through the form of asking *his* permission to take a log, knowing perfectly well that I should meet with a refusal. Of course I met with a refusal, but the fact of my having asked permission from a member of the household quieted my scruples a little, if not altogether. Having said good night, I closed my friend's door *securely* in order that he might not be obliged to wink at the irregularity I was about to be guilty of, or disturb me in the act. Then, selecting a good log, I shouldered it, and walked quietly out at the front door, passing close by the entrance to Sir Colin's room, the door of which was ajar, so that I could distinctly hear him conversing with Major Sterling, his brigade-major, or Captain Shadwell, his assistant quarter-master-general.

The log proved to be heavier than I expected, but it promised food and comparative comfort for one night at least; so I floundered on, sinking under its weight in the mud, up to my ankles at every step. I had got over about one-third of the distance to my tent when I heard steps as if in pursuit. This made me struggle harder, but, in spite of my frantic efforts, the footsteps sounded nearer and nearer every second, until at last they seemed to be close behind me, and almost at the same time a hand touched me on the shoulder, and a melodious Scotch voice saluted me in the following words:

'Bide a wee, an' I'll help ye. I'm Sir Colin's servant, an' saw ye tak' the log, an' I thocht tae mysel' that ye maun be sair putten tae't when ye'd dae the like, sae I've jist brocht ye anither log, an' I'll carry't tae yer tent for ye.'

This was a relief indeed, and my friend and I plodded on side by side until we reached my tent. I offered him a tip, of course, but he put aside my hand, saying, 'Na, na, I canna tak' it; for am I no yer ain namesake? And what for suld ae clansman rob anither?' He quite forgot, apparently, that both he and I had just robbed a countryman, but probably thought that a namesake and a clansman had a prior claim on his loyalty and consideration to one who was simply a countryman, and his master for the time.

It is said that wherever Scotchmen meet, they are ever ready to hold out the hand of brotherhood and assistance to each other. The story I have just told confirms the saying, and so does the following one; and, though it is not a reminiscence, strictly speaking, connected with my military service, the circumstance happened while I was still in the service. It occurred in London some years ago, and was as follows :

I wanted a couple of ash leaping-poles for my boys, and, after searching for them during several days without success, was at last informed that they might be procured at a certain shop. On arriving at the shop, I found it was an ironmonger's, and not a likely place in which to find what I required. Entering the shop, however, I asked the very respectable man who was standing behind the counter if he 'had any ash-poles?'

'Na, I dinna keep sic things,' was his reply.

The broad Doric in which he spoke sounded pleasant to my ears, and I ventured to remark, 'You are a Scotchman, I perceive.'

'Weel, an' what o' that?' angrily replied my countryman, at the same time bristling up like a Skye terrier.

'Oh, nothing,' I said, mildly, 'only I am a Scotchman too.'

'Are ye so, man?' replied the good fellow, while a kindly smile lighted up his face. 'Then I'll get ye the poles. I dinna keep them, as I said, but I'll send for them for ye.'

And he did get them for me, and took some trouble, too, to get them. We have been friends ever since, and I often pay him a visit, and have a chat with him, and thus revive memories about our common home, which appear to be as agreeable to him as they really are to myself.

Another story, of a somewhat similar kind, I must tell, as it shows that this feeling of brotherly kindness exists in the hearts of those in even the highest ranks of society.

A certain Scotch nobleman was requested by one of his friends, also a Scotchman, to use his interest in behalf of a third person, who was also Scotch.

'No,' said the peer, 'I cannot interfere in the matter.'

'But,' said the applicant, 'the man is a countryman.'

'No,' persisted the peer, 'I cannot do it even for a countryman.'

'But,' said the other again, with equal persistence, 'he is not only a countryman, but is from your own county!'

'Oh! is he?' said H——s G——e. 'Then that alters the case somewhat, I suppose; and I'll have to help him.'

Doubtless it is the rule that Scots do stand by each other, and, as far as my own experience goes, it is the rule; but the greatest wrong that was ever done me, amounting in its consequences almost to ruin, was by a countryman, a man who was indebted to me in various ways, as he often acknowledged, and who professed to be my *true* friend, but who cast me aside as soon as I had done all that he required of me, and failing me at the last, was silent while I was being wronged, almost ruined.

The claims of kindred and nationality may be strong, for 'blood is thicker than water,' as they say; those of friendship are considered binding amongst honourable men, but the claims of justice are sacred, and he who, being in a position of authority, knows that wrong and injustice are about to be committed against his friend, or against any man who comes within the pale of his authority, and does not raise his voice in remonstrance or protest, is as guilty of the commission of the wrong and injustice, as he or they who perpetrate them. If he lack the courage to protest, he is unfit for the position of authority; but, if he lack the will, he cannot be considered just and upright; and, however he may try to stifle the whisperings of conscience, he must in his heart feel that he is untrue to the man who was loyal to him in thought, word, and deed, and who has suffered for that loyalty.

But I must revert to the year 1854, and to my Crimean reminiscences.

Very early in the winter, one of the few houses left standing in Kadikoi and the church were converted into hospitals, the former for officers of the Highland brigade, and the latter for the men of the 93rd. The house gave shelter to many a sick officer during the first winter, but was eventually used for other purposes. The sick of the regiment were accommodated in the church; but this was always filled to overcrowding, and the poor fellows lay packed as close as possible upon the floor, in their soiled and tattered uniform, and covered with only their worn field blankets.* There the surgeons bravely worked and toiled by day and night, with little power and less hope of doing good, for they had only a very scant supply of medicines, and no bread, or soup, or wine, or any single article with which to nourish the starving sick. By day and night, at every hour, men came from camp, from guard, from picket, and from fatigue-duty, wet, cold, benumbed, with life just flickering in their feebly-beating hearts; and only warmth and nourishment were required to rouse the flicker into a flame and bring them back to life. But all that could be done was to lay them gently down and watch life ebb away, often without a struggle or a moan.

And yet the British soldier, in all this misery, never uttered one word of complaint, and was an object to be looked at with admiration and respect. Though lean and hungry-looking, with unkempt hair and beard, with pale and hollow cheek, and clad in rags that scarce kept out the wind and cold, his step was firm and free, his bearing proud, nay, even majestic, and he looked the picture of a man braving trial and adversity; and from his sunken eye there shone a light which told that his courage still beat high, and that sustained by the courage of his race he would endure without a murmur further

* Before the end of the winter, boards and trestles were supplied in lieu of hospital-cots, but these were not more comfortable than the wooden floor of the church.

suffering still, and conquer in the end. During that awful winter I came to know him well, to understand his virtues and his faults, and willingly gave up mind and body to his service. Food, shelter, and proper clothing were all that he required to enable him to undergo any amount of labour and exposure, but these were not supplied in time to save many a life.

Whose fault was that? Who was to blame for all his unnecessary suffering during the winter of 1854–5?* I do not know if, with all the inquiries that were made, that was ever decided. It certainly was never made known clearly to the general public. Perhaps it will be better not to allude further to the subject, and to hope that we have learned such a lesson from the past as may help and guide us in the future. Yet, though so frequently at war, and with so many opportunities of gaining experience, we are never ready for an emergency, but, whenever such arises, have to begin to make our preparations in a hurry.

When our countrymen at home woke up to the knowledge that their army before Sebastopol was reduced to nearly half its strength, and that what remained of it was sorely pressed and in urgent need, they sent, in ship-loads, hundreds of necessary things; and in their great charity—God bless them!—many that were unnecessary and even useless, and in their sympathy vied with each other in spending money liberally, deeming nothing too good or too expensive for their

* See Mr. Kinglake on this subject, in his sixth volume.

ABUNDANCE AT LAST.

gallant soldiers, who, in their turn, were deeply grateful for such thoughtfulness.

Among the many articles that reached us for general distribution were blankets and coats lined with fur, also cotton and woollen underclothing, and woollen socks and gloves. The underclothing was in such superabundance that we could afford to make frequent changes, to put on new and throw away what we had worn only for a week or so, which, though new and good, and only soiled, it was considered too great a trouble to wash.

For hospital use came large supplies of wine and spirits, soups, milk, soft biscuits, jellies, and preserves, all most necessary and acceptable; but one generous charity sent a number of round, red, Dutch cheeses, hard almost as cannon-balls and indigestible as leather. I need hardly say that these were not suitable for men whose teeth were loosened in their swollen, bleeding gums, or for those who were ill with fever, or dying from protracted dysentery. Still the present of Dutch cheeses for sick men showed that the good people at home had exhausted their ingenuity in their selection of articles on which to spend money.

A large consignment of buffalo robes also was sent us, but they took up too much room in the tents, and, besides, harboured vermin to such an extent that on more than one occasion I had to order that they should be burned. These robes must have been expensive, and I fear that the purchase of them was money thrown away, for they all disappeared, and during the second winter there was not one of them to be seen.

The distillers of Campbeltown (as I heard afterwards), mindful of their countrymen, sent out for the Highland Brigade a large supply of whisky, but whether this ever reached us I know not. If it did, some fortunate individual must have received a double allowance, for none ever came to me. However, if I had received my share, most probably I should not have used it, for during the whole of that winter I never touched my ration of rum, an article, by the way, which never failed. Doubtless my ration was issued, but possibly my faithful soldier servant thought that it 'might na be guid for me,' and appropriated it himself.

I had personally to undergo great bodily labour and much anxiety during that first winter; for a regiment, circumstanced as mine was, was a most responsible charge. Often I sought the assistance of my commanding officer (Lieutenant-Colonel Ainslie), who generally gave, but sometimes withheld, his support. Perhaps I was too anxious, and therefore too exacting in my requests; or possibly, being a young surgeon, and only just appointed to the regiment, he did not feel inclined to place implicit confidence in my suggestions until he knew me better. On one occasion he declined to see the necessity of following my recommendation in a certain matter which I considered urgent; and, though I endeavoured to convince him, he failed to see either the necessity or the urgency. At length his persistent refusal to act irritated me to such a degree that I forgot myself—lost my temper, in fact—and remarked to him 'that he was the only commanding officer I had ever served under who appeared to me to be indifferent to the welfare of his regiment.' This was a thoughtless, insubordinate remark; and, even if there had been the slightest shade of truth in what I said, I had no right to say it at all, and certainly not in angry mood, and in disrespectful word and manner. The colonel flushed perceptibly, but said not a word in reply, and simply pointed to the door of his tent, through which I passed, still angry. In this mood I foolishly and wrongfully continued for a couple of days, during which I never went near him. On the afternoon of the second day, as I was seated in my tent 'nursing my wrath,' the colonel's servant presented himself, and delivered the following message:

'The colonel's compliments, an' he'd be glad if ye'd step up, an' drink a glass o' champagne wi' him, which he's jist gotten frae ane o' the ships.'

In a moment my anger vanished; for I was completely taken aback by this mark of generosity—not at the unselfishness of his offering me half of his champagne at such a time of scarcity, but at the kind-heartedness which prompted him to be the first to offer reconciliation, though the *amende* was due to him from me. As I said, my anger vanished in a moment, and with the impulsiveness of youth (I was a young man for my position in those days—just thirty years of age) I started from my seat—the bare ground—and set off at a run up the hill, determined to offer my apology, and thank him for his consideration before accepting his hospitality. On my entering the tent, the colonel held out his hand, and, before I had recovered breath to speak, said to me,

'Not a word about what happened the other day. Do not speak of it. Do not think of it. Perhaps I was more in the wrong than you were; so tell me again what you want me to do, and, if I can help you, I will.'

My old colonel is still living, and I hope may read this, and believe that I felt very keenly the reproof conveyed to me in his quiet, kindly dignified manner; that I profited by it, and never forgot myself in a similar way, or failed in respect and duty to any of his successors in command.

I may here mention that in those days a medical officer was not expected, and was not required, to express opinions except upon purely professional matters. His duties were to cure disease, not to make suggestions to prevent disease. Rules and regulations enjoined the most rigid and unquestioning obedience from him to his commanding officer, and as a rule this was as rigidly enforced. It was thought sufficient; and a medical officer was considered efficient if he attended his hospital regularly, and treated his patients skilfully. Nothing more was expected of him, and, if he did this, those in military authority over him thought that he had done enough, and the surgeon, trained in this idea, generally thought so too, and did not venture upon a wider range of duty.

CHAPTER V.

Duties—Road from Balaklava to the Front—Carrying Shot and Shell—Housing the Regiment Underground—Cossacks Dressed in Red—Drafts from England—Young Kirby—Sir Colin's Visit—Constantinople—St. Sophia—The Sultan Abdul Medjid—Turkish Ladies—Return to Crimea—Sir Colin resigns his Command.

DURING the winter of 1854-5, the duties which devolved upon the troops at Balaklava were not to be compared in severity with those performed by the army before Sebastopol. The former had no trench-work and no fighting, but had to throw up their own entrenchments, to furnish large out-lying and in-lying pickets, and were oppressed by constant fatigue-duties. These last consisted of hard labour in landing and storing commissariat supplies for the army generally, and in bringing up everything for their own use from Balaklava to their respective camps. But there was one fatigue-duty which pressed heavily on them, which the men of the 93rd detested, and on which they were employed almost daily for upwards of two months.

The road from Balaklava to the head-quarters

on the Chersonese heights, which we were forced to use after the battle of Balaklava, had become impassable for wheeled carriages, and the government transport animals were completely knocked up from want of forage and over-work, and, as ammunition for both artillery and infantry was absolutely necessary, the 93rd (and I think the other Highland regiments also) was required to furnish large fatigue-parties daily to carry shot and shell from Balaklava to the front. The men grumbled fiercely as they left camp for this duty, and loudly anathematized, not only the heavy loads, but the unhandy or clumsy means of transport afforded them. So many loose shot or shell were placed in a field blanket, and two or four men, grasping the blanket by the corners, swung the load along between them. Many of the men preferred slinging the loads over their backs, and staggering along under the weight of two or more shot. To carry heavy loads over a good road would have been severe labour of itself, but to flounder under them through deep, tenacious mud, into which at every step the men sank halfway up to the knee, and out of which it required a considerable amount of muscular effort to drag their feet, made the labour ten times more severe. It was too much to require from men exhausted by starvation and by previous disease, from which many had barely recovered, and from existing disease, from which many suffered, but of which they made no complaint, until they were unable to drag one leg after another.

The parties generally returned to camp, after performing this duty, perfectly done up, their great-coats soaked through by the rain or sleet, their underclothes saturated by the profuse perspiration caused by the violent exertion of carrying heavy loads over such ground as I have described, and their well-worn boots and trews thickly coated with mud. They had no change of clothes, no dry things to put on instead of their wet ones, and were obliged to sit or lie down in their wet things on the damp ground within their tents, and shiver from cold until the next issue of grog.

The results of this duty were severe bowel complaints, fever, aggravated scorbutic symptoms, and often cholera. Indeed, many a man died from the consequences entailed by this particular duty who might—nay, probably would—have lived to do good service of another kind.

There was another duty on which the men were employed when not on shot-and-shell fatigue, and which ended in failure, after much toil and labour had been expended on it, affording the men opportunity for a good grumble. The regimental camp was placed on the southern slope of Highlander's or Sutherland Hill, and thus was sheltered to some extent, but, for military reasons, the tents were so pitched that their doors faced to the north, the quarter from whence the cold, cutting Crimean wind blew, driving rain and sleet, and often snow, before it into the tents, converting the ground within them into a bed of mud, and keeping the men's clothes and blankets in a constant state of damp. Sir Colin, always watchful, observed this, and gave orders that a long, deep, broad trench, large enough to accommodate the whole regiment, should be dug on the slope near the crest of the hill, behind the principal earthwork, in which several guns were mounted, and which was the key of our position. This trench was to be roofed over with planks, on which a thick layer of clay was to be laid and well beaten down. The men worked most unwillingly, as they appeared from the first to have had an instinctive knowledge that the trench would not answer the purpose for which Sir Colin intended it. Besides, in clearing out the earth, a quantity of human remains (bones) were exhumed, and this not only increased their unwillingness to work, but excited a feeling of disgust, or, as the men called it in their own phraseology, 'a scunner,' at the prospect of having to live amongst the dead.

The trench was finished, however, and occupied, but, within a very few days after occupation, it was flooded by a heavy downpour of rain, and the men had to abandon it in haste, and return to their tents, grumbling and laughing alternately—grumbling at the waste of labour, and laughing at the bad engineering, and for many days jocularly speaking of the whole work as 'Sir Colin's folly.'

The fact was, that the great trench was dug on the slope of the hill, so that there was a constant oozing of moisture through the upper bank or wall, and all the many openings, made large so as to admit of rapid ingress and egress, looked to the north, the same military reasons applying here as in the case of the tents, viz., that in the event of alarm or attack the men might ascend easily and quickly to line the defences. But these large openings facing to the north gave free ingress to the rain and snow, which there was no way of getting rid of except by the slow process of percolation, and they admitted the piercing cold wind also, which blew fiercely in, and rushed, howling dismally, through the great cavern.

There was no reason why the men should not have been hutted securely underground. The mistake was in having made one large excavation instead of many, each one of the many large enough to hold half a company or a section of a company, and with only one opening or door, facing to the south instead of to the north.

A detachment of sailors made two small burrowings at the foot of Highlander's Hill, one for their officers and one for themselves, in which they lived warm and comfortable for some time. The Sardinian army also was hutted underground during the winter of 1855–6. Their huts, though simple, were carefully constructed in the following manner. Square or rather oblong holes were dug down to the depth of six feet, and over these pent roofs, thatched with reeds or straw, were erected. There was a door at one end, approached by a flight of half a dozen steps paved with stone, and opposite the door was a fireplace, with well-built flue. Each hut was large enough to accommodate from ten to twenty men, and in tolerable comfort—in greater comfort, indeed, than many of the wooden huts sent out from England for our own army afforded.

Soldiers are like children, easily roused to anger, and as easily excited to mirth. Even in the midst of discomfort and danger, a trifle will rouse their wrath or move them to laughter. I have heard them quarrel with each other, and speak angry, threatening words, and in a few minutes afterwards, apparently having forgotten their cause of dispute, joke at each other's expense. I have seen them when under fire laugh at a comrade for endeavouring to dodge a ricochetting round shot, chaff another loudly for ducking his head at the sound of a passing bullet, or for throwing himself flat on the ground to escape the splinters of a shell which had fallen near them with its fuse still hissing and spluttering, and have seen them even when under a hot fire play off practical jokes on each other.

Officers also, in the days of which I write, were much given to practical joking, and the following incident, which occurred in the month of December, 1854, was considered a practical joke, and I was accused of being *particeps*, or, rather, *origo criminis*, though nothing was further from my thoughts at the time than to jest. Indeed, in the whole course of my service, I never

F

perpetrated a practical joke; for life has always been too serious a matter with me, and it was especially so at that time. The exact date I have not noted, but it was towards the end of December. I remember that it was an awful night. The darkness was intense, and a bitter cold wind blowing from the north-east drove the rain and sleet before it in sheets, and the mud was more than ankle deep. In spite of the darkness, wind, rain, and mud, however, I found my way to the hospital about midnight, and was in the act of preparing some medicine for a patient in a small room in a cottage situated within the enclosure of the church which was the regimental hospital. The cottage had been the priest's dwelling, but I had converted it into a refuge for the worst cases of illness, and for special cases, and one very little room I used as a surgery. While so employed, two young cavalry officers entered, and one of them addressed me as follows:

'We are the officers of the cavalry picket; I have drawn my men within the enclosure here, and I propose to take up my own quarters for the remainder of the night in this hut.'

I told him that 'such a thing as his taking possession of the hut, as he called it, was impossible, as it was part of the hospital of my regiment.'

'Well, then,' said he, a little peremptorily, 'I must have a corner somewhere, and you must spare me one.'

'I cannot make room for you,' said I; 'but you

may look round, and, if you see a vacant corner, either here or in the church, you may occupy it until it is required. But,' I continued, 'may I ask who you are?'

'I am —— of ——' (mentioning a noble name); 'I have just arrived from England, and this is my first night on picket duty.'

I felt sorry for him, more especially that his first experience of picket duty should have been on such a night; and, as he threw open his great-coat or cloak, he looked so neat and trim, and his gold lace shone so bright compared with my own, which was worn and tarnished, that I felt I must try to help him. I offered him the shelter of a bell-tent which was pitched on a spot of dry ground just behind the cottage, and which was unoccupied at that moment. I told him plainly, however, that it 'was possible the tent might be required during the night, and that if it were he would have to turn out.' This he promised to do. I then called an orderly, and desired him to show the officers where the tent was. But, as they were leaving the little surgery, I overheard my noble friend ask the orderly 'if he thought there was any probability of the tent being required.'

'I'm no jist shure,' was the cautious reply of the Scot; 'there's naething intilt the noo, but there's twa or three o' the men vera bad, but it's possible that nane o' them'll dee the nicht.'

'Good gracious!' said the officer, 'do you use the tent as a dead house?'

'Ay, sir, jist that, but ye needna be feared, ye'll no be disturbed if we can help it.'

I had not intended that my friends should have heard all this, being really desirous of helping them to the only accommodation there was, and thinking, or, at least, hoping that there might not be a death during the night. However, having recovered from the first shock of surprise, my friends, like sensible fellows, made up their minds to occupy the tent, thankful to have any shelter over their heads, and for a spot of dry ground to sit or to lie down on. Fortunately they had a quiet and undisturbed night.

I never mentioned the circumstance, in fact I forgot all about it, and was surprised some days afterwards to hear that somehow or other it had got wind in the cavalry brigade, and that it was looked on as a practical joke, and gave occasion for a good deal of amusement and laughter, in which my two friends joined, though it was at their own expense. I never saw my friends again, and, though the cavalry picket for weeks thereafter occupied regularly every night a corner of the enclosure round the hospital, I never was applied to again for a night's lodging.

One day in February, 1855, I nearly got into a serious scrape. The afternoon happened to be fine, and being weary with overwork, and in need of a breath of fresh air, I mounted my horse, and accompanied by poor Menzies, one of my assistants (since dead), rode out on the plain in front of our camp, and as far as our vidette, who was posted on one of the chain of low hills which had been No. 6 of the redoubts held by the Turks up to the day of the battle of Balaklava. We had a long talk with the vidette, who was an old soldier of the Greys, about the heavy cavalry charge. He told us that our men felt as if they were 'riding the Rooshians down,' and that while *they* sat erect in their saddles, 'the Rooshians cooered doun,' as if to avoid the sword cuts that were made at them.

On our return to camp, we rode down the Valley of the Six Hundred, intending to turn into the Balaklava plain round the base of the hill which had been No. 5 redoubt. But we either missed the way, or forgot where we were going, or what doing, and continued to ride on slowly straight down the valley. Suddenly two mounted men, dressed in red coats, appeared within a couple of hundred yards of us, riding slowly in our direction. I am a little near-sighted, but, seeing red-coats, I thought, and remarked to Menzies, that the two men belonged to our own cavalry, and continued to ride on until we were within fifty yards of them, when, to our dismay, we perceived that they were Cossacks. We wheeled round immediately, and galloped back as fast as our horses could go, and, being well mounted, were soon out of danger. The Cossacks did not attempt to give chase, for they were mounted on very small ponies, while I rode my handsome (captured) Russian charger, and Menzies a good stout pony.

Never after that did I venture beyond bounds.

During the winter, several officers joined the regiment with drafts from England. One of these, Ensign Kirby, a young, delicate-looking lad, remarked to me at our first meeting,

'This is a terrible place, and I fear that I have come out only to lay my bones here.'

He evidently spoke quite seriously; and, as I looked at him, I could not help feeling that he would not be able to endure the hardship and privations to which he would necessarily be exposed. Poor young fellow! he died of fever within a couple of months after arrival, and he lies at rest in the valley of Kadikoi near the very spot on which he was standing when we first met him.

I was not with him during his illness; for almost at the same time I was myself suddenly taken ill with fever. Before taking to my cot (and I struggled against this as long as I could stand), I desired that it should be placed in a small room in the cottage, next to that in which I had been in the habit of putting the most serious cases of fever.

During the first days of my illness I was delirious, at least I was told so afterwards. Certainly those days have ever been a blank in my memory. On returning to consciousness, the first thing I was sensible of was a pressure on my shoulder, and a voice saying,

'Poor fellow! I am afraid he'll die.'

I recognised the voice, and looking up into Sir

Colin's face—for it was he—as he leaned over me, said faintly, or tried to say,

'No, sir, I shall not die.'

It was a weary time though during which I lay helpless there—five weeks—and during all those weeks I could hear the poor fellows in the next room (only a thin partition, with a door in it, separated us) raving in the delirium of fever. More than once I knew, from the short, laboured, sobbing respiration, that some poor comrade's life was drawing to a close. I even recognized the shuffling noise of feet as the dead was carried out from amongst the living, whose lives, too, were trembling in the balance.

But these sounds did not cause me to feel any alarm. I never thought that death was near myself, though I was prostrated by the same fever of which I had seen so many die, and of which I knew that others lying within a few feet of me were dying daily. There was one man lying ill in the room next to me, Sergeant Graham, who thought that I had been kind to him in some way, and who during his delirium constantly called me by name, begging piteously that I would go to him. When he recovered consciousness, and heard that I was ill also, and lying in the next room, he tried to stagger to his feet, poor fellow, 'to come and nurse me,' as he said.

We both recovered, served together for many years afterwards, and always had a true affection for each other.

When it was considered safe to move me, I

was put on board ship and sent to England. I remained at home three months, and then returned to the Crimea ; but on the voyage back was so crippled by an attack of acute arthretic rheumatism as to be very lame for a time after rejoining my regiment. Before the setting in of cold weather, however, I had quite recovered. I knew several other officers who also suffered from severe rheumatism after illness such as I had had.

In October, 1855, Sir Colin resigned the command of his division for reasons well known (supersession by a junior) ; but before embarking for England he was kind enough to send for me to say good-bye. He returned to the Crimea in the spring of 1856, for the purpose, I believe, of commanding an army corps intended for special service in the event of the war being continued. He met with a hearty welcome from his old Highland brigade, and it was pleasant to see how the veteran chief's face brightened up at the enthusiastic reception given him.

On my way home to England I spent nearly a week in Constantinople, during which time I saw as much of the great city and its environs as a convalescent could. For the first two days my strength only admitted of my being rowed in a caique on the Bosphorus; but as health returned I visited Therapia, the Sultan's new palace of Dolme Baghtche, which at that time had not been occupied, Scutari and its large hospitals, and Renkioi, where my old friend Dr. George

Beatson was in charge. Afterwards I spent a forenoon in the Mosque of St. Sophia, to which I found no difficulty in gaining admission, and on my return from thence met the Sultan Abdul Medjid, on horseback, on his way to prayers; but on attempting to enter the mosque in his train I was forcibly ejected.

My last two days were spent at the sweet waters of Europe, and at those of Asia. In both I saw many Turkish ladies, some sitting beneath the shady trees feasting on *love's delight*, and others being driven in gilded arabahs drawn by oxen; but all were jealously guarded by great, fat, hideous-looking beings whom one can hardly call human.

The ladies wore the yasmak, but of so thin a texture that their faces could be distinctly seen. Many were very beautiful, and did not object to be looked at by the Giaour—at least, they did not turn away their heads, or draw their yasmaks closer, or even cast their eyes upon the ground, but quietly returned our stare doubtless out of curiosity.

On my ride back from the sweet waters of Europe I met three carriages of English build, and drawn by English thoroughbreds. They were filled with beautiful women belonging to the Sultan's harem. The ladies seemed to be very happy, for they drove with open windows, chatted and laughed, and made no effort to conceal their beauty.

Of all the places in the world that I have

visited, Stamboul is the most unsavoury. The streets are narrow and paved with boulders; and running down the whole length of each is an open sewer, the odour from which is overpowering. As I said in a former chapter, the appearance of Stamboul from the sea is beautiful—like a fairy scene; but one should be contented with a distant view, for, the moment one lands, all enchantment is dispelled. But in spite of noxious odours, which one can become accustomed to, I suppose, one sees strange sights and hears strange sounds at every turn. Dignified Turks, showy Albanians, sombre Persians, and fierce Khurds, all arrayed in their picturesque, national garbs, many of them armed with terrible-looking knives and handsome-looking pistols. Also fat pashas, in European dress and glittering with orders, riding along on their handsome little Arab horses, preceded and followed by nimble runners, shouting to make way for the great man.

Shopping was a difficulty, as we English have not the tact and patience to make a bargain, and these virtues are necessary in all dealings with Orientals. The shopmen sat cross-legged behind their wares, inhaling the smoke of the fragrant weed through long cherry sticks (the chibouque), or through the narghilie, and taking the world easily. The grand bazaar is a sight worth seeing, but even there business was carried on languidly, and I saw but few customers, except shrouded figures purchasing scent or gay articles of dress.

In walking along the streets, one has to be constantly on the alert to avoid being ridden over by horsemen, or by strings of mules, or laden donkeys, or smothered beneath the load of some sturdy porter carrying piles of boxes on his back, and walking easily, though bent nearly double, under an enormous weight.

CHAPTER VI.

Spring of 1855—Fall of Sebastopol—Preparations for second Winter—Highland Camp—Valley of Vanutka—Spring of 1856—Tartar Villages—Baidar Valley—Baghcheserai—Palace of the Khans—Gipsy Village—Russian Monastery—Jewish town of Tchoufut Kaleh—Simpheropol—Hospitals—Sisters of Charity—Evening with Russian Officers.

THE dreadful winter of 1854-5, with all its sufferings, came to an end at last; and spring returning, brought with it health and strength to those who were spared, and who had borne the heat and cold and burden of the past year. The shattered regiments having been recruited, and a large increase made to the army, the siege was renewed with vigour, and went on through all the summer, in spite of a severe check in June; and in September, after two more bloody battles had been fought (in which the English took no part), to relieve the straitened garrison, the allied armies mustered their full strength for another effort; and then the great fortress fell, the Russians fiercely fighting to the last amid 'a heap of blood-stained ruins.'

Then autumn came again, and, taught a lesson by the previous winter, we made preparations to pass a second in the Crimea. Christmas found the British army hutted safely and comfortably, in wooden huts sent out from home. Thus housed, and with abundant stores of all things necessary to health and comfort, and with piles of books (which had been sent out to us from home) to read, and no hard work to do, we cared not for floods of rain, nor for the bitter north winds with their driving clouds of snow and sleet; and while the storms raged fiercely without, and we lay secure under comfortable shelter, we felt that our lives were being passed in ease and even in luxury, when compared with the previous year.

Thus passed our second winter in the Crimea, and as another spring came round the great emperor died, and his successor being averse to war, or perhaps without the means of continuing war, an armistice was agreed to, preparatory to a peace.

During the armistice, permission was given to the officers of the allied armies to visit places of interest in the Peninsula. Of this permission the English took advantage freely, but not so our allies; for in all our wanderings we never met a French officer. In every nook and corner, go where one would, the British subaltern was met with, riding his little bat pony, seeing and being seen, and spending his money liberally.

The Highland encampment was situated in a narrow gorge at the entrance to the Vanutka

Valley, eastward of the village of Kamara, and our wooden huts were erected on a spur, facing east, and sloping down to a little stream, which flowed swiftly along a rocky channel. On the opposite side, cut deep along the face of the hills, was the Woronsoff road, which, commencing at Sebastopol, ran through the valleys of the Tchernaya, Vanutka, and Baidar, and along the southern coast of the Crimea. The gorge where we were hutted was deep and narrow, and shut in by hills of mountain limestone, the sides of which, intersected by little wooded glens, and deeply scored by many rushing streams, were densely clothed with dwarf oak and scrub, amongst which several of our young officers looked in vain for game. During the first months of winter the weather was so wet and stormy that we scarcely ventured beyond our camp, but on the return of genial sunshine in the spring, both officers and men joined in the national sports of quoits and shinty, and got up Highland games; and the officers made excursions to the glens and villages in our immediate neighbourhood.

In the vicinity of our encampment were many Tartar villages, hidden amongst trees within the lesser valleys, and to these, with Adrian Hope— of whom I shall have more to say by-and-by—I frequently paid visits. We were always accompanied by a Polish gentleman, Mehemet Bey, an officer in the Turkish army, and attached to our division as interpreter, I think. This officer spoke a number of languages fluently, knew English fairly, and could converse to a certain extent with Russians and Tartars.*

Under his guidance and with his assistance we were always welcomed by the Tartars to their houses; and there, surrounded by the whole family, including the women, we used to sit cross-legged upon the floor, and chat freely of the country and their history, public and domestic, but not so freely of their Russian masters, of whom, in fact, they spoke little and unwillingly. The women sat or moved about unveiled, and handed us tea in little tumblers, and lighted our chibouques. The Crimean Tartars are a comely race, with fair skins, straight open eyes, and well-cut features; and several of the women whom we saw were very pretty, with large, lustrous eyes, blooming cheeks, and regular, white teeth, all evidences of good health, and probably also of some admixture of other blood, perhaps Turkish or Jewish.

I got to be on such friendly terms with one family from my frequent visits that the good dame offered to show me her wardrobe. This was extensive, and composed of a great variety of garments; amongst them was her wedding dress, a handsome white robe, made of soft woollen stuff, and thickly braided and ornamented with silver. She had never worn it since the day on which she came as a bride to her hus-

* I never called on Mehemet Bey, but I found him studying the *Times*. This he did to improve his knowledge of English.

band's house. I understood that it was a sort of heirloom, and came to her from her mother and grandmothers from remote generations, and would descend to her own daughter and grandchildren for generations to come. All the articles produced for my inspection were taken from a large chest, which was stowed away in the best room of the house—one apparently not usually occupied—and were so carefully folded and wrapped up that, even if she had not told me, I should have known that they were never used.

We frequently visited the Tartar villages in the Baidar Valley also. This is a wide extent of undulating pasture-land, rich and well-watered by many streams, and enclosed by rugged hills, especially on the east and south, in which game of many varieties abound. But our visits thither were more frequently on horseback to enjoy the paper-hunt instituted by the brothers Gooch, one of the 92nd and the other of the 93rd. On one of these occasions the meet was numerously attended, and the run, longer and more exciting than usual, took us far from our camp, and as the whole field went along at a rattling pace, in full cry, we came suddenly upon a French outpost, who, I presume, taking us for a body of marauding Cossacks, turned out in haste and stood to their arms. But when, on our near approach, they discovered who and what we were, an old corporal contemptuously saluted thus: 'Sacré, ces sont les Ecossais, ils s'amusent.' To him it was, I presume, inexplicable how the English could take pleasure in 'la chasse au papier,' in which he could see neither pleasure nor amusement.

Shortly after the armistice was proclaimed, and while the preliminaries of peace were being settled, officers of the allied armies were permitted to travel about the Crimea, under the protection of a Russian passport given by the military authorities. Having obtained this necessary document, a large party of us decided to visit Baghcheserai. We started on horseback at an early hour, galloped across the Balaklava plain, crossed the Tchernaya by the Tracktyr bridge, which had been the scene of a deadly struggle between the Zouaves and Russians in the autumn of the previous year, and ascended the Mackenzie heights, from whence we rode quickly and merrily over the grass-covered steppes, and by noon arrived at Baghcheserai, the ancient capital of the Crimean khans.

The town or city lies in a deep and narrow valley, which is enclosed by limestone hills. This valley opens out wide at the point of entrance, and contracts gradually, until at the farther or eastern extremity, it becomes a deep fissure or cutting, closed in by precipitous rocky cliffs. Through the length of the valley flows a small but rapid stream, on both sides of which, and almost in the middle of the valley, stands the town, whose only object of interest or attraction is the palace.

Having tied up our horses under a shed attached to the hotel, we started off at once to inspect the palace, for many centuries the abode of the Gherais. It is a gloomy pile of buildings, enclosing several small paved courts, in which grow shrubs and flowering plants, watered from a handsome central fountain. The rooms are numerous and small, dark and comfortless, except the hall of audience, at one end of which, raised high above the floor, is the seat of judgment—a sort of balcony, from which the khans in former days administered justice to their people—rough justice, perhaps, but still according to their lights, and as such accepted by their subjects. From thence we walked up the valley to the gipsy village or encampment, formed by burrowings under and amongst the rocks; from thence we retraced our steps, and ascended by a long flight of wooden steps to a Russian monastery, consisting of a number of chambers or galleries cut in the face of the cliff, interesting to us as displaying the result of labour and perseverance only, but held in great veneration by the orthodox. Here we saw Russian peasants at their devotions, which, as far as we could understand, consisted in humble but passionate adoration of some pictures of saints, and in their repeatedly kissing the glass cases within which these pictures were enclosed.

From the monastery we crossed the valley, and ascended to the Jewish town of Tchonfut Kaleh, built along the very edge of a stupendous cliff, and overhanging the valley. On entering the gate, we were accosted by a young Jew, who, speaking French fairly, invited us to his father's house, and, after treating us to sweetmeats and cold water, offered to escort us to the synagogue. We were invited to enter the humble but sacred building by a handsome and venerable rabbi, and permitted to look at a copy of 'The Law,' written on vellum and rolled up in a case covered with purple cloth and bound with silver, which had been brought hither centuries ago by the fathers of the tribe, or rather portion of the tribe. The Jews who inhabit this town, and those who dwell in Mungoup Kaleh, situated on one of the lofty cliffs which enclose the pass of Coralie, in the vicinity of Balaklava, are the Karraim Jews, so called, I believe, from the Hebrew word *kara*, signifying scripture. They differ from other Jews in their repudiation of the Talmud and rabbinical commentaries, and by their strict adherence to the letter of 'The Law' as laid down in the Pentateuch.

They are, I believe, descended from, or rather belong to, the tribe of Judah, and are the descendants of those families of the tribe of Judah which remained in Babylon after the return from captivity to their own land of the main body of the tribe. Subsequently, however, those families also left Babylon, travelled in a northerly direction, settled in different countries, and some few of them in the Crimea. It is supposed that they built the town of Tchoufut Kaleh, that they were expelled from it for a time by the Tartars, but allowed to return to and re-occupy it after Baghcheserai was completed.

Our last visit was to the Jewish cemetery, the Vale of Jehoshaphat, as it is called. It is extensive, surrounded by a belt of fine trees, and filled to over-crowding with tombstones, many of them very old, as shown by the almost complete obliteration of inscriptions, while others of later date had Hebrew characters cut deeply into them. At sunset we returned to our hotel, weary with our long day's work, and prepared to accept thankfully whatever there might be to eat and drink. The substantial portion of dinner was animal food certainly, but it was tough and tasteless, and the style of cooking did no credit to the chéf; but whatever it was, in compliment to our nationality doubtless, it was offered to us as beef steak à l'Anglais. The only liquor we could induce our host to produce—perhaps there was no other in his cellar—was an execrable fiery spirit, which the Russian loves, called bodki, not unlike in taste and smell to bad Irish whisky. Hunger and thirst compelled us to eat and drink, and the power of youthful digestion saved us from any after unpleasant consequences.

Our party at the hotel was a large one, consisting of Russian officers, several Jew contractors, and ourselves; and as the whole accommodation amounted to one public room—the bar, in fact—and a closet, both without beds or couches, and with only a very limited number of chairs, we all had to sleep together on the floor and endure throughout the night the persecution of unpleasant neighbours of several kinds. This got us up betimes, however, on the morrow, and, after a meagre breakfast off some scraps remaining from our evening meal, four of us—Burroughs, Ewen Macpherson, Gordon-Alexander, and myself—started in a telega for Simpheropol. We should have ridden thither had we been wise, but we were anxious, for once, to travel à la Russe, and regretted it when too late, for our conveyance was primitive and uncomfortable.

It was simply like a large barrel resting on a wooden frame-work set on four wheels, without springs of any kind. On either side of this barrel was a square opening to get in and out by, which could be closed by a curtain, and inside bundles of straw (fresh and clean fortunately) were arranged as seats. We had a team of three horses yoked in the usual Russian fashion, three abreast, and these were changed once during a drive of twenty-four miles.

Our Jehu was a merry, or at least a noisy, fellow, clad in *scented* sheep-skin, and without other covering on his head than a thick thatch of yellow hair. His tongue was never quiet, and the use he made of this organ appeared to exercise a greater influence over his horses than the cruel whip he carried; which, however, I must do him the credit to say he made use of less to urge his horses on than to flourish as a sign of office.

The road along which we travelled was much

cut up, and full of ruts and deep holes, so that in our springless carriage we were bumped and shaken terribly, but arrived at our destination without accident and in time for lunch.

Simpheropol in reality consists of two towns, old and new, the former oriental in style, but a poor specimen of an oriental bazaar. The narrow street through which it was necessary for us to drive was thronged by Jews and Tartars, and, to judge from the noise they made, trade appeared to be brisk around the little shops or booths which lined the street, and which were kept by the clever, accumulative Hebrew for the benefit or convenience of the thriftless, or at least less calculating, Gentile.

The new town is built in European style, stands in the open plain in the vicinity of a small stream, and covers a considerable extent of ground, many of the houses being detached, and each having its plot of garden in front and rear. Almost in the centre of the new town stands a handsome church or cathedral, St. Isaac's, which, with its dome of green and gold, is a striking and imposing building, and is seen to advantage, as there is a considerable extent of open ground around it, part of which forms a public promenade 'where the citizens do congregate' in the cool of evening to listen to the military band.

We spent the afternoon in strolling about the streets and visiting the principal shops, in which we found chiefly English goods exhibited. We purchased a few gold trinkets and charms made, as we were informed, of the gold found in the Ural Mountains. This may have been the case, but they had much the appearance of English manufacture. We also visited several of the cafés which were thronged by Russian officers drinking tea and smoking cigarettes, and who, with great politeness, introduced themselves and rendered us assistance in various ways.

In the evening we followed in the stream to the promenade, and there saw the beauty and fashion of Simpheropol. Amongst them were some really pretty girls, who seemed, like the sex all over the world, to be aware of their good looks, and who were evidently not disinclined to be looked at and admired by the red-coated strangers. One *pater familias* addressed us and introduced us to his pretty daughters, with whom, after the promenade, we walked home and enjoyed a refreshing cup of tea, followed by sweetmeats and cold water; the former, acid jam or jelly, were handed round in crystal dishes, from which, with the same spoon, each person conveyed a little of the preserve to his or her mouth, and washed the morsel down with a sip of cold water, the same tumbler being used by all.

The family spoke French and German, but as they all had dark hair and eyes, and aquiline features, and gave us sweetmeats and cold water as the Jew in Tchoufut Kaleh had done; and as they did not tell us that they were Russian, and did not appear to know, or at least to be known by any of the Russian officers at the promenade, we concluded that we were being hospitably entertained by a Hebrew family.

As we walked about the new town, we came to several large private houses in use as temporary hospitals, and, on entering, found them occupied by soldiers suffering chiefly from scorbutic affections. They had neither cots nor bedding, but lay, many of them in a helpless condition, upon the floor, packed closely together, dressed in tattered uniform, the long, brown great-coats, worn by officers and men alike of the Russian army when on active service. They had no other covering whatever. As I walked from room to room, a private approached, and, addressing me in French, offered to give me any information I required. Surprised to hear a Russian private soldier speak French, I asked him if there were many soldiers in the ranks who could speak other languages than Russian. 'No,' he answered; 'but I was an officer once and noble, and though I had served long and with distinction in several campaigns, and been wounded more than once, I was degraded for a little fault, and shall probably end my career in the ranks; but I am weary of life, and care not how soon the end may come.' What had been his little fault of course he did not say; but he must have fallen low, poor fellow, and forgotten all his noble breeding in his degradation. He asked us for money 'to buy tobacco,' as he said; but there was a tremor of his lips and hands, certain signs of intemperance, and most probably the money which we gave him was spent on vodki. While we were within the building, two young medical officers entered, but they took no notice of us, not even by a courteous salute. We were afterwards informed that they were not Russian, but of another nationality, which I refrain from specifying.

As we parted from the private soldier, he pointed out another building as the regular military hospital, to which we sought and obtained admission. We found it full of convalescent wounded, most comfortably cared for. To this establishment was attached a large staff of Sisters of Mercy, several of whom had served in Sebastopol during the greater part of the siege. These received us with great courtesy; and, on learning that I was the surgeon of a British regiment, one of them, a little, elderly lady, took possession of me, and led me round the wards, explaining the cases in French, which she spoke fluently, and asking my opinion.

One of their ward arrangements struck me as peculiar. It was this: The cots, instead of being placed round the wards with their heads towards the walls, were arranged in the middle of the rooms, with their heads turned to each other, and about six feet apart. On my asking for an explanation, my little conductress said, 'By this arrangement we remove our patients from the hot and dusty walls to where they get most fresh air; and the sick, instead of looking at each other, and thus witnessing many a sad and painful sight, can look out at the windows and doors, and see the trees, and flowers, and God's blue skies.' I learned a lesson from this, and years afterwards introduced the same arrangement in my own regimental hospital in India during the hot and rainy seasons.

One thing surprised us greatly in our intercourse with the Russian officers whom we met in Simpheropol, which was that so many of them spoke our own language well. I asked one of them, who spoke it perfectly and without the least trace of foreign accent, how he had acquired such complete mastery of the language. 'Oh! in my case,' he answered, 'it is easily explained, for before this war I lived quietly during many years in Scotland, and married a Scotch lassie.'

We spent that evening merrily in a café, with a party of Russian officers, who entertained us at supper, during which they endeavoured to persuade us to try the (to us) novel mixture of champagne and porter (XX). But for the politeness of these officers, we should have gone supperless to bed, for the café attendants were not overcivil or attentive to our wants, and appeared to value the English current coin less than the much-thumbed, dirty Russian rouble notes, and to heed our requests, mildly expressed, less than the frowns and peremptory orders of their own officers.

CHAPTER VII.

Ride to Yalta—Early Start—Tartar Villages and Vineyards—Ruined Villas—Alupka—Prince Woronsoff's Palace—Oreander, the Summer Palace of the Empress—The Emperor's Room—Yalta—Rides without Passports—Cossacks—Pass of Coralie—Jewish town of Mungoup Kalch—Valley of the Tchernaya—Sebastopol in Ruins.

SHORTLY after our return from Simpheropol we made up another party to take a three days' ride along the southern coast. There were four of us,* and we decided to follow the Woronsoff road, and ride as far as Yalta, or farther, should our short leave allow us.

We started very early in the morning, to make the most of time, and as we rode along the Baidar valley the sun, just peeping over the distant hills, tipped with golden hues the forest trees, clothed luxuriantly in their young foliage, and caused the dewdrops, clinging to each blade of grass that carpeted the earth, to sparkle like brilliants. The still air, laden with the scent of violets which grew in wild abundance, resounded with the

* Burroughs, Blake, and Munro, of the 93rd, and Williams, of the commissariat. Blake and Williams are long since dead.

melody of many birds, which, perched on every twig and spray, and hidden in the thick, leafy hedges, poured forth their gladsome morning song. We, young, full of health, and free from care, rode on in the full enjoyment of the beautiful objects around us, and of the sweet sounds that fell upon our ears.

At the southern extremity of the Baidar valley, which I have described as being shut in by lofty hills, the road ascended gradually for some miles, winding round hill and spur, all clothed with forest trees, and passing over the summit of the chain of hills, through a deep rent (the Pass of Phoros) spanned by a noble arch of masonry, descended due south, through wild and rocky ground, to the shores of the Black Sea, and then, turning east, ran along a narrow stretch of undulating plain lying between the sea-shore and a long line of noble cliffs.

After clearing the broken, rocky ground, and riding some miles due east, we found that the plain became wider and more open, though it still retained its undulating character. On its northern margin, to our left, opened many little valleys, on whose densely-wooded slopes we could discern the red-tiled roofs of Tartar villages, and on the level space below extensive vineyards planted on either side of the little streams, which, rising in the mountain range above, had found a rocky channel for themselves through which they sought the sea. On the south side of the plain, perched on little wooded heights and knolls, were many handsome villas, the summer retreats of the Russian nobility.

We visited several of them, but found them tenantless. They were, or rather had been, comfortable, if not luxurious, dwellings, and were surrounded by extensive grounds, laid out in orchards, vineyards, shrubberies, and flower gardens. But all around there were evidences of wanton, wilful destruction. The buildings themselves were in a ruinous condition, the fruit-trees cut and injured, the vines, torn from their trellis work, were creeping along the ground, and the shrubberies and flower-gardens were trampled down and choked with weeds; gates were broken from their hinges, classic statues, broken and torn down from their pedestals, were thrown amongst the shrubs and weeds, and the wreck of marble fountains lay around. Not a living thing was visible, not even a dog was there to bark a welcome or resent intrusion!

Within the houses we found the same ruin and desolation. The handsome furniture was broken and thrown about, pianos were destroyed, pier-glasses, torn from the walls, were smashed in pieces; books and music, and little articles of ornament, which betokened women's presence, were heaped together on the polished oaken floor. Why and wherefore all this wreck and ruin, and by whom the savagery was perpetrated, was never known. It was not by the British soldier, for he was never there, and besides he is not much given to vent his anger in this way, or to find pleasure in wantonly destroying what he does not require or cannot carry away with him. Our allies were blamed, perhaps unjustly; but, by whomsoever it was done, it was done completely.

Towards evening we reached the village of Alupka, and found accommodation at the little roadside inn, kept by an Englishwoman, daughter of an English *femme de chambre*, brought out years ago by the Woronsoff family. She was a child at the time of her arrival in the Crimea, but in her maidenhood had married a Russian domestic—probably a serf—and, though still speaking her mother tongue, had quite forgotten tidy English ways, had assumed the customs and manners of her new home and people, and kept her house as comfortless as any other Russian wayside inn. However, she gave us accommodation and food, such as they were; but while informing us of her English origin—which she did not do at first—she had no smile of welcome for her countrymen, and showed no pleasure at the sight of the red jacket which probably was once familiar to her.

Having deposited our greatcoats and saddle-flaps in the public room, the only one available for visitors, and having stabled and fed our own horses, we started to visit the palace of Prince Woronsoff, which is within a short distance of the inn. The palace is a large, irregular pile of buildings, partly of gothic and partly of Saracenic architecture. It has a dark and gloomy appearance externally, due in a great measure, I think, to the dark-green sandstone of which it is constructed. The rooms which we were allowed to inspect are small and badly-lighted by small, irregular-shaped windows. The library is large and well stocked with many handsomely bound books, arranged in oaken cases, which, being closed and locked, prevented our ascertaining the character of the literature or the languages in which the books are written. The grounds around the palace are extensive, well laid out, and watered by several artificial streams of crystal water rippling through pebbly channels and flowing into the Black Sea. We had not the pleasure of seeing our countryman, the Scotch gardener, by whom the grounds and gardens were arranged, and under whose care and management they were at the time of our visit.

In the evening we returned to our inn, and, after a late dinner and post-prandial pipe, stretched ourselves on the couches in the dining-room, on which were spread cushions covered with strong-smelling leather and of very doubtful cleanliness. Being tired with our day's ride and excitement, we were soon asleep.

There are no bed-rooms in the Russian wayside inns, and generally only one public room, which all travellers must share, and make the most of its accommodation. Baths and basins are things unknown, but on the early morrow we used the Black Sea as our bath.

We were early in the saddle next day, and rode

along the coast, following an excellent road, which winds through thickly-wooded valleys, between groups of huge ivy-covered rocks heaped fantastically upon each other, and under the shadow of thick hedgerows of pomegranate and myrtle, the former bright with its large single scarlet flowers, and the latter with its bunches of modest white blossom.

By noon we arrived at Oreander, the summer palace of the Empress. Without hesitation, we entered the grounds, rode up the avenue to the main entrance, and, fastening our horses to the trees, sought permission to enter, having heard from our landlady of the previous day that visitors were admitted. The door was thrown open by an aged domestic, who, bowing low, said in German that 'it was the Empress's pleasure that English officers should be allowed every opportunity and facility to inspect both the palace and the grounds, and that each one who sought the privilege should only be requested to sign his name and rank in the hall book.' This done, we were conducted from room to room, admiring everything, but surprised at the simplicity apparent in all arrangements. The public rooms were large and lofty, with inlaid oaken floor and carved oaken ceilings, and plainly furnished. Her Majesty the Empress's private rooms were in no way superior to the ordinary boudoir and bed-room of an English gentlewoman; and the Emperor's bedroom was small, uncarpeted, and furnished very much in the style of an English subaltern's barrack-room, even to the little narrow iron cot.

We did not inspect the grounds, as it was late in the afternoon, and we were desirous of reaching Yalta before evening. Mounting our horses, therefore, we followed the road, and riding leisurely, so as to enjoy the picturesque scenery on either side of it, and in the far distance also, reached Yalta late in the afternoon. This town, or rather small straggling village, is prettily situated at the head of a wide open bay, the site having been selected as a convenient and suitable one for those engaged in the fisheries along the southern coast—at least, so we were informed on the spot.

Riding straight up to the hotel or inn—a better one than usual, as far as external appearance went, and, as we found, affording superior accommodation to those we had hitherto visited —we drew rein at the entrance. A buxom dame came forth to meet us on the threshold. Smiling over her whole face, and holding out both hands, she gave us a kindly welcome, and addressed us in English as follows:

'How are you, gentlemen? I am so glad to see you, for you bring with you memories of the old home and of old friends. Come in, and I'll order dinner for you, and give you *cod's head and oyster sauce* just as if you were at home.'

It was pleasant to be greeted thus, and so unexpectedly, in our own English, spoken fluently. We asked her history, and heard that she had come out from home, as a young woman, with her

H

father, who had been a carpenter in the service of Prince Woronsoff; that she had married a Russian freedman shortly after arrival; and that she was now well-to-do and mistress of the inn. But, though prosperous and contented, she still remembered with affection, and longed to re-visit, her old English home.

There was literally nothing to be done or seen at Yalta. Stagnation, perhaps temporary, owing to the war, seemed to rest on all around and in the place. The few people whom we met moved listlessly about; if free from care, apparently oppressed by idleness. There was no stir, no work, no active life. Even the young were silent, for we saw no boys at play, and heard no children's merry noise and laughter; there was no sound even to break the stillness, except the ripple of the little wavelets on the shingly beach beneath the village, and as the shades of evening settled down, we ourselves, oppressed by a feeling of weariness, sought our inn and the promised dinner, which we found ready, and which the good landlady herself served up in fair old English fashion, and with an evident desire to please.

On the morrow we were stirring early, having to ride the whole distance back to camp in one day. This we accomplished, arriving late at Kamara, exhausted by the heat, which was excessive, and by a ride of thirty miles, but delighted with all we had seen.

As we became familiar with the geography of the surrounding country and with the Tartar population, we made many other short excursions, and as these were often got up on the spur of the moment, so to speak, we forgot to apply for the needful passport. On the very first occasion on which we went without this necessary document we stumbled on a Cossack picket, which barred the way at once, one of the picket making signs at the same time, which at first we failed to understand. But it occurred to one of our party that he was demanding the passport; so, feeling in his pocket, he drew forth an old official letter, and handed it to the Cossack who was making himself most conspicuous by gesticulation. He took and opened the letter, and, holding it upside down, gravely pretended to read. The perusal of the document seemed to satisfy him, for he returned it with a reverential bow or nod, and let us pass. In other rides, however, we found an English silver coin slipped into the Cossack's dirty hand as useful and efficacious as a Russian passport or an English official letter.

Those Cossacks were the dirtiest human beings I ever saw in any part of the world. They were clad in greasy sheepskin coats, coarse, wide, woollen trousers, and long leather boots. On their heads they wore flat sheepskin caps. Their hair and beards were thick and matted, and seemed to be one continuous growth. Their faces, begrimed with dirt, were broad and flat, with high cheek-bones, and small, snub noses; and their small, restless, grey eyes appeared to be always half closed. They were not pleasant-looking fellows, more especially as they were armed to the teeth, while we were without weapon of any kind. I always felt that it would not have been prudent to run the risk of meeting them quite alone, and in an out-of-the-way corner.

About six or seven miles from our camp was the Pass of Coralie, a wild, deep, winding, rocky glen, shut in by lofty, almost perpendicular cliffs, deeply serrated from top to bottom on both sides of the pass, just as if the hill through which the path runs had been suddenly rent asunder by some powerful convulsion of Nature.

A good road runs along the bottom of the pass, and affords an easier route for wheeled traffic from the southern coast to the interior than the road leading from Sebastopol and the Valley of the Tchernaya up the Mackenzie heights. Perched upon the summit of the eastern cliff, almost hanging on the very edge of the dizzy height, and looking as if about to topple over and down into the abyss below, is the Jewish town of Mungoup Kaleh, alluded to in the preceding chapter.

A party of us rode through the pass, and afterwards, by a narrow zigzag path cut in the rock, up to the town. We did not meet a living thing or hear a sound of life therein. It was like a city of the dead, and the silence that reigned in the long street, and within the courts and houses, and the large burial-ground close to the wall, overcrowded with old, grey tombstones, heightened this impression, and made one hasten away from the dreary spot.

I spent one day only amidst the ruins of Sebastopol. It was such a mournful visit that I never went thither again, for as I moved along the desolate streets and amongst the shattered, crumbling buildings, I could not help feeling that all the destruction and ruin had been in a great measure the doing of my own people. Sebastopol in ruins was one of the saddest sights I ever saw.

I often wandered about the Valley of the Tchernaya, and along both shores of the harbour of Sebastopol, visited the great forts Nicholas and Alexander, and the chambers and galleries cut in face of the northern cliffs. But my chief object in these wanderings was to collect fossil shells, which are to be found in great numbers and of different varieties imbedded in the sandstone rock, from which they are easily removed.

CHAPTER VIII.

Tartar arabah Driver—Assault by a Man of 93rd—Threats—Warning—Sixteen Months Afterwards—A Struggle—Sudden Death—Court-Martial—Charge of Murder—Medical Evidence—Guilty of Homicide—Penal Servitude—Communication from Prison Official Sixteen Years Afterwards.

I INCLUDE in my reminiscences the details of an unfortunate affair which occurred in the regiment in the spring of 1856, and which necessitated the assembly of a general court-martial, before which the medical evidence required was given by myself. For reasons which I will explain further on in this chapter, the affair made a great impression on myself and on all connected with the regiment. There is no one serving with the regiment now, however, who is aware of all the facts, though there are still two officers present with it who may remember the court-martial.

On landing in the Crimea in the autumn of 1854, the army was almost, if not quite, without the means of transport. But the Tartars either came forward voluntarily or were pressed into our service with their arabahs or bullock-carts for the purpose of conveying supplies of food for the troops, grain for the horses, and the few hospital and other tents which were allowed to be carried with the army.

As a rule, these Tartars were treated with every kindness, but in one or two instances may have been rather roughly handled by individual soldiers, who possibly thought that they were giving their services unwillingly because they did not understand what was said to, or required of, them; and possibly, too, because our men had grown irritable and impatient from inaction and illness in Bulgaria, and from exposure, over-fatigue, and semi-starvation after landing in the Crimea.

There was one, perhaps there were several; but I know there was at least one of these Tartars, with his arabah, attached to my regiment to carry our food supplies, the meat portion of which was under the charge of one of the regimental butchers.

The day after our arrival at Balaklava, I was standing near the hospital tent, when I saw a Tartar, a slight young lad, running towards me, pursued, and being rapidly overtaken, by a soldier of the regiment, who carried and brandished a large stick.

The Tartar threw himself on the ground before me, and clasped my knees, just in time to escape a savage blow aimed at him by his pursuer, and which, had it taken effect, might have killed, or at least seriously injured, him. The soldier, quite regardless of the presence of an officer—for he was in a perfect frenzy of rage—seized the trembling Tartar by the throat, and, uttering a dreadful oath, threatened to kill him. I immediately called to a non-commissioned officer and several privates who were standing near to secure the madman, for such he was at that moment, and they succeeded in doing so, but with difficulty.

On looking down at the unfortunate Tartar, who still clung to my knees, I saw that blood was flowing from his nose and mouth, and that he bore several marks of blows upon his face. I pointed to the poor lad, who was trembling in every limb, and asked the soldier 'if he had inflicted the injuries.' He at once replied,

'Yes; and he had better keep clear of me, for I'll kill him, if I ever catch him.' And then he struggled with the men who held him, to free himself and put his threat into execution.

I desired the non-commissioned officer to take the man off to the guard-tent, and there to hand him over as a prisoner; but, at the same time, remarked to the man himself that 'it was a cowardly thing to strike a creature who did not understand him, and who was but as a child in size and strength compared with himself; and that for the future he had better try to curb his temper, or some day, when in a fit of passion, he would commit murder, and be hanged.' He answered, savagely,

'I don't care.'

He was a butcher by trade, a powerful, hulking fellow, with a hard, cruel expression on his otherwise handsome, swarthy face. He was punished next day, both for his insubordinate behaviour to an officer, and for his cruel treatment of the poor native.

Even after sending the soldier to the guard-tent, I had some difficulty in allaying the fears of the Tartar lad, but succeeded at last, and passed him safely beyond our lines. He disappeared, and I never saw or heard of him again.

The soldier did not come under my notice again during the first year we were in the Crimea, and not indeed until the spring of 1856, when I was one day called suddenly to see a man of the regiment who, I was informed, had either been stunned or killed in a fight with another man, also of the regiment. On arriving at the spot where the fight had taken place, I found a man lying on the ground—dead, and, on looking up, was startled to see, standing close by as a prisoner, the very man from whose fury I had protected the Tartar little more than a year previously.

I repeat that I was startled; for the former savage scene came before me, and I recalled to memory the warning I had then given him, 'to try to curb his temper, or some day he would commit murder;' and I remembered his answer, too: 'I don't care.' And now there appeared to be every probability that he had killed the man lying dead on the ground, almost at his feet, at least, nearly a certainty that he would be tried on a charge of murder. And he *was* tried on that charge; for *he* had forced a quarrel on his unwilling comrade, had roused his anger by bitter taunts, and was the first to close in the struggle which had ended so fatally. The medical evidence which I was able to give at his trial, however, saved him from being found guilty of murder; but, strange to say, his own words condemned him. Six little words, uttered in his anger as he was being marched as a prisoner from the scene of the struggle to the guard-room, were quoted in evidence against him, and he was found guilty of 'CULPABLE HOMICIDE,' and sentenced to penal servitude.

This happened twenty-seven years ago, but the whole occurrence and everything connected with the assault upon the Tartar, the fight, and the trial, are as fresh in my memory to-day as if all had happened yesterday.

On entering the hut where the court-martial was assembled, I looked round, and my eye fell upon the prisoner. He was a pitiable object to look at, an image of despair, and apparently overwhelmed with a horrible fear. His limbs trembled, as if scarce able to sustain the weight of his body, although it was bent and shrunken like that of an old man. His face was pale and haggard, his teeth were firmly clenched, and his lips, drawn tightly over them, twitched horribly, and the muscles of his neck jerked his head backwards convulsively. Poor wretch! he was a coward, after all.

He did not see me—at least, he did not look at me—as I entered the hut and took my place at the bottom of the table, almost facing him; but, when he heard my voice, he raised his bloodshot eyes and cast a wild, imploring look on me for just a moment, as if to entreat me to have mercy, and then he turned his eyes upon the ground again, and inclined his trembling, jerking head towards me, as if to catch my words.

My evidence was very short and very simple. I stated that I had most carefully examined the body of the dead man, and found thereon no mark of violence whatever, no swelling, no scratch, not even a trace of discolouration, to denote the pressure of an arm or hand, but that, on further examination, I found the heart and large artery close to the heart extensively diseased, to such an extent that any powerful emotion, such as a fit of anger, might have arrested the action of the one or caused rupture of the other, and so sudden death.

After a short pause, and in reply to a question of the court, I stated that ' in my opinion sudden cessation of the action of a diseased heart had been the immediate cause of death, and that a fit of anger, followed by sudden and powerful bodily exertion, had been the remote cause; but that had his anger not been roused, and had he avoided sudden great exertion, the man now dead might have been living still.'

When I had ceased to speak, there was a little stir amongst the members of the court, expressive, as I thought, of relief from a painful position and from a great responsibility, and, as I turned to leave the hut, by permission of the president, the wretched prisoner stood erect for a moment, and, through tears that glistened in his eyes, cast a look of gratitude upon me, as if he felt that my evidence would clear him of the awful crime of murder, and at least save his life.

I have said, however, that six little words, spoken incautiously, and before his wrath had subsided, were brought in evidence against him, and condemned him. As he was being marched to the guard-room from the scene of the struggle, one of the escort said to him, 'I am afraid you've killed him,' and in reply the prisoner said, loud and angrily, and with horrible profanity, 'I hope to God I have!'

The finding and the sentence of the court were no doubt right—'Not guilty of murder, but guilty of culpable homicide.' Though he did not kill his enemy, there is little doubt he would have done so if he could; in his blind, ungovernable wrath, his desire, his intention was to take life; but he was mercifully saved from the actual commission of murder by the hand of God. He was sent home to undergo the penal servitude to which he was sentenced—for twenty-one years.

Sixteen years afterwards, on my return to England from India, I received a letter from an official of one of our convict prisons, informing me that a convict, then undergoing penal servitude, often spoke of me with gratitude and affection as having been the means on one occasion of saving him from the possible commission of a great crime, and on another occasion of having, by my medical evidence before a court-martial, saved him from sentence of death. In the same letter a message was sent to me from the poor fellow, to the effect that he was now a changed man, that he could control his temper, and that he was looking forward hopefully to being of some use on his release, whenever that might happen. More than that I have not heard either of or from him.

CHAPTER IX.

Embark for England, June, '56—Land in Portsmouth, July, '56—Aldershot—Her Majesty's Inspection—Dover—Prepare for India—Sudden Orders for China—Presentation of new Colours—Head-quarters, under Leith Hay, sail for China—Arrive at the Cape—Ordered to Calcutta—Calcutta—Sir Colin's Visit—Chinsurah—Cawnpore.

IN June, 1856, the regiment embarked at Kamiesch Bay on board H.M.S. *Sidon*, Captain Inglefield (now Admiral Sir E. Inglefield), and sailed for England.

We had a pleasant voyage, but were much crowded on board. The officers of the regiment were distributed as follows: The seniors messed with the captain, the next in seniority with the ward-room officers, and the juniors with the midshipmen. At night we slept in cots or hammocks slung between decks, and several of us on our own bedding laid out under a gun.

The men slept on deck in their uniform, which they divested themselves of only once during the voyage, and that was to bathe in the sea, the captain kindly stopping the ship to enable us to do so.

We landed at Portsmouth in July, and proceeded thence by rail to Aldershot, where, on the day after our arrival, the regiment, with a number of other corps (which had landed from the Crimea before us), were reviewed by Her Majesty the Queen, accompanied by the Prince Consort.

From Aldershot, a few days after the review, we proceeded by rail to Dover, and were encamped on the western heights with the 42nd Royal Highlanders, and several other corps. What the object was for which this encampment was formed I never could understand, unless it was to give the people, and especially the Londoners, who came down in crowds, an opportunity of seeing some five thousand men in camp, a sight which in those days was very rare.

We remained in camp until the end of September, when part of the regiment (head-quarters) was ordered to occupy the Castle, and four companies the Western Heights Barracks. After settling in quarters, we commenced to make our preparations for service in India, for which part of Her Majesty's dominions we had been detailed before leaving the Crimea, and whither we expected to proceed during the winter of 1856–7.

Early in the spring of 1857, however, the regiment received sudden orders to prepare for immediate service in China, as war with that nation had been determined upon.

It was decided that before leaving England the regiment should receive new colours, and these

H.R.H. the Duke of Cambridge consented to present, as the regiment had formed part of his division in the Crimea. This imposing ceremony was performed in May, 1857, and was followed by certain festivities customary on such an occasion.

A few days thereafter the regiment proceeded by rail to Portsmouth, and on June 1 three companies under Lieutenant-Colonel the Honourable Adrian Hope were conveyed by sea to Plymouth, embarked in H.M. troopship *Belleisle*, and sailed for China.

On the 16th of the same month the headquarters of the regiment under Lieutenant-Colonel Leith Hay embarked at Portsmouth in the hired steam transport *Mauritius*, Commander Donald Cruickshank, and on the morning of the 17th steamed out from Spithead for China also.

A few days before embarkation the regiment was paraded in the Clarence victualling yard, Gosport, for Her Majesty's inspection. The Queen on that occasion was pleased to express her satisfaction at the appearance of the regiment, and to wish us God's speed.

We commenced our voyage with pleasant weather, but though the *Mauritius* was a full-rigged ship, with only auxiliary steam power, the wind did not admit of our making sail, and we went under steam only. But, as she did not carry coal sufficient for a long voyage, we were obliged to call at the island of St. Vincent, one of the Cape De Verde group, and the coaling dépôt of the West Indian and South American Lines, for a supply, to enable us, if necessary, to steam the whole way to the Cape.

While at St. Vincent, the consul, Mr. Miller, received us kindly, inviting several of us to his house, and entertaining us hospitably. He was the only Englishman, indeed the only white man, on that side of the island where the coaling depôt was established. His very comfortable cottage was situated high up on the side of the hill overlooking the anchorage, and from the summit of the hill a good bird's-eye view of the whole group of islands could be obtained; but it does not repay one for the trouble and labour of the ascent. After struggling to the highest point and looking round, I was constrained to acknowledge that I had never seen anything that appeared so like desolation.

In the course of conversation, our host described to me the horrors which had attended an outbreak of cholera amongst his negroes some years previously. They died in such numbers that at last the few survivors refused to dig graves for the dead. He was consequently obliged to construct a large funeral pyre, on which the dead were placed. Having set fire to this he rode off to his home; but before entering the house he turned to look at the conflagration, and, as he did so, saw, or thought he saw, one of the dead sit bolt upright in the midst of the flames. He was, of course, much shocked, and accused himself of having been too hasty in disposing of the dead, and told me that the terrible sight was constantly recurring to his memory, and caused him great uneasiness.

I explained to him, to his satisfaction and comfort, that what he had seen was, I had no doubt, a dead body contorted into a sitting posture, or what appeared to him a sitting posture, by the sudden shrivelling or contraction of that portion of skin in front of the body over which the flames had first swept. I further explained to him that if the man had only been in a state of syncope or collapse, he would have been smothered by the dense pungent wood-smoke long before the flames could have reached him.

If my visit to St. Vincent afforded no other pleasure, it gave me the opportunity of removing a painful doubt and calming the troubled conscience (troubled unnecessarily) of our host.

Having taken in a supply of coals as quickly as possible, at my urgent entreaty, we proceeded on our voyage. The urgency of my entreaty was caused by the arrival of one of the South American liners, with yellow fever on board; and, as I had had some experience of this terrible disease previously, I dreaded the possibility of its appearing in our ship, with its freight of upwards of eight hundred men.

From St. Vincent we carried fine weather with us until we got far enough south to meet the south-east trade and a heavy sea. Having made sufficient southing, we bore up for the Cape, still under steam, but with sails set for the first time during this part of the voyage, not so much to increase our speed, as to steady the ship, and prevent her rolling in the high seas, which struck her almost abeam.

When nearing the Cape, a small brig, racing before the trade, passed close to us, and surprised us not a little by letting fly her topsails, and dipping her English ensign repeatedly. These complimentary proceedings on the part of the brig gave rise to all sorts of surmises amongst us, and a feeling became prevalent (I do not know with whom it originated) that we should hear some startling news on arrival at the Cape; probably an order cancelling our further voyage to China. Several bets were made upon the subject, and I had to pay one of £5 because we did *not* continue our voyage to the celestial empire; and I confess I was very glad to pay it.

After anchoring in Simon's Bay, we found that the *Belleisle* was there, the naval officer who boarded our ship having informed us of this, and also of the mutiny of the Bengal Native Army. We had not been many minutes at anchor before Colonel Adrian Hope, with several officers of his detachment, came on board our ship, our arrival having been intimated to him by our buglers sounding the regimental call. From Hope we received a confirmation of the report of the mutiny in Bengal, and from him also first heard that orders from the Governor of Bombay had been received at the Cape to send the 93rd on to Calcutta, instead of to China. This probably was the news which the master of the little brig had meant to prepare us for by his signals.

The *Belleisle* sailed next day, and as soon as we had taken in a supply of coal we followed.

On the second day after leaving Simon's Bay, one blade of our screw gave way, and sank. The loss of this interfered with the ship's speed in a heavy sea, and rendered it necessary for us to run for the Mauritius, in the hope that we might there be able to fix a new blade; but, on arrival at Port Louis, we found that it would not be possible to do so, therefore, after taking in a further supply of coal, we steamed for Calcutta. To our great surprise and relief, we found that in smooth water our one blade propelled the ship nearly as fast as the two blades had done in a rough sea.

We entered the Bay of Bengal early in September, before the south-east monsoon had quite subsided. Consequently we had occasional heavy rain, with lightning and thunder, during the day, and magnificent meteoric displays at night.

One very dark night, while several of us were seated on deck, the ship was suddenly brilliantly illuminated, every spar and rope standing out in clear relief. Turning quickly in the direction from whence the light appeared to shine, I saw a meteoric body, of great size and of the brightest green colour, shooting rapidly from east to west, at some distance astern of the vessel. I never saw so large a meteor, or one of the same colour, or one that shone with such intense brilliancy. It was visible for several seconds, and disappeared suddenly, rendering the darkness deeper than before, and causing us to feel eerie and uncomfortable.

On September 20 (the anniversary of the battle of the Alma), we entered the Hoogley, and as we steamed up the river, and past Garden Reach to the anchorage, ladies and gentlemen waved a welcome to us from the balconies of the palatial residences which lined the eastern bank. We, in return for their kind reception, treated them to pipe music, which, though it might not have been appreciated by all, was listened to by some with pleasure as the sounds were heard in Calcutta probably for the first time, and brought back to their minds long-forgotten memories of their old home.

Very shortly after we had come to anchor, Sir Colin Campbell came on board. His appearance was a great surprise to us, for we were not aware of his presence in India, or of his having been appointed commander-in-chief. He was evidently very glad to see us, not only for the sake of auld lang syne in the Crimea, but also because nearly eleven hundred British soldiers, veterans in splendid health and condition, increased his power and immensely strengthened his hands.

We received orders to land and store our heavy baggage in Calcutta forthwith, retaining only such things as were absolutely necessary for field service. Accordingly all impedimenta were quickly sent ashore, and a large party of the regiment, dressed in their kilts, was landed, so as to get the baggage stored without delay.

This party caused quite a sensation in the city of palaces, for a kilted soldier had never been seen there before. The natives gazed in silent wonder at the peculiar dress and the stalwart figures of the new sahibs, or gagra wallahs (petticoat men) as they called them; and Scotchmen, who had been long exiled from home, rose from their desks, and came out and stood at the doors of their offices to look with feelings of pride at their countrymen, and listen, with a smile of pleasure on their faces, to the sound of their own northern tongue long unfamiliar to their ears. Some even brought out tankards of cool beer and invited the men, as they passed along, to drink, and *they* certainly required no pressing, for the sun was hot and exercise made them thirsty, or 'gey an' drouthy,' according to their own vernacular.

To my great surprise I found an old schoolfellow in Calcutta, James Hall, now laird of a handsome property in Argyllshire. We then and there renewed our schoolboy friendship, have kept up a constant communication ever since, and of late years I have often been a guest in his hospitable home, and his companion on the moors on the 12th.

After we had succeeded in relieving the Residency of Lucknow, I wrote him a short description of the part played by the 93rd in the operations, and he has several times told me that he still has that letter in his possession. It was one of the first private letters, giving an account of the fighting, that reached Calcutta, and my friend received it while in the midst of a party of Scotchmen, to whom he at once read it aloud, and by whom the information which it contained was received with a storm of cheers.

Having stored our baggage, the regiment was sent up to Chinsurah, and from thence proceeded by detachments to Cawnpore. There the regimental head-quarters staff remained during several days in order to allow the different detachments to meet, so as to cross the Ganges into Oude in an imposing body.

While at Cawnpore numbers of us visited Wheeler's entrenchments, the building in which the women and children had been butchered, and the well into which their bodies had been thrown. The slaughter-house had not at the time been quite cleared out, nor the well filled up. The floor of the former was covered over with scraps of women's dresses, and women and children's slippers and shoes, amongst which I observed long locks of dark and golden hair. There were stains of blood still visible upon the floor and on the whitewashed walls; but there was one stain upon the wall the sight of which sickened me. About six feet from the floor a large, sharp hook was fixed into the wall, which, on examining, I found to be covered with congealed blood, and on the wall immediately round it were many marks of blood which, on close inspection, I saw were the prints of infant hands. Evidently a wounded child had been hung upon the hook, and the poor thing, in its feeble struggles, had left the impress of its little bleeding fingers on the wall. This was horrible to think of or to look at, so I hurried from the room.

But as I was passing out of the enclosure my attention was attracted by a knot of Europeans and a number of natives standing round a wooden frame-work, from the cross-beam of which dangled two looped cords, and immediately beneath which stood two wooden boxes. On inquiry I learned that two of the murderers of the women and children had just been condemned to death, and that they were to expiate their guilt on the gallows erected on the scene of their brutal crime.

In my horror and anger at what I had just seen, I determined to remain and witness the execution, hoping that one of the monsters might be he who had tortured the child. The wretches were brought into the enclosure with their hands pinioned behind their backs, and made to mount upon the wooden boxes with their faces turned to the building in which they had perpetrated the murders; the ropes were then adjusted and drawn tight around their necks, the boxes kicked without ceremony from beneath their feet, and, after a few convulsive struggles, they were dead.

I had never seen a human being hanged before, and, though at any other time I would have avoided such a sight, on that occasion I remained to look on without the least feeling of pity or compassion. Many of the men of the regiment visited the slaughter-house and well, and I believe what they there saw filled their hearts with bitter hatred, with a burning desire for revenge, and it was long before that feeling of hatred was allayed or the desire for vengeance satiated.

The cantonment of Cawnpore was then a scene of ruin and desolation, for not a house which had been occupied by a European had escaped destruction. Many years afterwards I revisited the station, but did not recognize the place, so completely was it altered and improved. The grounds where the slaughter-house had stood were laid out as extensive gardens, and, over the spot where the well had been, I found a beautiful statue of a woman, with palm leaves in her hands, head bent and eyes cast upon the ground, as if sorrowing over the dead below. The statue is surrounded and hidden from general view by a high fretwork wall, which in my humble opinion is a mistake. It should stand exposed to view, so that it might be a prominent object to attract every eye, and show to the natives of India how Englishmen mourn for the innocents who met a cruel death, and how they respect and cherish the memory of those helpless ones who perished near the spot in the mutiny of 1857.

CHAPTER X.

Cases of Presentiment—The little Army for the Relief of Lucknow—Parade for Sir Colin—His Address to the 93rd—Lord Sandhurst—Sir Hope Grant—9th Lancers—The Advance—Death of Lumsden and Dalzell—Funeral Services at Midnight—Recognising an old brother Officer by his Wounds—Meeting a relative of Lumsden's, and describing his Death and Burial.

I FIND in my journal several remarkable examples of presentiment, or foreknowledge, of death described which came under my own observation, and it appears to me that there is close affinity, if not actual identity, between the conditions, mental and physical, under which presentiments and nostalgia (or home-sickness) occur. Of this latter distressing disease also several interesting examples are noted.

Both are attributable to a greater or less degree of prostration of the nervous system, and consequent physical exhaustion, or, on the other hand, physical exhaustion depressing the nervous system; and either condition, or both, may be induced by the immediate presence of danger, by frequent recurrence of danger, or by prolonged labour or excitement either of mind or body. It is hardly possible that the conditions under which presentiments or nostalgia occur ever do or can arise during perfect health and vigour. They result from some previous derangement, either mental or physical.

My opportunities of observation have led me to believe that, though a presentiment of approaching death may have complete hold of a man's mind, it does not influence his conduct when in the presence of danger, or when life may be imperilled, or in any way prevent his acting with calmness, courage, and discretion under any circumstances, even of the most momentous nature, and that this is equally true of men under the influence of nostalgia, even complicated with delusion.

I propose to give the details of several cases of presentiment and nostalgia which are described in my journal, and which are written at some length, affording interesting information of some great events which occurred under my own observation, and in which the friends to whom I shall allude were actors. In each case I shall state what I find described as to the fulfilment of the presentiment, and the result of the nostalgic condition.

Besides the assistance which my journal affords me, I have a perfect recollection of the different cases, and, without reference to notes, could give the particulars connected with each from memory alone.

The little army assembled for the relief of the Residency of Lucknow in November, 1857, paraded for the inspection of Sir Colin Campbell, the Commander-in-chief, on the evening of the 13th of the month, on the plain around the Alum Bagh, some miles to the west of the city of Lucknow. It mustered scarce five thousand men, including all arms of the service, both European and native, and also the Naval Brigade, under Peel. With this small force the brave old chief determined to cut his way through the besieging army of about fifty thousand regularly-trained native soldiers by which the Residency was completely surrounded, and rescue our countrymen and women shut up within their imperfect defences, hardly pressed by the enemy, and sorely straitened for food.

Of the five thousand men composing Sir Colin's army, all were veteran troops, who had seen war already, some in the Crimea, and others during the first stage of the mutiny, and especially at the siege and capture of Delhi. The infantry was made up of the wrecks of several regiments which had already done splendid service at Delhi and elsewhere, of detachments of several other British regiments which had been recalled when on their way to China, portions of which were already within the Residency, having entered it with Havelock's column, of one or two weak Sikh battalions, and of one complete regiment which had just arrived from England. This regiment, the 93rd Sutherland Highlanders, stood in column on the extreme left of the line. It was a solid mass of upwards of one thousand men, all in the very prime of manhood, in magnificent condition, and dressed in the full Highland costume. It had been one of the regiments of the Crimean Highland brigade.

As the old chief rode along the line, commencing from the right, the men who did not know him, or, at least, who had never served under his command, scanned with eager eyes his bearing and appearance, but allowed him to pass along their front in silence. As he approached the solid mass of Highlanders, however, who knew him well, he was received with a shout of welcome, which he acknowledged by a salute, and then addressed them thus:—

'My lads, there will be work of difficulty and danger to be done to-morrow, for we must relieve our countrymen and countrywomen shut up in the Residency, but I rely upon you.'

Ipsissima verba, for I was standing close to him, and heard him speak them in his own peculiarly quick, sharp way. He was answered by another shout, and then the whole line followed the example and cheered right lustily; and the old chief, as he rode away, must have felt that his little army was in 'good trim,' ready to follow him wherever he might lead, or advance whithersoever he might point the way.

Years afterwards I heard a distinguished general officer, Lord Sandhurst, say that Sir Colin never got sufficient credit for his daring and brilliant generalship on that occasion. With a small force hurriedly collected he had advanced to attack an army in position ten times the strength of that he led, knowing that in his rear there was another army five times as numerous as his own, well organised, and with a powerful artillery.

I omitted to mention that besides infantry Sir Colin had, on that occasion, a brigade of cavalry, of which one regiment only was European lancers. The 9th Lancers was the smartest cavalry regiment that I ever saw on active service; they were splendidly mounted on beautiful little arabs, and while on service in the field the men always turned out as well-dressed, and with their accoutrements and horse equipment as clean and trim, as if they had been in quarters.

The colonel of the regiment was the late Sir Hope Grant, as grand a soldier as ever lived. During the operations for the relief, however, he was not in command of his regiment, but either of the whole cavalry brigade, or of the whole force under Sir Colin's own immediate direction.

The artillery consisted of several batteries (three, I think) of horse artillery, one of field artillery, and Peel's heavier guns. I do not profess to be exact, however, for I do not intend or presume to write a description of the military operations for the relief of the Residency, but only to describe several incidents which came under my own observation regarding some of my my friends and comrades.

On November 14, 1857, we were fighting early,

and by the close of the day had driven the enemy from several of his outer works and positions, and established ourselves close to his second line of defence. We passed that night and the following day and night in the open air without our tents, but sheltered to some extent from the heavy dews of night and from the blaze of the noonday sun—for even at that time of the year the weather was hot—by shady trees within the enclosure of the Martinière College. We were kept constantly on the alert, and frequently exchanged rifle-shots with the enemy, who was in considerable strength immediately in front of us.

During the night of the 15th, officers and men alike lay stretched upon the ground fully accoutered, so as to be ready for attack or for an early move on the morrow. Many were stirring and making ready long before sunrise of the 16th, and, as the air was chill and cold, we lighted little fires, and stood in groups around them. Three of us stood at one of these little fires and spoke of what all knew was to be enacted on that day, and though apparently cheery enough we spoke with bated breath, for no one can be insensible to the fact that a certain feeling of solemnity arises in the hearts of all during the hours which immediately precede a battle.

While we stood and conversed, the great bright orb of day appeared above the horizon suddenly, as is the case in those eastern and in all tropic climes, and we turned and gazed at it in silent admiration. Just then one of the group,

Captain John Lumsden, an officer of the Indian Army, but temporarily attached to the regiment to which we other two belonged, touched me on the arm, and said, in saddened voice, 'That is the last sunrise that many will see, and God knows to which of us three standing by this fire it may be the last.'

He was a Scotchman, a large, powerful man, and apparently in perfect health; but there was at the moment he spoke an expression of sadness, perhaps of anxious care, upon his face, for he had just returned hurriedly to India, having left his wife and bairns at home in Scotland; and there was a mournfulness not only in what he said, but in the manner of his saying it, which led me to believe that he was alluding to himself, and to the probability that it would be the last sunrise that he should see.

A few minutes after he had spoken, the order was given for the regiment to fall in preparatory to an advance, and, as we turned to obey, we three grasped hands and said good-bye.

We never met again, for scarce two hours thereafter two of the three were dead, killed in the very fore-front of the battle, behaving with a gallantry that called forth the admiration of those who followed them. The one (Lumsden) who, while we stood by the fire, had spoken of the probability of approaching death, was killed while endeavouring to break a way into the Secunder Bagh (a large fortified building held in strength by the enemy, and which it was necessary to take before we could advance nearer the Residency); and as he stood in front of all, looking the picture of a man and soldier, and thundering with a hatchet upon a barricaded window, a bullet, fired from a loop-hole just above him, passed through his heart. Thus were fulfilled his own prophetic words.

The other of the three who had stood by the fire (Captain Dalzell of the 93rd) was killed in the open plain which lay on the east side of the Secunder Bagh.

Poor Lumsden had evidently been under a presentiment of approaching death, yet was apparently in the full vigour of mind and body, and had not been exposed previously during the campaign to danger or to depressing influences either mental or physical. But doubtless he was distressed at having parted with his wife and little ones so short a time before, and under such circumstances; and this had made him thoughtful, anxious—the very conditions of mind and feeling under which, when in the midst of danger, a presentiment of approaching death might throw its shadow over a man.

This presentiment, however, had no power to turn him from the path of duty, to affect his courage, or to prevent his acting the part of a gallant soldier and brave leader when he stood in the actual presence of danger, of the very danger in which he felt he should meet his death.

Before describing other cases of presentiment, I must follow these two friends to the closing scene of all. That 16th of November was a bloody day, though crowned at its close by victory, and followed by the successful relief of the Residency. Until a late hour at night we were busy with the wounded; but, having finished this often sad and painful duty, I thought of my two dead brother-officers and resolved that their bodies should be laid together in one grave, which the pioneers of the regiment were directed to prepare close to the breach through which the stormers had entered the Secunder Bagh. When it was ready, I turned aside alone to take a last look at my old friends and comrades, and, gently raising the covering, looked down on the dead faces on which rested a calm and peaceful expression, sure evidence that there had not been any bodily pain or suffering as life passed away; but it occurred to me that, had it not been for the peculiar pallid hue which overshadowed the *rigid* features, one unaccustomed to such sights might have thought that he was looking upon the faces of men hushed in the sound sleep of weariness and not of death. But it *was* the sleep of death; so, tenderly replacing the covering on the faces I should never look on again in this life, I murmured a farewell until the time when we shall all stand in that Presence where shall be no darkness and no death, but life and light for ever.

We raised the bodies of our dead comrades from the ground, clad in uniform just as they had fallen and swathed in military great-coats, and silently and reverently lowered them into their

A SOLEMN FUNERAL.

last resting-place—dust to dust and ashes to ashes,—laying them side by side in death as they had stood in battle during life.

It was the most solemn and impressive funeral, even for soldiers', that I ever witnessed, for we buried them '*at the dead of night*' close to the breach and not far from the spot where both had fallen. Around us lay many of our own dead comrades, and close by, within the enclosure of the Secunder Bagh, lay some three thousand of the rebel dead who had fallen under the fire and by the bayonets of our own men, of the 4th Punjab Rifles, and of a detachment of the 53rd. A wounded brother-officer (Lieutenant Cooper of the 93rd) stood at the head of the grave and read the beautiful English burial service by the light of candles held by wounded men, and all, save one (myself), who stood around and mourned by the grave, had been wounded in the fight that day.

While *we* thus paid them fitting honours, the boom of the enemy's guns sounded clear and sharp in the still night air, as if to pay a last tribute of respect to the gallant dead, and to remind *us* who still lived, and were performing the last sad offices to them, that there were work and danger yet before us, and that our dead comrade's prophetic words might have further fulfilment ere another sun should rise and set.

After the lapse of many years, I returned to England, and find the following remarks, with reference to the incident I have just described, entered towards the close of my journal:

Lately I was introduced to a lady at a social gathering, who in the course of conversation asked me if I had ever been in India, and, on my informing her that I had served many years in Bengal with the 93rd Highlanders, she said, sadly, 'My brother was killed when with that regiment at Lucknow,' and at the same time she mentioned his name.

'Ah, yes,' I said, 'I knew him, and saw him nobly act and bravely die.'

'Yes,' she continued, 'we heard of his brave deed and of his noble death, but it has been a cause of great sorrow to us all during these many years to think that his poor body was so mutilated by the rebels.'

'Then let me comfort you now,' I said. 'Such was not the case, for no hands except those of friends and comrades touched his body after death.' And then I told her with what respect and honour her brother had been buried, described the whole scene to her, and told her also that 'of all those who helped to lay him in his grave only Lieutenant Cooper and myself survive and know the spot where he lies.' I promised her an etching of the spot, and, I am glad to say, have been able to fulfil that promise, and have seen the little picture framed and hanging in her drawing-room.

During the day several of my brother-officers were wounded, viz., Ewart, Cooper, Burroughs, Macnamara, Wood, Welch, and Goldsmith. Cooper's wound was a sword-cut right across his forehead.

After the fall of Lucknow, he (Cooper) exchanged with Knollys of the Scots Guards, and returned to England, and from that time till 1876 we never met again. In June, 1876, however, we met in the waiting-room on the occasion of a levée at St. James's, and I found him so changed that I only recognised him by the scar of his wound.

Poor Welch was very badly wounded—a bullet entered his body; and, though I was able to trace the course it had taken, I was unable to find and extract it. The wound healed, but he was incapacitated for the duties of a regimental officer, and therefore left the regiment. He served for several years afterwards on the staff in Canada, but suffered from constant pain and was unfit for any exertion. After his death the bullet was found imbedded in one of the bones on the left side of the pelvis.

On the same day Colonel (now General) Sir A. Alison had his left arm shattered. Amputation was performed by Clifford of the 9th Lancers, who was in charge of the head-quarters staff, while the chloroform was administered by me.

CHAPTER XI.

Another case of Presentiment—A man Reports himself sick to Avoid Battle—Refuse to Excuse Him—Behaves Bravely during two Days—Killed on the Third Day—His Last Words—Malingering—Frequent in Olden Times—Causes—Common Soldier—The Soldier's last gift for his Mother.

THERE was a certain non-commissioned officer in my regiment, Sergeant D——, whose courage was looked on with suspicion by his comrades, who believed that he disliked and endeavoured to avoid duty in the trenches before Sebastopol, and that, when on such duty, he never exposed himself unnecessarily to danger.

I was aware of the existence of this suspicion, and possibly to some extent was influenced by it; but there was not a single occasion during the war which I could refer to as having come under my personal observation on which the man showed any real want of courage; still the suspicion did exist, and I think the man was sensible that such was the case.

On the day before we commenced the operations for the relief of the Residency of Lucknow, this man reported himself to me as sick and unfit for duty; but, as he appeared to be in robust health, the old suspicion recurred to my memory, and, after careful examination, I came to the conclusion that he was not ill, and told him that such was my opinion. He insisted, however, on his inability to do his duty and to accompany the regiment into action on the following day, but I adhered to my opinion, and desired him to join his company.

During the fighting on November 14 and 15, his behaviour under fire was perfectly free from reproach, but late in the evening of the 15th he again reported himself sick, and again, after a more careful examination than on the 13th, I refused to excuse him from his duty, and he went away evidently much disappointed, and remarked, as he turned to leave me, 'I shall not be able to go through the work before me, and shall not survive to-morrow.'

He was in his place in the ranks on the morning of the 16th, however, and went through all the severe fighting of that day, never flinching under the hottest fire, and was one of those who entered the breach of the Secunder Bagh, and fought as bravely as any man of the regiment. But just at sunset, when we all thought that the fighting was at an end for the day, and were congratulating ourselves on being alive, the company to which this man belonged was detailed to drive the enemy from a certain position, from whence they kept up a constant and annoying fire.

The Naval Brigade was directed to open fire from their heavy guns, and, under cover of this, the company was to rush forward, close with the enemy, drive them out, and seize and hold the position.

I was standing in rear of the guns, saw them open fire, and saw the company start to their feet—they had been lying down behind the guns—and advance at the double, with a cheer. But one of the guns had missed fire, or something, I know not what, went wrong with it; and, just as the company got well in front, this one gun went off, and the man of whom I write fell forward, struck by a piece of wadding or grazed by the shot itself. I saw him fall, and, on running up, found him lying on his face in mortal agony, for his back was broken. He lived only a few minutes; but, ere he breathed his last, he held out his hand to me, and said, 'I knew it would be so, sir.'

Was this man really a coward, and had he always been one, as suspected? I think not—at least, he was no coward during the last three days of his life, during which he exhibited as much power of endurance under fatigue, and behaved with as much courage under a constant and heavy fire, as any man. He never once attempted to avoid danger, or to leave the ranks to seek cover, or to hang back, which he might have done without being noticed or missed. Was I wrong in believing and insisting that he was quite well, or was he really ill after all? No, I do not believe that I was mistaken, for had he not been quite well he never could have undergone the excitement and fatigue, the hardship and exposure of those three days and nights—the days spent under the constant excitement and fatigue of battle, and the nights under the hardship and exposure of out-lying picket, with very little food, and scarcely time to eat it. Was he under the influence of a presentiment of approaching death? I believe so, for his words at our two last interviews implied that such was the case— viz.: 'I shall never be able to go through the work before me, and shall not survive to-morrow,' and 'I knew it would be so, sir.'

He was a Scotchman, a handsome, well-made fellow, and was, I am convinced, in good health, had not been exposed, physically, at least, to any depressing influence previously to November 13, the day on which he first complained to me of being ill. To my knowledge there was nothing to cause distress of mind or depression of spirits; and further, being unmarried, he could not have had any anxiety about his domestic affairs. Probably the feeling that he was about to be in the presence of danger, and in peril of life, may have caused a sudden nervous depression, followed by as sudden a presentiment of approaching death; and, though for a moment shrinking under the influence of fear, when he really found himself in the presence of danger he faced it courageously, and met death bravely—at least, without any show of fear, and in the performance of his duty. True, his death was the result of accident, an accident which probably was not known to anyone but myself; but still he had borne himself bravely, and by his gallant conduct during the last three days of his life, and by his death upon the field of battle, had wiped out the foul suspicion under which he had lived so long, and was mourned for by his comrades, who felt ashamed of their former cruel injustice and openly expressed their regret for it.

It may be thought that this was a case of malingering, or pretended illness; but to malinger is to simulate disease, to feign the symptoms of a particular disease. This man did not do so, but merely stated that he was ill, and felt that he should not be able to go through his duties, and survive a certain day on which he knew that he should be exposed to danger. But, even if he had been malingering, he adopted this method of avoiding the danger which under the pressure of a presentiment he felt constrained to shrink from.

In olden time malingering was a science, and the treatment of it was a part of scientific medicine, to such an extent that treatises and books on the subject have been written in every civilised language, and by able members of the medical profession. Time was indeed when a great test of professional ability in the army was to be well-informed on this subject, and to understand how to discover and unmask the malingerer, often after watching him patiently, and torturing him during weeks and months, which watching and torturing were as patiently endured.

While I write, there lies before me a treatise on this subject, extending over four hundred pages. At the time I entered the army this was compulsorily an item in a medical officer's small amount of literary baggage, but it is unknown to the present generation. So completely unknown is it that I doubt if there are a score of officers of the army medical department who have ever seen or heard of it, although innumerable authors are quoted, and cases of feigned illness referred to as far back as the *Sacred Writings*.

But why did the soldier have recourse to malingering? Was it in consequence of unlimited service? No, but because of the life-long drudgery and misery which at one time attended unlimited service—misery during expatriation for years in unhealthy climates, where he was forgotten. No proper care was given to his bodily comfort or recreation, or to his mental improvement; he was left to doze away his days in crowded barrack-rooms, with no refuge save the baneful one of the canteen, and no amusement save what he could find in the demoralising excitement of the society to be met with in the wretched streets and alleys round or near his barracks. In the dull misery of such a life hundreds, nay thousands, perished from drunkenness or by pestilence.

He had not then, as he has now, spacious quarters, with dining-room apart from his dormitory, and with lavatories, bath-rooms, and other hygienic comforts. He had not then, as he has now, libraries, with reading and recreation rooms, gymnasia and regimental games, and schools where he can improve his mind and obtain certificates of proficiency, the first step in the general system of competitive examination; and he was not then accustomed, as he is now, to feel that an interest is taken in his welfare by his own officers, by the public, and by the 'noblest and highest' in the land.

It can hardly be a matter of surprise to us now that he then rebelled against the miseries of his life, or that he adopted any and every means of deception to escape from them.

Even in England in former days men were herded together in barracks, without regard to comfort or sanitary requirements. It was not uncommon to find soldiers and their families placed in the same rooms with a score of single men, separated from each other only by a sheet or linen screen suspended by the wife herself to afford some protection and privacy to herself and her children.

All this is now changed, however, and the soldiers' health and comfort are matters of the first consideration. Common decency is respected and ensured by the provision of separate quarters for the married men.

It was not uncommon in former days—and I fear it is not uncommon even in the present—to hear people speak, perhaps in ignorance, but sometimes in contempt, of the 'common soldier.' He was, in their view, a creature to be shunned by the good and virtuous of society, to be excluded from certain places of public amusement, an outcast not to be thought of or considered until his services were required to fight his country's battles. Then he was expected as a matter of course to act bravely, and to think only of the duty which *he* owed to his country. 'Common soldier!'—a term which all who know his virtues have resented, and always will resent. He is a Private soldier, a member, though the humblest member, of an honourable profession, an honest man, with chivalrous and often refined feelings, who only requires encouragement and assistance to show that he does possess such feelings, and that he is capable of rising to the higher ranks of his profession.

I have been associated with the soldier for nearly forty years, under every circumstance of service, and my experience has taught me that, as a rule, he is truthful, generous, and chivalrous, grateful for any kindness, and repays those who think of and care for him with gratitude and affection.

But malingering has almost disappeared from the army—indeed, I think I may say quite disappeared. At the commencement of my military career I saw something of it, but only two undoubted cases during the last thirteen years of my regimental life.

Both were non-commissioned officers who had

served throughout the Crimean war. They were brave men and did not malinger from fear, but because they were weary of the service and did not want to go to India. Strange to say, both were killed on the same day, and while doing their duty nobly.

Another remarkable case of presentiment was that of a young private, David R——. As the regiment was falling-in for the assault of the Begum Koti at Lucknow, he took his Crimean medal off and handed it to his brother, who was a sergeant in the regiment, saying, as he did so, 'Here, John, send this to our mother—I shall be killed to-day.' He *was* killed, while fighting bravely, and scarcely half an hour after he had handed his medal to his brother.

I will conclude this chapter by mentioning two instances of courage and devotion to duty. They were as follows :—

Lieutenant Deans Campbell was on the sick-list, suffering from ulceration of the feet, which were so swollen and painful that he could not wear either boots or shoes. The night before we went in to relieve the Residency he begged me to take him off the sick-list, and get permission for him to take his place in the ranks in *slippers*.

'But,' said I to him, 'you cannot walk any distance even in slippers.'

'No,' he replied, 'I cannot, but you might lend me a dhoolie, in which I can be carried close to my company, and, when we begin to fight, I'll get out and fall into my place.'

I made the necessary arrangements, and he went through all the operations for the relief in his slippers, carried with his company in a dhoolie, and getting out and falling into his place when there was fighting.

The other instance was that of a private. He was in hospital, but not necessarily confined to bed. The night before the assault on the Begum Koti he begged me to let him join his company for one day only. I consented. He joined his company, fought bravely during the day, and came back to hospital in the evening.

CHAPTER XII.

Adrian Hope—March to Rohilcund—Attack on Fort Rohca—Hope Killed—My Belief that he Laboured under a Presentiment of approaching Death—The great Love the men had for Him—His Burial—Window in Westminster Abbey—Recklessness of Young Officers—A Wounded Brother.

I PROPOSE in this chapter to write, as fully as my journal, aided by memory, will enable me, of an officer whose memory is still cherished by those who knew him, and whose name is still mentioned with the respect due to the memory of a great man and brave Christian soldier. He was a Scotchman, young and of noble birth. During the last few months of his career, he held a position of high command.

Of all the leaders of men whom I have served under, he was the calmest and coolest under fire, and the most gentle and courteous in his manner to all with whom he was associated. He never uttered harsh or unkind words, but was generous in thought, speech, and act. He seldom found fault, yet, when he did so, his reproof was conveyed in the fewest words, and with the most refined consideration for the feelings of the offender; so that all, from the highest to the humblest, who served under his orders felt that he was a leader in whom they could trust, and a friend to whom they could willingly and unreservedly give respect and love. No position of danger ever seemed to move him in the least, no one ever saw him hurried, or knew from his demeanour if he were anxious under difficulties or not. He spoke to those around him in the hottest fire of battle in his usual gentle, courteous manner. Nothing escaped his notice, what had to be done by himself or at his order was done without hurry, at the right time and in the right way. One great peculiarity of his was that he often seemed to be asking advice while giving it.

He was one of Sir Colin's selected and trusted leaders during all the operations for the relief of the Residency and for the subsequent siege of Lucknow. He so fulfilled the duties of his command as to gain the confidence of his great chief and the devotion of his officers and men. I was honoured with his friendship, and this, and the position in which I served, brought us into such constant and intimate intercourse that I believe I had the fullest opportunities for forming a judgment of him, and yet possibly I may have failed in forming a sufficiently high estimate of the nobility and greatness of his character.

After the capture of Lucknow, at which he acted a prominent part in command of a brigade, a force of some five thousand men was dispatched to another district, under the command of a general of division. With the force, as second in command, I think—at least, in command of his old brigade—was sent the officer of whom I write; but on our way thither we somehow turned aside from the straight road, and, if I mistake not, in disobedience of orders (of this, however, I am not quite certain), to attack a little native fort, which we failed to take after wasting a whole long day beneath its walls, and losing a number of both officers and men.

The afternoon before our failure this officer sent for me, and complained of feeling unwell. He could not describe exactly what he felt, but could only say that he was weak, depressed, and 'out of sorts.' He expressed a hope that it might not be necessary to fight upon the morrow, though he thought there was a probability that we should attack a small fort belonging to a petty rajah, who it was known had been in correspondence with the rebel army in Lucknow, and who had not yet sent in his submission, though summoned to do so. After careful questioning and examination, I could not discover that my friend was suffering from any particular illness. But it was evident that his late great labour and watchfulness during the relief of the Residency and subsequent siege of Lucknow, and the anxiety, though not apparent at the time, attached to high and responsible command assumed for the first time by a young man, and the exhaustion to a frame not naturally robust caused by want of sleep and by exposure to the great heat during the months of March and April in that part of India, had weakened and exhausted him, and that this physical exhaustion, reacting on his nervous system, had been followed by a certain degree of mental depression.

He lay stretched upon his camp-bed, while I sat beside him and talked to him, in as cheerful a strain as possible, of many circumstances connected with the late siege, intending and endeavouring all the time to lead our conversation gradually but entirely into other channels and to subjects unconnected with his late life and duties. In this I partially succeeded at first; but, unfortunately, my own thoughts and words assumed the character and complexion of those from which I was trying to lead my friend's, and instead of rousing him from his state of depression I only increased it.

Our conversation turned to Shakespeare, and we repeated to each other many of our favourite passages from different plays; but I know not why it was that either of us referred to 'Romeo and Juliet,' or what induced *me* to quote the following line:

'The bloody Tybalt festering in his shroud.'

The moment the words were uttered, they brought back to my own memory, and doubtless to his, the terrible scenes of war through which we had so lately passed. I saw him shudder either at the words or at the memories they recalled and, starting up into a sitting posture on his bed, he said, 'Let us change the subject; or, as we are tired, let us rest a little.' He then laid himself down again, and closed his eyes, as if in weariness or sleep. I sat silent by him and watched him, breathing quietly and slowly, till he really slept. Then I rose and silently left the tent, impressed by a belief, but most unwillingly, that he was labouring under a presentiment of approaching death. Yet I found it difficult to admit that there was even a possibility of his being taken from us, for he was so beloved by all, and his life seemed so necessary to the public service.

Next morning, long before sunrise, we were under arms, and I sought him out. I was glad to find him apparently quite recovered from the feeling of depression, and cheerful because busy with his preparations for whatever might happen during the day; but he still expressed a hope that the day might pass over without fighting. In this hope we all cordially agreed with him, for we were tired of bloodshed. After all that people who know no better think and say, it is a mistake to suppose that the more accustomed men are to fighting the more they like, or, at least, the less they dislike it. On the contrary, men show a greater desire to fight and more daring in their first than any after battle, because they have had no previous experience of the danger, and have not seen the horrors of a battle-field. 'He jests at scars who never felt a wound,' is not more true than that 'He who never was exposed to danger has no idea what danger really is'; or that 'He who never saw a battle is most eager for the fight.' This, too, is certain, that frequent exposure to the risks and dangers of battle does not make men less brave, but it inclines them to be more prudent.

There was an old brother-officer of mine (since dead, alas!), a brave young fellow, but who was much given to vapouring—I know not a more suitable word to use—and talking lightly of war and of its dangers before his first campaign, but on the first occasion when he came under fire a round shot passed so close to him, and committed so much havoc amongst those around him, that he looked on with astonishment, and remarked to a brother-officer, 'Why, after all, it is not fun, as I expected it would be.' He lived to have enough of war, and, though he always acted bravely when he had to fight, he learned to practise prudence also.

But imprudence under fire is a common fault with young officers, and the following very painful example of this occurred in my own presence. It was as follows:

Two brothers, the elder a surgeon of a regiment, the other a combatant officer,* who had parted many years before, when both were boys,

* The one was surgeon of the 93rd, the other a lieutenant of the 53rd.

and had never seen each other since those happy days, met in the dark on the night before the attack on the Secunder Bagh. Next day the younger, in this his first engagement, commanded a company of his regiment, which, extended in skirmishing order, covered the advance of a small column. He was perfectly cool and collected, knew well what was his duty, and, as he advanced, made his men take advantage of every available covert, while his pride, or his imprudence, as I thought it, prevented his doing so himself, even though warned and remonstrated with by his old sergeant. The consequence was that he fell pierced through the body by a bullet. The elder brother was near him as he fell, and helped to carry him from the field, and watched and tended him, and was the first to communicate the sad news to the aged parents at home. He heard afterwards, from one who was present when the hurriedly-written letter was received and read, that the old father (himself a soldier) merely bowed his head and murmured, 'Thy will be done;' but that the grey-haired mother, though her heart was well-nigh broken under the agony caused by the sudden announcement, 'thanked God that her boy had done his duty bravely,' and that this was the only remark she made at the time or afterwards, when friends attempted to sympathise with and comfort her in her great sorrow.

This was not the first bereavement she had suffered. She had passed through a similar trial previously, and there were others equally severe awaiting her, for in her extreme old age all her other loved ones passed away before her, save one, and he, a soldier also, was absent in a far-distant land when the poor heart, weary with its many trials and sorrows, and broken at last, ceased to beat for ever.

But I resume my narrative, with an apology for this short digression.

We were under arms before daylight next morning, as I have already said, and, as soon as the first streak of dawn appeared, commenced our advance, moving slowly and cautiously in the direction of the enemy. Just then I met my friend again, and for the last time. He stopped for a moment to speak, and told me that the general in command had determined that, if the rebel chief did not tender his submission before we arrived within cannon range of his fort, an assault should be made. Even then, as he rode away (and they were the last words I heard him speak), he expressed a hope that the rebel might submit, and thus prevent unnecessary bloodshed. It was not to be, however. Within an hour our heavy guns, of which we had several with us, opened fire, under cover of which a portion of our infantry, both European and native, advanced quickly, and took up positions close under the walls. Meantime the enemy also opened fire from several small guns, and commenced a brisk fire of musketry on our advancing regiments.

I do not presume to describe the military operations of the day—indeed, I have purposely avoided touching upon purely military matters in these reminiscences, as such are supposed to be beyond my province, which is that of a non-combatant, who nevertheless has seen more of war, and been present in more battles and engagements, than very many of the combatant officers in the service. I will only remark, and without fear, for military critics have said the same, that we committed a series of unpardonable mistakes throughout the day, and retired at the close of it, jeered at as we did so by a small garrison of irregulars, from a wretched mud fort, which had only three sides of defence, the fourth side (for it had been square at one time) being not only undefended, but indefensible, and lost a number of valuable officers and men. Amongst the former was our gallant leader. He was killed in the very front of all, close under the wall, while calmly examining the defences preparatory to an assault which we felt confident he had resolved on making, without waiting for any further orders or instructions.

He did not live to know that the day had ended in failure. He fell before the order to retire was given, and was thus spared the pain and—must I say it?—the disgrace which we all felt had fallen on us. But, when it became generally known throughout the force that he was dead, each officer and man sorrowed as for his best friend. We could have mourned for him with a feeling of pride had he fallen on a well-fought field leading his Highlanders to victory,

as he had so often done before; but that his life
should have been sacrificed in a moment of de-
feat, or at least of failure, before a contemptible
mud fort, which one third of our force, under
proper management, could have taken, roused
such a feeling of indignation, such a storm of
wrath amongst the men, that they spoke openly
and savagely, and cursed the folly and stupidity
that had caused the death of their gallant leader.

That he laboured under a presentiment of approaching death on the evening before he was
killed I felt certain, for, during the many months
of campaigning in which I had had the privilege
of daily, hourly intercourse with him, I never
before had seen him depressed, or heard him
utter a single wish to avoid battle.

No doubt on the occasion to which I refer his
temporary depression was the result of prolonged
strain upon both body and mind, and of exposure
to climatic influence. This state of depression
induced a presentiment which caused him to give
expression to the hope that there 'might be no
fighting on the morrow.' But he did not allow
this presentiment to exercise any influence over
his conduct or to affect his courage; and I do
not believe he even for one moment thought of
self or anything but *duty* during the whole of
that disastrous day until the moment when he
fell.

His death was almost instantaneous, and his
last whispered words to his aide-de-camp, Archie
Butter, of the 93rd, were, 'Say a prayer with me,'

and then he closed his eyes in death. Thus, in the performance of his duty on the battle-field, and with a prayer upon his lip, passed suddenly from life to death, in the very prime of manhood, as modest, as noble, as brave a Christian soldier as ever lived. Lieutenant Dick Cunningham, now Sir R. Dick Cunningham, I think, was also present. He (Cunningham) had been badly wounded in the leg at the battle of Kudjwa, and I have no doubt, had he wished it, might have gone home invalided. But he preferred to remain and see the campaign finished. When he rejoined the regiment, though his wound was healed, the muscles of his leg were stiff and painful, and he was unfit to do duty on foot. He could ride, however, and therefore, with Colonel Leith Hay's consent, acted as extra orderly-officer to our brigadier, and continued to act as such to Leith Hay himself when *he* succeeded to the command of the brigade. I know it has been said that our gallant leader was in the act of turning to proceed to the rear in quest of the officer in supreme command when he received his mortal wound. This could not have been the case, for the bullet struck him fair in front, and must have been fired from a height not many yards from where he stood, as it entered his neck above the inner extremity of the left collar-bone, and passed straight down to his heart. I am able to state this with such exactness because I was the first to touch and examine the wound, and while employed on this painful duty had frequently, and I am not ashamed to acknowledge it, to brush the tears from my eyes, for I had loved the man.

The body lay during that night and all the following day till nearly sunset in a tent in the very midst of the men, who had so often followed where he led, who had been so proud of their leader, and who, by the hush and silence which reigned throughout their camp, wished to show their deep respect for the lifeless body of their late brave and honoured chief.

In the cool of the evening their last sad duties were performed. Just before sunset a long procession of Highlanders was seen winding out of camp, following in measured tread the bodies of their dead leader and of the officers who had fallen round and with him on the previous day.

Slowly and silently the funeral-party moved to the wailing strains of the bagpipe and the mournful notes of the muffled drum, and, passing through the long lines standing in respectful and reverent attitude, paused beside the grave which had been prepared in a secluded spot in a dense grove of forest trees. Gently as a mother lays her sleeping infant in its cot, they lowered the bodies, hushed in their last, long sleep, into their final resting-place, and then by these lone graves, as the shades of evening closed round us, and amidst the deepest silence, arose the solemn voice of prayer, offering up thanksgiving for those departed this life, and making petition for the living that they might be ready whenever and however the final summons should come.

I never witnessed such signs of deep and universal sorrow as were then apparent, but could also observe that on the faces of his men there was a rigid sternness, and that from their eyes flashed angry, ominous glances, as if they sought for some *one* on whom to cast the blame of this great sacrifice. For myself, I felt that I had lost companion, friend, adviser, and though many years have passed away since then, and I have made other friends in the army, I have never known his equal.

I am not aware if any monument marks the spot where he was buried; but in the north transept of Westminster Abbey is a modest window, on which, and on a slab immediately beneath it, is inscribed the name of

ADRIAN HOPE.

CHAPTER XIII.

Home-sickness—Old Reserve Battalions—Transfers—Case of Home-sickness and Court-Martial—Home-sickness in an Officer—Strange Delusions.

OF many cases of nostalgia, or home-sickness, noted in my journal, I find several very remarkable ones, and therefore shall give a short description of one or two. One of these, I think, is especially interesting, and, as the sufferer was a medical officer, we may be confident that the details he supplied as to his peculiar sensations and feelings are reliable, and not over-coloured.

Many years ago a few regiments of the line had what were then styled Reserve battalions. These Reserves were numerically as strong as the First battalions, both in officers and men, but when first raised had no Lieutenant-Colonels, being under command of the senior Major of the regiment. He, to some extent, was under the control of the Lieutenant-Colonel commanding the First battalion, with which the colours and band remained, consequently an appearance of inferiority was attached to the Reserve, and from this a certain amount of jealousy arose, which I do not think was ever allayed.

It was a singular system, the intention being to make two regiments out of one, and thus to increase the strength of the army without making this apparent; and, though the system was improved so far as to make each battalion a separate command under a Lieutenant-Colonel, still it never worked satisfactorily and was abolished.

While it lasted, the system was as much disliked by the regiments concerned as the late linking of battalions, or as the present territorial distribution, and the substitution for the old well-known sacred numbers by territorial titles, which many of the regiments feel they have no title to at all, and by which many have no desire to be known.

If in our old army organization there was anything good at all, it was our regimental system, and this we have ruined in the attempt to assimilate our little army, which serves by regiments in every quarter of the globe, to the great armies of continental nations, which are divided into army corps and divisions that remain in special provinces or districts, and never serve beyond their own frontiers except in case of war.

It has been asked many times, and the question may be repeated: Why did we not leave our active and foreign service army as it was, retaining voluntary enlistment for long service, filling the ranks of our regiments with men and not boys, thus keeping them always in a state of efficiency and maintaining the old *esprit-de-corps*? Was it not possible to have converted our militia and the whole nation's strength into a Territorial Army and Reserve?

The man who has been born free should be trained to protect and keep his freedom, so that he may hand it down pure and unsullied as he received it. He should be taught the use of arms to ensure this, and to ensure his willing and gratuitous service for home defence, and his services for pay if required in war elsewhere.

Might we not have increased our Militia and trained and disciplined them better, encouraged and enlarged our Volunteer army, and made use of the money which we spend in endeavouring to form slowly and keep up a doubtful Reserve, in creating what we require out of the whole strength of the nation?

Many years ago the First and the Reserve battalions of the same regiment (the 91st) were serving in one of our distant colonies (the Cape). On the First being ordered home to England, instructions were received to complete the Reserve to its full strength by drafting all the young soldiers, men under ten years' service, who in those days were considered young. Amongst those selected to be transferred was a fine young fellow of eight years' service, who had enlisted in the regiment before the Reserve was formed, and who never thought of the possibility of transfer to what he looked on as another regiment altogether; and further who, after six years foreign service, was most anxious to return home, partly because he longed to be home again, and partly because of the entreaty of his old widowed mother.

On learning that he was to be transferred he sought his captain (Wright*), who made known the particulars of his case to the colonel, who would not, or perhaps could not, listen to the poor fellow's appeal. Accordingly, against his will, he was transferred. But from that day he was an altered man. From being a smart, clean, active soldier, he became slovenly and careless, and from being a big, burly, merry fellow, he shrank into a moody skeleton, and at last presented himself at hospital with a maimed right hand, the fore (or trigger-finger as it was then called) having been chopped off close to the knuckle. He was of course tried by court-martial; but, though the nature of the wound gave rise to strong suspicion, he told a story having a possibility of truth, and as there was no evidence to bring against him, and his 'record' showed previous good character, he was acquitted and sent home to be discharged. To be sent home was the sum of his desire. He had no wish to be discharged, but knew that if discharged he would be able to earn a living in civil life without the finger, the loss of which rendered him unfit for military service; at least, so thought the authorities in those days.

* Who afterwards distinguished himself on the occasion of the wreck of the *Birkenhead*.

After arrival in England he was discharged and soon got well, as big, and burly, and merry as ever, and easily found employment. We were all glad to hear of his well-being and well-doing, for he had been a general favourite, and we had thought that, at the time and under the explanation he had given, his transfer might have been avoided. Indeed, it has always been acknowledged in the service that to transfer a man from one regiment or battalion to another against his wish is impolitic and harsh.

Generally men are invited to volunteer from one regiment to another, but in the case of those First and Reserve, and lately in the case of Linked battalions, there was no option in the matter. Transfer was compulsory, and was of course a cause of much discontent.

The case which I have just described was a well-marked one of nostalgia. Under the intense yearning for his home the man's health had completely given way; and as a last and certain way of attaining his object, and gratifying his intense longing, which he had not power to resist, he did not hesitate to maim himself. This was not, could not be proved, but I had no doubt on the subject myself, nor had I any doubt that, if he had failed in attaining the gratification of his desire, he would have died.

Another remarkable case of home-sickness was that of the medical officer I have alluded to. He had passed his childhood, boyhood, and early manhood amidst the mountains and glens in that part of Argyllshire which look out upon a range of mountain-islands, and on the great blue restless ocean lying far beyond them. He had entered the army at the age of twenty-one, and from that time until he reached his forty-eighth year had 'knocked about the world,' as the common phrase is, and served in every quarter of the globe. He had shared in all the miseries and dangers, and glories too, of four campaigns, and of twenty-six years of foreign service had spent fifteen continuously in India. During all these twenty-six years he had only twice re-visited his home, for a few days only on each occasion. His health had always been good, no matter what the climate was where he served, or what the duty on which he was employed; but sometimes in India, when the great and prolonged heat of the upper provinces blanched the ruddiest cheek and weakened the most robust frame, he, too, used to suffer from exhaustion. When in this condition, if he sat idle for even a little while, memories of the old home would come floating before his mind, and he would see his rugged mountains looming dark under the leaden wintry sky, or capped with their clouds of driving mist, or faintly visible through the drizzling rain or the whirling snow-storm; and he would hear the roar and wash of the great ocean waves as they dashed against the black rugged rocks, piled in fantastic heaps on the wild open shore. At other times his sense of hearing would be so morbidly acute that he could hear the wind soughing through the clumps of rugged pine which crowned the low hill-tops, and of larch and hazel which lined the deep narrow glens. But, what was more painful than aught else, he often heard distinctly the rippling, tinkling sound of running water, as if he were sitting on the rocky bank of one of his own mountain burns in the calm and still of summer evening. But he never let those feelings get the mastery over him; he would fly to work, and, working hard, would regain his usual frame of mind. He often told me that he could bear it all, and derive pleasure from the whole delusion, but that, when the rippling sound of running water fell upon his ear, the pleasure was turned to pain, the sound was so home-like.

This same officer suffered afterwards from a remarkable delusion, which he thus described: His wife and children had been with him some eight years in India, but the climate began to tell upon the wife and elder girls. They were growing thin and pale and weakly. The Doctors said a change was necessary for them, so they were sent to Scotland to his own old home. Then he lived alone in a large, half-empty house, which had to be closed and darkened day after day while the Indian sun glared fiercely down, and hot winds blew, and clouds of dust whirled by. At times, when he sat beneath the waving punkah and let his thoughts wander to his home and absent ones, the cheery voices and merry laughter of his bairns would sound distinct and sweet as music in his ears, making his soul weary for his home and for the companionship of those he loved and missed.

At other times, 'when tired sitting still' (as his native servant was wont to say), he rose and paced slowly up and down the large empty rooms 'to rest himself.' With no one by to say a word to, and no companion but the children's old pet dog, a vision of a little dead child, swathed in white shroud, appeared before his eyes. No matter how he turned or where he looked, it still was visible, and seemed to be real, until, mastering his feelings, he approached the spot and reached out his hand to touch it, and then the vision faded from his sight. This did not happen once, or even twice, but often, and daily towards the end of the hot season, when he had become weak and weary of his solitude.

But strange to tell, after an interval of four years, during which his wife had returned to him, and another child had been born, the vision of the little dead child became reality, for this last born was taken suddenly away, and in the very house and room in which, four years before, he had so often seen the vision; but on this occasion there was no illusion, no vanishing of the vision at his approach, but, as he stretched forth his hand, it touched the cold dead face of his little child lying shrouded in his cot.

He had never made any secret of the vision he had so often seen, but noted it in his journal, and spoke of it to his wife long before its singular fulfilment. He also mentioned it to another medical officer, and quite understood that it was a mere illusion created by a weakened nervous system, and a mind oppressed by the solitude in which he lived.

He never was oppressed during the cold season or by the feelings or illusions described when vigorous and strong, and engaged in outdoor occupations and amusements, but always towards the end of the hot season, when he was necessarily much alone, and mind and body were well-nigh exhausted by the long-continued and oppressive heat. Had this vision, and the apparent fulfilment of it, occurred some two or three generations ago amongst our Highland kinsmen, it would most probably have been considered an instance of second-sight.

The wife also of the officer during her absence suffered from a somewhat similar illusion. She told me that sometimes, when sitting in the gloaming quite alone, she felt as if her absent husband were really beside her; and that at other times when she walked alone in the still evening by the sea-shore under the great, black mountain which overshadowed her home, she felt as if he were walking by her side, or thought she heard his rapid footfall following close behind. So very real were these feelings that with a beating heart she would turn to look at him and speak, and was only then convinced that imagination was playing her false.

This same lady, at the end of one of the hottest

seasons ever known in India, suffered greatly from exhaustion. While in this state she was one day taken to see a tame leopard, which was kept in a small room, fastened by a chain long enough to admit of the animal moving about to any part of the room. For many days afterwards, if sitting alone, or moving about her house, she fancied that she saw the cat-like leopard with its green eyes fixed on her, stealthily creeping round her chair, or following her from room to room, crouching low, and making ready for its spring, and, though it made her heart throb and her pulse beat faster, she said that she never felt any alarm at the illusion, but that, fixing her eyes upon the spot where she saw the spectre, she stood still until it slowly faded from her sight.

CHAPTER XIV.

The Residency Relieved—March to Cawnpore—Cross Ganges under Heavy Fire—Enemy try to break down the Bridge of Boats—Removal of Wounded to Allahabad—Battle with Gwalior Contingent—Pursuit to Serai Ghât—Nana Sahib's Palace—Ride to Cawnpore—Battle on the Kalch Nuddee—Return to Lucknow—Reception of the 93rd by Peel's sailors.

THE operation for the relief of the Residency occupied seven days, during which time every man of the army was constantly on duty day and night.

By the afternoon of the seventh day all the sick and wounded of the relieving army and of the Residency garrison had been sent to the field hospital, established at the Dill Koosha; the women and children safely removed from the Residency; the treasure secured; all supplies that could not be made available were destroyed; and the guns which could not be taken with us bursted or spiked. Then the little army retired quietly during the night without the knowledge of the enemy, and encamped within the vicinity of the

Martinière. There the good and brave Sir Henry Havelock died.

On the morning of November 24 the relieving army, with an immense convoy of sick and wounded, and of ladies, women, and children, under its escort, commenced to fall back on Cawnpore, while the Residency garrison was formed into a corps of observation, under the command of Sir James Outram, and left encamped on the Alum Bagh plain, for the purpose of watching and holding in check the rebel army within and around Lucknow.

The distance between the Bunnee Bridge (where we were encamped on the 26th) and Cawnpore is thirty-four miles, and on starting from thence on the 27th we quite expected that in consequence of the immense convoy under our protection we should take at least three days to perform the distance; but were not a little disappointed as we passed the first camping-ground, and continued to move on during the forenoon until we were in sight of the second. About 1 p.m., having marched at least sixteen or seventeen miles, the army was halted, and orders issued for the men's dinners to be got ready. While halted for this purpose we were surprised to hear the low rumbling sound of a distant cannonade, and to see Sir Colin with his staff gallop past; but were still more surprised to find that after the men had had their dinners we were ordered to resume our march.

As we moved on, the sound of heavy guns

became louder and more frequent, and we began to think that Sir James Outram had been attacked by the Lucknow rebels. We were not long left in doubt, however, for an aide-de-camp was sent back by Sir Colin, with orders to hurry on the whole force, leaving a strong guard to protect the convoy, as the Gwalior contingent was besieging Sir Charles Wyndham and his brigade in the entrenched camp on the western bank of the Ganges, and close to the city of Cawnpore.

On hearing this intelligence the men forgot that they were weary, that they had already marched twenty miles, and they braced themselves to perform the remaining fourteen, quite believing that immediately on their arrival at Cawnpore they would have to fight a battle.

The day was intensely hot; the roads were ankle-deep in dust, which, stirred by the long lines of men, sick-bearers, baggage animals, vehicles, artillery, and cavalry, hung around the column in a dense, suffocating cloud. The sick and wounded, and the women and children, suffered terribly, not only from heat, dust, and thirst, but also from swarms of flies which followed them; and those men who had undergone amputation, and those with broken limbs and severe wounds, suffered excruciating pain from the jerking and jolting of the dhoolies as the exhausted bearers staggered under their burdens.

During the last two hours of the march, many of our men fell out, quite unable to keep in the ranks, some from exhaustion, others from footsoreness; and at last, when we arrived at our destination at ten p.m., scarcely three hundred out of eight hundred men were with the colours; all were present, however, by midnight. The sick and wounded also were brought in by that hour, and myself and my assistants were occupied with them till three o'clock on the following morning. By that hour every wound had been carefully dressed, and every sick and wounded man fed. Many of the men suffered much from galled and blistered feet; some of them were so bad that, on trying to take off their hose, the skin of their feet and ankles peeled off with them.

At daybreak next morning we were under arms, and not a man was absent; even those with bleeding feet were in their places, so anxious was every one to take his share in the expected fight.

As soon as daylight permitted objects to be seen, the enemy opened fire on the entrenched camp, and on the bridge of boats also, so as to break the latter and prevent our crossing; but Peel, on our side, took up a position with his heavy guns on some sand-hills which overlooked the river, and commanded the enemy's batteries. Under cover of this cannonade, we crossed the bridge exposed to a heavy fire; but fortunately not a shot struck the bridge, though many fell into the river very close to it.

Having gained the left bank, the regiment marched quickly past the face of the fort under a rapid musketry fire from the enemy. We had only one casualty (Lieutenant Dunlop Hay, slightly wounded in the leg). After passing the fort, we turned to the right, and got under the shelter of a number of ruined buildings, from whence we debouched upon the plain opposite to the rebel position in and around the city of Cawnpore, and by this movement secured the road to Allahabad. On the afternoon of the same day the wounded were brought across the river, and during that night and next day the ladies and women and children crossed also, and were encamped at some distance in rear of the troops, out of danger.

I secured a large building (which I afterwards heard was, or had been, the cavalry officers' mess-house) as a hospital for our own wounded—we had no sick—and had them all comfortably settled within a couple of hours after their arrival. The doors and windows of the house had all been destroyed, but the roof was uninjured. How it had escaped destruction, I could not imagine, for the thick thatch might easily have been set on fire, as had been done to all the other buildings round. The house afforded space and comfort, but was unfortunately within reach of the enemy's guns, and as their shells frequently burst near and over it, I was in constant dread of seeing the dry thatch in a blaze. However, it gave shelter to the wounded, protection from the heat of the sun by day and from the keen, sharp night air, and therefore I risked the danger, knowing that in the event of fire we could easily remove the men before the burning roof could fall-in.

We remained encamped on the plain of Cawnpore while arrangements were being made for the despatch of the women and children, and of the worst cases of the sick and wounded, to Allahabad, supposed to be the safest refuge for them. On learning that the wounded were to be sent in open bullock-carts (rough conveyances for men who had suffered amputation, or whose limbs were broken, or who had been shot through the body), I went to Brigadier Adrian Hope and remonstrated, and he, concurring with me, proposed that I should go with him to Colonel Mansfield (afterwards Lord Sandhurst), chief of the staff. On hearing what I had to say, viz., 'that in my opinion the serious cases of amputation, fractures, &c., should not be moved as directed,' he got very angry, told me that 'I had no right to express any opinion, as the order for their removal had been issued with the approval of the principal medical officer, and that I had nothing to do but to obey, as no responsibility rested upon me.' I replied that 'I should of course obey the order; but that I thought a certain amount of responsibility did attach to me where the wounded of my own regiment were concerned, and that I was bound to draw attention to any arrangements which in my opinion might be followed by serious if not fatal consequences to them.' This only made the chief of the staff more angry, and he ordered me 'to leave his presence;' but, seeing that I hesitated to do so, his anger turned upon Hope, whom he desired 'to remove me instantly.'

Accordingly, I was ejected from the tent, but as I was being hustled out, I turned and said,

'Excuse me, sir, but I have only done what I consider my duty.'

I never knew until two years afterwards that it had been proposed to try me by a court-martial for my conduct on that occasion. I heard it from Sir Colin himself one evening when he dined at our mess. He told me that while at Cawnpore the chief of the staff came to him, and said,

'I wish to try a medical officer by court-martial.'

'All right,' said he, in reply, 'try him. But who is he?'

'The surgeon of the 93rd Highlanders.'

'Oh! no, Mansfield, there must be some mistake; I know that fellow very well, for he was with me in the Crimea. You must forgive and forget his offence whatever it is, for I am certain he cannot have been guilty of neglect of duty.'

What the charges were to have been Sir Colin did not say; but he laughed heartily as he told me the story. No doubt, if Sir Colin had not known me well, I should have been tried; but I think I should have been acquitted.

While we were encamped at Cawnpore the enemy constantly sent shot and shell into our camp, and several of our officers and men were wounded by pieces of shell and by shrapnel bullets. Only one officer and one man were struck by round shot. The officer lost his arm—

but I shall speak of him directly—and the man, a Corporal, was only severely bruised.

One of the officers, Captain Cornwall, wounded by a shrapnel bullet, had a wonderful escape. The bullet struck him on the edge of the collar-bone, passed behind the large blood vessels, ran under his shoulder-blade, and was cut out by me from beneath the skin low down on his back. Had the bullet not touched the collar-bone, it would have cut the large artery and vein, and this would have caused almost instant death. Strange to say, Cornwall never felt the bullet strike, and did not even know that he was wounded until informed of the fact. The officer who was struck by round shot was Brevet Lieutenant-Colonel (now Lieutenant-General) Ewart, C.B. It was a terrible wound, the left arm being shattered above the elbow. Assistant-Surgeon Menzies, of the 93rd, who was near him at the time, got him into a dhoolie, or covered stretcher, and, placing his thumb on the large artery, brought him to me at the hospital.*

Ewart, when brought in, was almost in a state of collapse from the shock following such a terrible wound, and from the sudden gush of arterial blood which had followed. He was therefore not in a fit state to undergo an operation. He entreated me to operate at once, and though it was hard to refuse, I did so, knowing that in the state he was any further loss of blood, even

---

* Life was saved in this case by the pressure of the thumb on the artery.

the little which might occur during amputation, would have killed him. As soon, however, as I saw that he had rallied from the great shock, and from the sudden loss of arterial blood, and was fit to undergo an operation, I amputated close up below the shoulder. He suffered no pain during the operation, as it was performed while he was under the influence of chloroform. I may here state that I never performed any operation either during or after a battle, and I have performed many, without the use of chloroform.

I shall have occasion to mention my friend Ewart again.

On the evening of December 5, 1857, we were ordered to send all our wounded into the field hospital, and to strike tents and pack baggage. On the 6th we fought the Gwalior contingent, defeated it, took its standing camp, baggage, supplies, and forty guns. I do not attempt any description of the battle, though I saw a good deal of it, as myself and assistants were close up with the regiment during the whole day.

Several times during the battle I found myself close to Colonel Mansfield (Lord Sandhurst). Once when he was slightly wounded himself, again when his brother, Major Charles Mansfield, was severely wounded, and while I was attending him, and for the third time when I was dressing a wounded Rifle Brigade man. On this last occasion, just as I had bound up the wound, I was surprised to find Colonel Mansfield standing beside me, and much more surprised when he held out his hand, and thanked me for my conduct during the day, saying at the same time, while a smile played across his face, 'You must forget what occurred between us three days ago.'

During the remainder of the campaign, and for years afterwards, Sir W. Mansfield never met me without a kind word of recognition, and I must say I never knew any man who could speak and act more pleasantly or more kindly than he. In fact, to those who knew him, there was an irresistible charm and gentleness in his manner. In this engagement we had none killed, and only fourteen wounded; amongst the latter were Lieutenant Stirling and a Lance-Corporal, who were both struck by the same round shot. The former had his thigh shattered, and the latter his left arm.

While I was attending to the corporal, Stirling was carried off the field to the hospital at Cawnpore, where his limb was amputated, and where he died. The soldier's arm I amputated on the battle-field, and it was one of the most successful operations I ever performed, for within fourteen days the man was walking about with his stump quite healed.

The night of December 6 we bivouacked on the field of battle, and on the following day at noon the regiment formed part of a column sent in pursuit of a portion of the routed Gwalior contingent, which had fled in the direction of Serai Ghât. The column consisted of the 42nd, 53rd, 93rd, and 4th Punjaub Rifles, and of the 9th

Lancers, and one or two batteries of horse artillery, under the command of Brigadier Hope Grant.

We marched during the whole afternoon and evening up to ten p.m., when we were halted for rest and food, after which we went on again all night. Early on the following morning the artillery and cavalry overtook the enemy, quickly routed them, and captured some fifteen guns.

It was a weary march, and it was the only occasion on which I ever attempted to sleep on horseback; but I was so completely done-up that I made my syce lead the horse, and, twisting my great-coat straps round my wrists, slept, or rather dozed, for a couple of hours, waking up every few minutes with a start, as I found myself slipping over to one side.

After the action at Serai Ghât, we were ordered to Bithoor, the residence of the Nana Sahib. We destroyed his palace, and secured a large quantity of his gold plate, which had been thrown into a deep well for concealment.

We remained at Bithoor for some days, and while there a message was brought to me to the effect that my friend, Colonel Ewart, was very ill —'dying,' the messenger said. Therefore, on the following morning, I started with Blake, 93rd, and the Reverend Mr. Henderson, and rode into Cawnpore, a distance of about twenty miles. It was not prudent to ride without escort, but I could not let a brother-officer die without making an effort to try to save him when I was so near.

I found Ewart in a bad way. The stump, apparently, had not been dressed—at least, not properly dressed—since I left him. The ligatures were lying loose in the wound, though detached from the arteries, and the wound itself was looking unhealthy, the lower portion, or flap, being in a state of mortification. I at once removed the ligatures, carefully washed the wound, and applied necessary remedies to the gangrenous part. I then gave directions to the hospital attendant as to what further should be done, for I saw no medical officer, and desired him to say to whoever was in charge that, if possible, Colonel Ewart should be removed to some building where he would have fresh air and more comfort.

In the afternoon of the same day, I rode back to Bithoor, and reached our camp just in time to perform another capital operation. During the day my friend Nightingale (now Lieutenant-Colonel 93rd) had had his right hand blown almost to pieces, and I was obliged to perform amputation above the wrist.

Ewart made a good recovery, attributable in a great measure to the fact of his having been removed to a comfortable house, and also to the care and attention of his friend whose name is mentioned in 'Reminiscences of a Soldier's Life.' I have the great pleasure of meeting Ewart occasionally, and confess that I look upon his empty sleeve with much satisfaction, and with thankfulness that he still lives.

My friend Nightingale had some bad symptoms after the operation, but eventually made a good recovery. Alarmed at the danger Ewart had run after he had been left at Cawnpore, I determined not to part with Nightingale until his wound should be healed, and until I saw him walking about. Accordingly, to make certain that he should be cared for, I carried him with me wherever we went, kept him in one of my own tents, and watched and nursed him myself, and was glad I did so. He is still with the 93rd, and we often meet. I look with as much satisfaction at *his* empty sleeve as I do at my friend Ewart's. Nightingale used to get very irritable sometimes when I was dressing his wound, but instead of venting his irritability on me, he did so on Lamb, his faithful and devoted servant.

We remained at Bithoor until the headquarters of the army under Sir Colin arrived. Then the whole force moved on Futtehghur, an important station and dépôt, occupied by a considerable rebel force. This force came out to oppose our advance, and took up a position on the Kalleh Nuddee, a deep stream spanned by a suspension bridge. This the enemy had attempted to destroy to prevent or delay our advance. But we were too quick for them, and made our appearance before they were able to effect more damage than our engineers could repair in a couple of hours. As soon as the repairs were completed, the 53rd regiment was pushed across, and, getting quickly under cover, commenced the engagement. At the same time our guns opened fire, and after a time succeeded in silencing those of the enemy. One of these, which was very cleverly placed so as to be protected by some high mud walls, and which had caused us much annoyance during the day, was at last dismounted by a shot from one of Peel's guns, which Lieutenant Vaughan of the Naval Brigade had laid and fired himself.

Early in the fight, Captain (now General) Henry Maxwell, R.A., then attached temporarily to the Naval Brigade, was severely wounded, his thigh having been broken close to the knee by a musket or rifle bullet, which was thought to have lodged within his knee. Amputation was deemed to be necessary, but he demurred to that, and requested that the surgeon of the 93rd might be asked to come and see him.

I happened to be dressing my friend Nightingale's stump, when a very small midshipman, whose name I did not know, riding a very small black pony, presented himself and delivered a message from Maxwell, begging me to go and see him.

I went at once, and after carefully examining the wound—there was only one where the bullet had entered—with my finger, I found that the bone, though broken, was not splintered, and that the knee had not been injured, so that wherever the bullet was it was not in the joint. I therefore suggested that the injury should be treated as a fracture. He got all right, and upwards of a year afterwards the bullet was discovered, and cut out from amongst the tendons behind the knee. I have seen him twice only since that day, and very grateful I found him to the man whose advice saved him from being a cripple.

In the afternoon of the day, the 93rd was ordered forward either to relieve or to support the 53rd, I do not know which. I believe, however, that the 53rd were under the impression that it was to relieve them, and as they were the regiment in advance that day, and had commenced the action, they were not well pleased that another regiment should deprive them of the post of honour, or finish what they had begun, and what they were able and willing to complete. Accordingly, as the 93rd commenced to file across the bridge, a 53rd bugler sounded the advance, and the whole regiment sprang from their covert and rushed forward with a cheer, sweeping their officers, who vainly endeavoured to control them, along with them in their headlong charge, to encourage which the advance seemed to sound from more than one bugle.

It was a grand rush, before which the enemy fled in confusion, many of them to be cut up by our pursuing cavalry, and as they bolted they left two guns to be captured by the gallant 53rd. Sir Colin was really very angry, or pretended to be so, because, as I understood, this unauthorised advance of the regiment had somehow interfered with his plans; but, though he spoke very sharply on the occasion, I do not think the noble regiment suffered in his estimation. Certainly it did not suffer in the estimation of Colonel Mansfield, who had formerly been its lieutenant-colonel.

Having captured Futtehghur, the army remained encamped there for some days, and a brigade under Adrian Hope, of which the 93rd formed a part, was sent out into the surrounding district to assist the civil authorities in restoring order. In February this brigade retraced its steps to Cawnpore, crossed the Ganges, and moved towards Lucknow, to join the army assembling for the siege of that city. On our way thither we came up with our old friends, the 79th, which regiment had just arrived in the country, and had a cordial reception from both officers and men.

On the last day's march, as the 93rd approached the camp formed on the Alum Bagh plain, the men of Peel's Naval Brigade came out to meet us. They lined both sides of the road, and their fiddlers, I forget how many, placing themselves at the head of the regiment, played us to our camp-ground; the blue jackets saluting us with cheers, and with many singular pithy nautical phrases, expressive, I believe, of esteem, and used by sailors as terms of endearment, but which I think I had better not repeat here.

It was a most amusing scene. The strange musicians moved along with a rolling gait, raising their feet high, and stamping on the ground, while they fiddled away with an energy meant, no doubt, to show their desire to make their reception of the 93rd as demonstrative as possible. Our men accepted the compliment thus paid them by their sailor-comrades, but found it impossible to restrain their laughter at the novel sight of a regiment of Highlanders marching with a band of fiddlers at its head.

I had often seen Captain Sir W. Peel on the battle-field, but never had the pleasure of speaking to him, until the day on which he was wounded during the siege of Lucknow. He was struck by a bullet, which lodged in his thigh, and the young medical officer who was with the Naval Brigade either could not discover its position, or did not think it prudent to endeavour to remove it. Peel requested that I might be sent for, and on my presenting myself, asked me, in a very quiet manner, 'if I thought the bullet should be allowed to remain in his leg.'

'No,' replied I, 'if it can be found.'

'Well, then,' said he, 'will you kindly try to find it, and take it out.'

On examination, I found it lodged close behind the large blood-vessels, high up in the thigh, from which position I extracted it after a good deal of trouble.

I saw him only once after this, when he sent

for me to express his thanks. The wound was then healed, and he was preparing to start for Calcutta. On his way thither he died of small-pox, a miserable end for one who had so often been exposed to danger and death on the battle-field.

CHAPTER XV.

Fort Rohea—Enemy retired during the Night—Intense Heat—Skirmish at Allygunge—A Rebel Prisoner blown from a Gun—Joined by another Brigade—The Commander-in-chief assumes Command of the whole Force—Battle of Bareilly—Charge of Ghazies—Enemy's Cavalry attack Baggage—Narrow Escapes.

ON the morning following our unsuccessful attack of the rebel fort, described in Chapter XII, we found that the garrison had vacated it during the night, and on taking possession discovered, to the surprise of all, except of the few who had been aware of the fact previously, that the side on which we made no attack was perfectly indefensible, so much so that a body of cavalry might have entered. However, it is quite possible that the general in command might have been aware of the indefensible state of this side of the fort, and that he made his arrangements for the attack, expecting that the enemy, overpowered by our artillery and musketry fire, would endeavour to escape in that direction, and be overtaken by our cavalry as they fled across the plain. This may have been the case, but probably the enemy had seen our cavalry, and felt that, if they retired from the fort in daylight, there would be no possibility of escape.

On examining the imperfect defences, and the mud buildings immediately behind them, we could not perceive that any great damage had been effected by our artillery fire, and the charred remains of the few dead bodies which we found in the shallow ditch on the indefensible side of the fort was evidence that the loss of the enemy in killed at least had been small as compared with our own. The very fact of the enemy having burned their dead proved plainly that they had made their preparations to retire very leisurely.

There was no pursuit, and we remained encamped in the vicinity for a couple of days, occupied in the destruction of the fort. Having accomplished this, we resumed our march.

I do not remember to have been on any service where troops were so harassed or exposed to greater suffering and discomfort. We were disspirited by the shame of failure, for which the men felt they were not to blame; we were oppressed by the intolerable heat, scorched by a blazing sun, nearly suffocated by hot winds and by clouds of dust, wearied and exhausted by want of rest and sleep, and disheartened by the daily loss of comrades, who fell victims to heat-apoplexy. Our camps were generally formed in extensive groves of mangoes, under the grateful shade of which we were comparatively cool and comfortable during the day, but at night the hot air, radiating from the ground, and confined by the dense overhanging foliage, was oppressive and stifling, impeded respiration, and kept our bodies, in a state of feverish restlessness. Added to these causes of discomfort the noise made by the number of camels packed closely round our tents, and the sickening effluvium from their bodies rendered sleep impossible, or, at least, disturbed and unrefreshing.

We learned during that march that the protection and comfort afforded by the shade of trees during the fierce heat of day in the hot season, is far less in comparison to the discomfort experienced in the same position at night, and that it is preferable to pitch one's tent out on the open plain, and there to endure as patiently as possible the great noonday heat, with the certain prospect of enjoying a lower temperature and fresher air at night, in which respiration could be free, and refreshing sleep possible.

We were fast becoming a washed-out-looking lot. The bronzed hue of health had faded from our faces; these had become pale and haggard, showing great black circles round the eyes. The elasticity of step with which we had moved but a few weeks ago had changed into a weary, listless walk, in which we appeared to drag our limbs along. From being in a state of constant restless activity, we sought to lie down and rest at every halt, and during the few minutes that it lasted fell into weary and unrefreshing sleep. There was no jest or laughter in the ranks. The men did not seek comfort from their pipes, but from all quarters was heard the cry for water, and often also was heard the call for 'the doctor,' as some poor fellow was suddenly stricken down by heat-apoplexy. To increase our miseries and anxieties, small-pox appeared amongst us, and fever became prevalent, and we had to carry these cases with us, as we were not near any station where the sick might be sent to hospital.

On the fourth day after resuming our march, we were roused into something like our old energy for an hour or two by a skirmish with the enemy, in which they were quickly defeated, with the loss of their guns. Could we only have had such a skirmish every day, it would have done us good. It would have given us something to do, to think of, and to talk about.

A day or two after this skirmish a general parade of the whole force was ordered for the purpose of witnessing capital punishment. A native soldier, who had been in our service, but had deserted to the mutineers, and while with them had murdered an European, had been taken prisoner. He was tried, convicted, and sentenced to be blown from a gun. When the parade was formed up, the prisoner, a tall, handsome Sikh, was marched into the open square. He showed no sign of fear, but, walking erect and with a firm step, in the midst of his escort, straight up to the gun, placed himself with his back close to the muzzle. He was literally blown to pieces. It was a terrible sight; but this method of punishment was thought necessary at the time, I believe, especially where the murder of an European could be proved. I had seen many of the mutineers hanged, but this was the only case of blowing from a gun that I saw or heard of during that period of the mutiny through which I served.

About this time another brigade and a body of artillery, with several heavy guns, joined us, and the commander-in-chief, Sir Colin Campbell, took command of the whole force. We then marched on Shahjehanpore, and from thence to Bareilly, where a large force of rebels had assembled. We attacked this rebel force on May 5, defeated it, and on the following day occupied Bareilly, the capital of Rohilcund. The town or city was really occupied first by a force from Delhi, under General Jones, which had been ordered to co-operate with the army under the commander-in-chief. The principal medical officer of this force was my old friend, Kerr Innes.

Immediately after the occupation of this rebel centre, the force was broken up, and the 93rd and two other Highland regiments (42nd and 78th) were ordered to remain to occupy Bareilly, and hold the district.

The day on which the engagement at Bareilly was fought was the very hottest I ever experienced in India or elsewhere. The sun beat down upon us with tremendous power, and a withering hot wind blew clouds of dust before it, and, as we were out on the open plain, there was nothing to screen us from the one or shelter us from the other. Fortunately, we were near several large wells, and had an abundant supply of water, without which our sufferings would have been terrible.

During the greater part of the day the 93rd lay upon the ground, watching a thick belt of wood about eight hundred or a thousand yards to our front, which was held by a considerable body of rebels with several small guns. As we were out on the open plain, the enemy could see us distinctly, even though we were lying down, and occasionally brought their guns to bear on us. They had got the range accurately, and dropped their shot unpleasantly close to us, but not one took effect. Our men submitted to this at first in a pleasant mood, and jested and laughed equally at 'a bad shot,' or 'a near shave.' But at last they began to get out of humour, and to show signs of irritation and restlessness at inaction under this annoying fire. They thought that the enemy had had enough of their own way, and that it was time to make a forward movement and close with them. At last, late in the afternoon, when the sun was low down in the west, an A.D.C. galloped up and held a short conversation with Colonel Ross, of the 93rd (Colonel Leith Hay at the time commanded a brigade), who almost immediately gave the well-known order, 'Stand to your arms,'—an order the soldier likes well to hear when standing idle, while the roar of battle sounds on every side of him, and when lying down inactive under a heavy fire. He knows that it means a return to life and action, but never reflects that it may mean death.

On this occasion our men sprang to their feet with alacrity, and quickly got into their places, making their bonnets trim, and smoothing their kilts as they did so, for the Highlander is particular about his appearance. There was silence in the ranks, but the contracted grey eyes and a grim smile lurking on every face told that the men were angry, and boded mischief to the enemy should they cling to the wood a little longer. But there was a general fear that they would retire when they saw us coming on, for somehow, if they could avoid it, the rebel soldiery never during the mutiny cared to meet the sahib when anger was flashing from his eyes.

We advanced quickly with the old cheer, our flank companies leading in skirmishing order; but, as we feared, the enemy, with their usual nimbleness of foot, retired hurriedly, and escaped us, though we had made haste and entered the wood at a run. At one time of the day, a native dressed in white, and carrying what appeared to be a white flag, walked forth from the wood, and advanced boldly in our direction. We all thought that he was deserting from the enemy, and coming over to us, so paid little heed to him. Our quartermaster, Joyner, who happened to be riding across the plain on our left, seeing the man, turned to meet him. When they were within twenty yards of each other, the native halted, raised his matchlock to his shoulder, and, taking steady aim, fired, but missed. Joyner at once returned the compliment with his revolver, but missed also. The native then, throwing aside his matchlock, drew his tulwar, and advanced rapidly. Before he had time to strike a blow, he was surrounded, and cut to pieces by four of our own sowars, who had galloped up to the rescue.

At another period of the day we witnessed a charge of Ghazies (fanatic Mussulmans), intoxicated by bhang, and vowed to kill or be killed. About thirty of these suddenly emerged from some ruined buildings on our left, and advanced straight upon the flank of the nearest European regiment (42nd). They were dressed from head to foot in green, and armed with tulwar and shield.

I do not think that our people quite understood what they were, or what their intention was, for they allowed them to advance without attempting to oppose them, until they were close to them, in fact, close enough to use their tulwars and to inflict several wounds. Then, however, they were speedily shot down or bayonetted. They managed to wound and unhorse the colonel of the regiment (Cameron) and to wound several of the men, but failed to kill any. The enemy's cavalry almost at the same time swooped down upon our baggage-train. Though they caused some confusion, they inflicted no damage, and were driven off.

When I saw the enemy's cavalry galloping down in the direction of our line of baggage, I was alarmed for the safety of the sick, and especially of two brother-officers, Lieutenants Burgoyne and Grimstone, who were both ill with fever, the latter very ill. At the close of the day, however, I had the satisfaction of seeing all my patients brought safely into camp. They had suffered much during the day from want of proper attention and nourishment, from the discomfort of long exposure in dhoolies, the thin cotton coverings of which afforded very inadequate protection against the intense heat of the sun and the force of the withering hot wind. It appeared that Lieutenant Burgoyne, on becoming aware of the approach of the enemy, had wisely directed the sick-bearers to seek shelter within the line of baggage carts, and there he and the other helpless sick were comparatively safe.

I have great pleasure here in bearing my testimony to the courage and devotion of the Indian dhooly-bearers. I always found them faithful to their duty, and never knew them shrink from the dangers of the battle-field, or neglect or forsake a sick or wounded European. I have several times seen one of these bearers killed and many of them disabled while carrying a wounded soldier out of action.

CHAPTER XVI.

Our Army—Old Memories—The old Regimental Numbers—Long Service—Esprit-de-Corps—The Reserve—The Old and New Schools—The Regimental Surgeon of Old Times—A Sentimental Institution—The old Surgeon re-visiting his former Regiment—His own Arrangements still in Force.

WE hear that our army is now in a satisfactory condition. Doubtless it is, and will do its duty as gallantly as formerly. But old memories are clinging to it still, and a generation or two must serve and pass away before fresh honours and distinctions can be won by the territorial regiments to equal those entwined round the old respected regimental numbers.

In the olden times, recruits enlisted into the regiments of their choice, and served therein, as a rule, for twenty years and upwards. Young gentlemen sought appointments to their county regiments or to national corps, and followed the fortunes of these over the whole world, waiting patiently, and rising slowly step-by-step until at last they attained command of them.

In those olden times, officers and privates felt proud of the history of their corps, of their titles, badges, or distinctions won on great battle-fields; of crests and mottoes interwoven with the names of great campaigns or victories on their colours. They were even proud of sobriquets which had their origin in some chance expression of an honoured leader standing 'Firm' with his men in danger, or 'Dying Hard' with them when sorely pressed; or applied by generals or lookers-on at some brave deed performed in desperate fight.

In those olden times, every member of a regiment believed that his own possessed some peculiar excellence, and each vied with the other to add some further lustre to its honourable history, to maintain its discipline, and keep its credit free from stain. And there was good fellowship and kindly feeling. Officers and men, from constant intercourse during long years, came to know each other's good qualities, or little faults and failings, and made allowance for the latter.

Yes, in those days a kindly fellow-feeling reigned throughout all ranks, making the life of a soldier a very pleasant, happy one. The colonel was sometimes *feared*, but oftener looked up to with respect and love. The senior officers were the friends, companions, and advisers of the younger; and these younger, though not so crammed and learned as at present, were, as a rule, well-educated and often accomplished young fellows. A private was generally several years in the ranks before he got his stripe, and sergeants were men of long service and experience, and were therefore useful to, and trusted by, their officers.

Does this description of what existed in the olden times apply to our regiments of the last ten years, and will it apply to our army in its changed and present circumstances? During the past decade, have officers and men manifested the same confidence in, and the same reliance on, each other as they did when the regiment, with its well-known old number, was the unit of our army, and when long service bound all ranks firmly together, and created and kept up an *esprit-de-corps* which it is to be feared is now looked upon and treated as a matter of sentiment, or as a feeling that never did exist and is not necessary?

But we who spent our lives in the old long-service army know that *esprit-de-corps did* exist, that it was productive of much good, and we grieve to see that the feeling is discouraged or ignored. We have all read the arguments in support of short service with the colours, and the necessity for the formation of a Reserve. But, after ten years' trial of short service, what is the strength of the Reserve which we have formed? At most some fifty thousand men. At what cost to our fighting army has this Reserve been formed? It has filled the ranks of our regiments with lads, and caused a scarcity of efficient non-commissioned officers, and been followed by such a rapid current of change in our regiments that officers and men have not time to know how far they can rely upon each other. What are the conditions under which our Reserve can be made use of? In the event only of the nation being engaged in European warfare.

Can we feel confident that these fifty thousand men will again respond to any sudden call to arms after the experiences of 1877, when the men of the Reserve *did* respond so honourably and loyally? We must only hope they will, while the nation must be prepared to make better provision for wives and children during the absence of the men on service.

Yet though we of the old school thus write, and though we feel in our hearts 'that glory is departed,' we cherish the hope that *esprit-de-corps* will be kept up in our territorial regiments, and that a motto somewhat like that borne by one of our old distinguished corps may apply to the whole army of the future, 'Aucto splendore resurgam.' True, we of the old school are now in the sear-and-yellow-leaf period of life—old fellows who have lived our day, and now find ourselves upon the shelf, thrown there, or perhaps gently laid there, by the new school, which, more full of life and vigour than we are, with new ideas and aspirations, is bent on change, thought to be improvement, so as to keep pace (as they think and say) with other nations. Be it so; but the new school will acknowledge that we of the old long-service army bore the heat and burden of our generation gallantly, and will bear with us as we mourn over the destruction of old customs and institutions which we held in much respect, and under which we upheld our country's honour and renown, and, as we are passing from the scene of active life, will forgive us if, in bidding them God speed, we say to them, 'Go ye and do likewise.'

As I write these words, the glorious news of victory has been flashed home from Egypt, and all England reads with feelings of pride and exultation of the splendid valour of the *young* soldiers of our territorial regiments under their great leader, who has been and is the chief advocate of the new system of short service with the colours and transfer to the Reserve. All honour to the brave *lads*, and may the great victory of Tel-el-Kebir be the prelude to other and far greater honours than our noble army has achieved in the past.

But amongst the many changes which in recent years have been effected, not one has been felt more keenly by all classes than the loss of the regimental surgeon. We acknowledge that there were serious defects in the old army medical organization, and that something more suited to the requirements of modern warfare was a necessity. But the change that has been made was too sweeping and too sudden of accomplishment, and was deeply felt by all classes, especially by the medical officers themselves.

The regimental surgeon of all men had it in his power to make himself useful to and popular in his regiment by strict devotion to his duty, to which he often felt there was no limit, even when toiling beyond his strength; also by giving to and receiving from his brother-officers companionship and friendship, and by treating the men and their families with kindness and consideration, receiving from them in return confidence and even affection. His position, when he chose to make it so, was of all others in the regiment the most useful and the happiest. During long years of service, both in peace and war, he became the friend of all, and could exercise an influence for good on everyone and everything connected with the regiment, possibly unseen and unfelt, because ruled and guided by tact and judgment unmixed with selfishness. He was the willing recipient of little confidences committed to no other keeping. He was the adviser whom all sought in difficulties, and who often settled little troubles in a quiet way that proved satisfactory to all concerned. He was generally a good companion, too, and took part in all his brother-officers' amusements; was ready to boat and fish, or to shoot and hunt, with them, and even willingly gave advice about the purchase or the illness of a horse or dog. Then in accident or sickness, or on the day of battle, he was relied on with the most implicit confidence; for all knew, from the care and watchfulness they had seen him exercise in other cases, that *they* too would receive the utmost attention from one who was the thoughtful friend of all.

True, the regimental surgeon was not always

popular, but I can affirm without fear of contradiction that, when such was the case, the fault lay with the surgeon himself, and not with the regiment.

The regimental system, however, we have been told authoritatively, is now ' a thing of the past,' and time will efface the pleasant memories connected with the regimental surgeon, and may perhaps show that he was an unnecessary and even *sentimental* institution; but his former usefulness is still acknowledged and his absence deplored by the service generally. Is it too late to restore him even now? Does the service require it, and would the present medical officers themselves desire it?

In explanation of what I have said as to the usefulness and popularity of the old regimental surgeons, I may mention what occurred in my presence not very many months ago. A medical officer of administrative rank, as it is called, while making an inspection of the barracks occupied by the regiment of which he had formerly been the surgeon, observed several little hygienic arrangements still in operation which had been introduced at his own suggestion many years previously, and asked what was the object of them.

'Why, sir,' was the reply, 'these are your own old orders, and they have never been altered or interfered with since you left us, but now we have no one to tell us what to do, or show us how to do it.'

This may seem a trifle, but it was a trifle gratifying to the old surgeon, and showed that his presence and his thoughtfulness had been, and were still, useful to his old regiment.

The medical department was the first portion of the army to which Lord Cardwell's great scheme of reorganization was applied and carried to completion, but it was effected under many a protest and amidst intense dissatisfaction. Now, however, that the application of the scheme to the whole service has been accomplished, is our army system really perfect, and fit to compare with those of other European nations? No, it is not, and never can be so, until the nation consents to accept universal military training.

I have remarked already that in former days there existed generally, or almost universally, a friendly feeling, which extended throughout all ranks, but I think that in Scotch or Highland regiments there was something more than this. In these there was a friendly intimacy between officers and men which by strangers might have been looked upon as familiarity, but which was in reality the evidence of esteem and confidence in each other which knew no fear, and was the result not only of long companionship, but of a feeling of nationality. In those days of which I write Scotch regiments were intensely national; and in support of this assertion I may instance the 93rd Sutherland Highlanders, which, on embarkation for India in 1857, out of a strength of one thousand and seventy men, had nine hundred and forty-four Scotchmen in the ranks, and the great majority of these were Gaelic-speaking Highlanders.

I find in my journal many allusions to this feeling of friendly intimacy, and some interesting and touching instances of it, which are, I think, worthy of record, and which I will describe.

CHAPTER XVII.

I re-visit my old Regiment—Find few old Friends and Comrades—Kindly Greeting from the Few—The Sergeant-major—Drum-major—My old Batman—My Faithful old Orderly—His care of Me—The old Pipe-major—His Affection for 'the Doctor'—Some of his Sayings and Doings.

IN relating the following anecdotes, I do not adhere strictly to chronological arrangement, but tell them just as it suits my purpose, adhering, however, strictly to the text, and always quoting remarks or expressions in the very words which were made use of.

I will not refrain from mentioning the names of persons living—these, however, are unfortunately few—and of those who may be mentioned I will write nothing likely to give offence; indeed, I am confident that the publicity now given to the following old stories, detailing facts, will afford pleasure or amusement, and not annoyance, to the very few who know them. Of the living or of the dead I will write only what is kind, for I am happy to be able to say that in my long military career I found infinitely more that was good and noble than was base or mean in those with whom I was associated.

Officers of the old school—that is, those who served prior to the introduction of short-service with the colours—are often surprised and disappointed, on re-visiting their old corps, to find so few brother-officers remaining, so few old comrades in the ranks.

A friend, an old officer, mentioned to me lately that not very long ago he was serving in the same garrison with the regiment (a Highland one) to which he had formerly belonged, and that of all the officers present only two were old companions with whom he had served in the Crimea and in the Indian Mutiny, and that of six hundred men *there* present he found only half a dozen who knew him personally. These few, however, were men of the old stamp, who had grown grey with years and long and varied service, then just drawing to a close. He found the sergeant-major was one whom he remembered as a young soldier; the drum-major, now a tall, powerful man, he remembered as a soldier's son; and in his wife, now the mother of a family, he recognised an old acquaintance whom he had known from early infancy.

All were pleased to see him, grateful for his kindly recognition of them, and for the friendly offer of his hand. In conversation with the sergeant-major, he alluded to old times, to stirring scenes of active-service in which they had been together, and remarked that he 'looked back on those days as the most useful of his life.' In reply, and with a touch of what I have termed 'friendly intimacy,' his old comrade asked, 'Were they not the happiest, too, sir?'

Some days thereafter, this same officer, as he rode through the barrack-square, observed an old soldier stop to look at him, then walk a little way off and turn to look again; so he rode up to him, when the old private, saluting respectfully and clasping the offered hand of the officer, exclaimed, with apparent familiarity, 'Lordsake, sir, I thocht it was yersel', but I wasna jist shure o' ye wi'out yer beard.' Then he expressed his pleasure at the meeting, and asked 'how the lady was, and if the children,' naming them correctly and in their proper order, 'were alive and well?' A stranger, witnessing this meeting, might have wondered at the apparent familiarity on the part of a private to an officer; but there was no familiarity intended, only an expression of 'friendly intimacy,' the result of long companionship, for officer and soldier had served together during many years.

In 1857, the 93rd was marching hurriedly from Calcutta towards Lucknow, to form part of the army intended for the relief of the Residency.

One afternoon, while halted in camp, the officers were purchasing horses or ponies, and one of them had just effected a purchase; but, on mounting the little animal, it reared so viciously that the rider slipped off at once. This officer's old batman (or groom) happened to be looking on, and, after waiting for a minute or two, asked his old master,

'Are ye no gauen to munt agen?'

'No.'

'Then ye're gauen to let a bit beastie like thon beat ye?'

'Yes, I am.'

'Then I wadna if I was you.'

No disrespect was meant, only surprise that his old master, whom he knew to be a good horseman, should allow himself to be 'thocht feared for a bit *brute* o' a pownie.'

At the battle of Cawnpore, which was fought directly after the relief of the Residency, the following incident occurred to myself: The regiment was advancing in line, under a smart fire from the guns of the enemy. I followed immediately behind the centre, and, as usual, was accompanied by my old orderly, Private William D——. We were both old soldiers familiar with the hiss of round shot, the rush of shell, the crack of shrapnel, and the ping of the bullet, but I had never heard the whistling flight of grape. Suddenly, as we advanced on that occasion, it seemed to me that I heard the sound of birds in rapid flight above and around me, and at the strange sound I swayed my body round, so as to present my side to it. Immediately the old orderly touched me on the arm, saying at the same time, 'A'm ashamed for ye, doctor; haud yer front tae't, man, it's only grape ye're hearin'.' The good fellow was not ashamed of me, but for me, and explained his meaning thus: '*I* ken ye weel eneugh, but I wad think ill suld ithers suppose or say that "the doctor" was feared for a grape shot.'

This same orderly was as good and brave a soul as ever lived. He was true as steel to me, and often, as if unintentionally or accidentally, interposed his big body between me and danger on the battlefield. He had only one failing; but who is perfect? He was always strictly sober when he could get only water to drink, but had no objection to whisky or rum when he could get either; and, as he said himself, 'he liked the taste o' them baith weel.' He was generally rough in speech and act, but was fearless under danger, and always handled a sick or wounded comrade as gently as a woman could, and lowered his rough voice into a whisper to speak words of kindness and comfort. For ten years he was the devoted follower of his friend 'the doctor,' whom he looked upon as the great oracle of the regiment; but at last old age, failing strength, and those anomolous pains (of which old soldiers used to complain in their twentieth year of service) obtained for him his discharge. Not many years thereafter he was laid in his final resting-place in his own Highland home.

The Pipe-major of the regiment was a character, and a great favourite with both officers and men. He was a man of few words, at least English words, for he usually spoke and always thought in Gaelic, which I may say was the language spoken at that time by the majority of the non-commissioned officers, and by a large majority of the men. He was a plain-looking man, above the average height, broad and thick-set, and, blessed with a most enduring physique, was perfectly indifferent to heat or cold, feasting or fasting, and relished water when there was no whisky, though I never heard of his drinking too freely of the former. No word of satisfaction, no murmur of complaint ever escaped his lips, a smile seldom lit up his countenance, and he never laughed. He lived through all the hardships and privations of the Crimean campaign without one hour of sickness, and returned to England in perfect health. I feel a mournful pleasure in writing this short history of John McL——, Pipe-major of the 93rd, and in paying my humble tribute to his memory.

He had a great affection, I believe, for 'the doctor,' as I was styled in the regiment, and first showed his affection for me on the morning of the reconnaissance made (in February, 1855) by Sir Colin Campbell in the direction of the Russian position, in the valley of Tchorgoun, near Balaklava. The column detailed for this duty consisted of the Highland Brigade, with artillery, to be supported by a French division (Vinois'). It was ordered to leave the encampment at midnight, but was delayed by a heavy snowstorm, which came on suddenly, and, while it lasted, rendered any movement impossible. About two a.m., however, the storm abated sufficiently to allow us to make a start. Accordingly we moved quietly and silently out of our entrenchments. But, though it had ceased to snow, a cold, boisterous north-easterly wind was blowing, which drove into our faces showers of fine, dry snow from the ground, and of sleet, so fine and dense, that we felt as if enveloped in a cloud of needles, which pierced so sharply that it was hardly possible to keep our eyes open. We staggered along, however, across the open plain, and round the base of the low hills, which had been redoubts, in spite of snow and sleet and darkness, under the guidance of a friendly Tartar who knew the track, and could follow it without the use of eyes. Just as morning dawned we found ourselves on the top of a height overlooking the enemy's position, but, as no French division had appeared to support us, we halted, and watched the Russians as they hurriedly turned out of their huts, quite taken by surprise.

While halted, the Pipe-major observed that his friend 'the doctor' was limping about as if in pain, and, alarmed at his apparently crippled condition, approached, and thus addressed him:

'A'm sorry to see ye hurplin, sir. What's the maater we ye?'

'I have got a bad pain in the ankle.'

'Mebe ye're hungry, sir. Will ye tak' a bit o' wheat-bread and a bite o' tongue?'

'Thank you; with pleasure.'

'Than here 'tis; an' gude tae, an' it's frae the north; an' mebe ye'd like a dram?'

P

'Yes, awfully.'

'Weel, here's a drap o' the richt stuff, an' nane o' yer trash they ca' rum; an' it's frae ma freends in the north tae.'

In time John learned to like the trash he then called rum.

'The doctor' ate evidently as if he were hungry, and drank the 'richt stuff' as if he were cold and required it; and the Pipe-major stood and watched him with as much satisfaction apparently as if he were applying a quaich filled with whisky to his own lips, and remarked, 'A'm thinking ye'll be a' richt noo.' It was afterwards discovered that the Pipe-major had friends and admirers at home who had not forgotten him, but had several times sent him a box containing 'deelicacies,' as he called them, which he unselfishly shared with those for whom he had a special regard.

When a regiment returns to England from foreign or active service, everything requires brushing up—officers want new kits, the men new clothing, the band new instruments, etc., and, if it be a Highland regiment, the pipers require new pipes. The 93rd, on returning from the Crimea, was much in need of new equipment generally, for it was one of the first which had been despatched to the East early in 1854. And amongst other articles of new clothing, on its return to England after the war, it was decided by the officers that the pipers should be dressed in green cloth instead of red coats. This was to be done at the expense of the officers themselves, and one of their number was deputed to arrange as to style, pattern, etc.

This officer accordingly sent for the Pipe-major, and the following short dialogue passed between them :—

'McL——, the officers have decided to dress the pipers in green tunics, and *you* are to be dressed very handsomely and as befits a pipe-major.'

'Ay, an' hoo's thaat, sir?'

'You are to have a tunic trimmed with silver braid, and with silver buttons.'

'Vera weel, sir.'

'But you'll have to brush yourself up a bit, and swagger a little more than you do.'

'Na, I'll no do thaat.'

'Why?'

'A'm no a gude-lookin' enough man.'

'Very well, then, I'll mention what you say to the officers, and possibly they'll not dress you as they had intended.'

'Ah, then I'll try and swagger,' exclaimed McL——, with great emphasis.

To the day of his death, however, he either would not or could not 'swagger,' or show any of the conceit usually exhibited by a piper; and, though he was a first-rate performer, he always played as if there was 'no note of music in his soul.' To judge from his solemn appearance and motion while playing the most enlivening reel or strathspey, a stranger would have thought that he was performing a task in which he had no pleasure, and yet he was perfectly absorbed in the music, and thought his 'pipes' the queen of instruments.

CHAPTER XVIII.

John McL.—His Amiability—Isaac T.—His Love of Fun—McL——'s Illness, and Extraordinary Delusions on Recovering Consciousness—His gallant Behaviour at Lucknow—His Last Illness, and Last Message—The Regiment before the Assault—Young MacDonald—His Death—Surgeon on the Day of Battle.

McL——'S taciturnity, and, I may add, his amiability, were the means through which others often took advantage of him. There was one sergeant in the regiment, Isaac T——, a good fellow and true as steel, but in those days much given to fun and practical jokes, and often at the expense of honest John McL——.

One of his jokes was to make John 'foo,' and while in this state to draw him out, get him to unbosom himself, and actually tell stories, sometimes bordering on the marvellous, and at other times on the ridiculous. As John liked his liquor, and never shirked, despising 'heel-taps,' he easily fell into the trap laid for him. This happened so frequently that at last John had a severe illness in consequence, during which he was violently delirious, and, as this happened while the regiment was on the march in India, it was necessary to put him into a tent by himself, and to set two native hospital attendants to watch him.

Indian tents are large and lofty, and lined inside with dark-blue cotton. These, when lighted up at night by a couple of little earthenware lamps, very similar to the old Highland 'kreusy,' are dark and gloomy, and to a man awaking to consciousness from delirium would appear doubly so. 'The doctor,' anxious about his patient, visited him during the night, and as he stood by the cot or dhoolie, John opened his eyes, stared wildly round for a second or two, and then, fixing his gaze on his two sable attendants who sat crouched beside him, he seized 'the doctor's' hand and whispered,

'Whaur am I, sir?'

'Comfortably in your cot, and, I think, better.'

'Weel,' said John, again staring round the tent, 'a'm no in —— ony way, for *ye're* here, and I dinna see Isaac T——.'

The poor fellow, frightened at the gloom of the tent, and possibly at his dark, weird-looking attendants, and impressed, too, by the recollection of the troubled visions and terrible spectres which had haunted him during his delirium, thought that he was in *the* place of torment, but felt some degree of assurance from the presence of his friend 'the doctor,' and from the fact that his tempter was not visible; or perhaps he felt thankful for even the small mercy and comfort of his tempter's absence.

This was his only severe attack of illness up to that date, but on recovering he took to hard drinking, and had another bad illness, of which he died. His last words were, 'Gi'e ma love to the doctor' (I happened to be absent on leave at the time) ' an' to a' ma auld comrades.' Thus passed away one who looked on the regiment as his home, and on his comrades as his best and only friends. He was as insensible to danger as he was to heat or cold, to feasting or fasting, and it is but fair to his memory to put on record an instance of his courage and disregard of danger, which will be found at the close of this chapter.

At the siege of Lucknow the 93rd was detailed by Sir Colin himself as the storming-party for the assault of the key of the enemy's position (the Begum Koti). I shall never forget that day, with its crowd of incidents. Even now, though so many years have passed, the whole scene, of which I was an eye-witness, and in which in my own sphere I was an actor, comes back as vividly as if all had happened only yesterday. During the morning of that day, while a breach was being made in the strong defences which surrounded the enemy's position, the regiment occupied an enclosure surrounded by high mud walls, which in former days had apparently been a well-kept garden. Even then, amid the surrounding ruin, the orange and the citron blossomed, and the rose, the myrtle, and the jasmine bloomed. From this enclosure the regiment moved to take up its final position before the assault. As it passed out a brother-officer (Charles William Macdonald), a captain, but still a lad, whose right arm had been severely bruised early in the day by a splinter of shell, but who, though thus far disabled, had refused to leave the field, plucked a rose, and, handing it to me, said, 'Good-bye, old friend—keep this for my sake,' and then moved on. It was his last gift and last farewell, for within half an hour thereafter he was killed, two bullets striking him in quick succession as he entered the breach at the head of his company. His faithful old servant brought the body out upon his back, and laid it gently down upon the ground before the friend to whom he had spoken his last 'good-bye;' and as they stood together side by side, and gazed down on the pale, boyish-looking face, the eyes closed as if in sleep, and a smile upon the lip just darkened by a fringe of down, the old soldier turned away, and, brushing his rough hand across his eyes, murmured, 'Oh, pity me, but it was a shame to kill him!'*

The position of a surgeon on the day of battle is a peculiarly trying one, for he has none of the excitement of the fight, and, though quite as much exposed to danger as his combatant comrades, he must keep his head clear and his hand steady, in order that he may be able to exercise his calling

---

* Another officer (Lieutenant Sergison) was killed on the same day.

carefully and skilfully; but a scene such as I have just described is enough to shake the strongest nerves, and to make the heart throb and the hand tremble. While he has to care for the wounded only, he has the cheering expectation of being able to alleviate suffering and to save life, but when the lifeless body of brother, friend, or comrade is laid on the ground before him, he knows that there is no hope, and his feelings are almost akin to despair, no matter how inured to war and its incidents he may have become.

I had been with the regiment during the early part of the day within the enclosure, and followed it as it moved from thence to take up its final position, and there I stood watching the bearing of the men.

Behind some ruined buildings and battered walls, nearly opposite the breach, stood some eight hundred men, throughout whose ranks reigned a silence deep as death. Each man stood leaning on his rifle, wrapt in his own thoughts. What were they? Ah! who could tell? But the contracted brow, the flashing eye, the dilating nostril, and the closely-compressed lips told plainly that their blood was stirring fiercely; and the slowly-heaving chest, the quivering muscles of their naked, brawny limbs, and the slight forward inclination of their bodies, reminded me of greyhounds held in leash and straining to be slipped. Though each man knew that danger or perhaps death was very near, he knew also that he was not alone to face them; but that on either side and all around him stood old comrades, who, often tried before, had proved themselves staunch and true, who had never failed him, and who would now stand firm with him in any peril. In such companionship he was prepared to do his duty, or even to die. Such was the confidence engendered by long fellowship in the olden times, such was the faith each had in the other, and such was the *esprit-de-corps* in our old regiments.

Suddenly there was a slight movement in the ranks, just enough to break the previous stillness. Officers quietly moved to their places, men stood erect, pressed their bonnets firmly down upon their heads, stretched their arms and limbs, as if to test their freedom, and then, grasping their rifles tightly, stood firm and steady. Thus they remained for just a second or two, when the tall form of their favourite leader, Adrian Hope, appeared, and his right hand waved the signal for assault. Then a cry burst from their ranks. It was not a cheer which has a pleasant ring in it, but a short, sharp, piercing cry, which had an angry sound that almost made one tremble. I never heard the like before and never since. Then followed the rush and tramp of hurrying feet.

Who in the vigour of youth or manhood has not felt the many excitements of life—a day on the banks of silvery Tweed or other river, when the salmon leaped and plunged and rushed up stream, carrying out yards on yards of line; who does not know the excitement of the eight-oared race; who has not gloried in the hunting-field, when the pack with scent breast-high go racing on so close together that a 'sheet might cover all,' and when the music and melody of their deep-toned notes have stirred the blood to face the biggest pace? But, oh! nothing can compare with the wild cry and rapid tread of angry men rushing into battle; and the more so when those angry men are comrades tried and true, who know and trust each other, and who have fought and proved their courage on many a battle-field before.

With the leading party and amongst the foremost stormers was our friend, John McL——, who, entering the breach, tuned up at once, and, pacing up and down within the inner court of the enemy's works, perfectly regardless of his own safety, played the regimental gathering while the fight raged fiercely round him, thinking, as he afterwards said, that 'the lads would fight all the better when they heard the music o' the pipes.' This was never forgotten in the regiment, and greatly increased his popularity, and I have much pleasure in recording it.

He lived for several years after the mutiny, and passed away from amongst us as I have already described, universally regretted. He was buried with the usual military honours, and his favourite tune, which he had played so often and so well for many a dead comrade, was his own requiem. The 'Flowers of the Forest' never sounded so sad and plaintive as at poor John McL——'s funeral.

CHAPTER XIX.

Penalty attached to the writing of Reminiscences—The Memory of old Friends—Brave Acts—Surrounded by the Enemy—MacBean—His Receiving the Victoria Cross—Private George McK.—Refuses to be Attended to by Anyone but his 'ain Doctor'—Burroughs Wounded—Two Distressing Scenes.

ONE of the penalties attached to writing the reminiscences of a long military career is the painful necessity of recalling to memory old comrades who were taken suddenly away amid the din and shock of battle, or old friends with whom one had lived for years in closest fellowship, but who had passed silently away amid the still and calm of peace. And as the curtain closed over each of them we, who are still spared for a little longer, should accept the warning, and make ready for the last great muster. But, come when and how that hour may, it will be well for us if we have been true and upright in our lives, loyal to our friends, forbearing to our enemies; have striven to do our duty to the best of our ability, and are waiting patiently, strong in faith, and in the hope that as the veil is drawn suddenly or slowly before *our* closing eyes we shall hear the great Comrade, Friend, and Leader say, ' Well done, good and faithful soldier.'

Many brave acts were performed *that* day on which the key of the enemy's position at Lucknow was assaulted and taken; but amongst them one shone conspicuous, and the hero of it obtained the Victoria Cross. I now tell the story.

After entering the breach, one of our officers (MacBean) as brave a man as ever lived, and yet as simple as a child, found himself almost alone, and surrounded by the enemy. But he wielded his sword so dexterously, and made such good use of his revolver, that after a desperate struggle, in which he killed eleven of his foes, he stood unharmed. .Some time afterwards, a regimental parade was held for the purpose of presenting his well-earned cross, and as the general, Sir R. Garrett, pinned the decoration to his breast, he addressed him in the following words :—

' This cross has been awarded to you for the conspicuous gallantry you displayed at the assault of the enemy's position at Lucknow, on which occasion you killed eleven of the enemy by whom you were surrounded. And a good day's work it was, sir.'

' Tutts,' said my gallant and simple friend, quite forgetting that he was on parade, and perhaps a little piqued at his performance being spoken of as a day's work. ' Tutts, it didna tak' me twanty minutes.'

These are the very words he used, spoken in

his own braid Scotch too: I who tell the story heard them, for I was standing by his side.

This old friend lives in my memory only. He was one of my brother-officers, who had escaped death on many a battlefield, and who passed silently away to the last muster in the still and calm of peace, surrounded and tended to the last by soldiers, which had always been his wish; and I, who had been his friend for years, and his companion in many a danger, was the only one of all his old comrades that was near him at the last, except the old soldier who had been his servant, and who was sent over from Ireland through the kindness of Colonel Knollys (then commanding the regiment) to be with his old master and to nurse him during his illness. Our first meeting was when he had just been gazetted to a commission, our last at the close of his earthly career when he was a General.

I believe that no man ever lived who tried more honestly to do his duty than William MacBean. Whatever were his little failings, all who knew him will acknowledge this. From the humblest position in a regiment he had risen to the command of it, and shortly before his death was promoted to the rank of Major-general.

After the capture of Lucknow, Sir Colin offered to recommend him for a company in another regiment. Before deciding, however, he consulted Adrian Hope, who advised him to decline it, and wait for a vacancy in the 93rd. Strange to say, he got his company in the regiment by poor Hope's death.

Another incident connected with this assault will exemplify the friendly feeling and intimacy which existed between officers and men in the olden times, and the confidence they had in each other.

Amongst the wounded was a private, George McK——, a fine, big, manly fellow, full of life and fun, who had been one of the great promoters of the drama, and one of the best actors in the regiment in former days. His right arm was shattered at the elbow, and, as I stooped over him to examine the wound, he looked up in my face, and asked,

'Is't a' ower wi' me, doctor?'

'No,' replied I, 'but it will be necessary to take off your right arm.'

'Ah, man, if I dee, what'll become o' ma puir auld mither?'

After arranging the shattered limb as gently and as securely as possible, I gave orders that he should be carried at once to the regimental hospital, distant about a mile, and at the same time sent instructions to have everything ready for several other operations that would be necessary.

By some mistake, this man, and this man only, was taken to the *field* instead of the regimental hospital, and there the surgeon on duty, after a careful examination of the wound, told him that the operation should be performed without delay.

'Na, na,' said the poor fellow, 'no till our ain doctor comes; he said he wad come, and a'm shure he will.'

As soon as the fighting was over, and all the wounded men collected, I returned to our camp, and on arrival my first inquiry was for George McK——, but just at that moment a message was brought to me from the *field* hospital to the effect that a man of the regiment had been admitted there, who was very badly wounded, but who refused to allow anything to be done for him except by his own surgeon. I hastened to the *field* hospital at once, desiring one of my assistants to follow. On arriving there I found George McK—— in such a state of prostration that it was impossible either to operate on his arm, or to remove him to the regimental hospital. He looked up into my face as I stood by his cot, and whispered,

'Ye were lang o' comin', man. They wanted to cut aff ma airm, but I wadna let them, and tell'd them that naebody suld cut ma airm aff but our ain doctor; but ye're come noo, an' I ken that I'll be taken care o'.'

I was obliged to leave him again, to attend to the others that were to be operated on in the regimental hospital, but desired my assistant to remain and watch McK——, and to give him frequently small quantities of stimulants and nourishment, promising to return as soon as possible.

In the early morning, having completed all the

other operations, I returned to the *field* hospital, and found that McK—— had completely rallied, and was in a fit state to undergo the operation; so, under chloroform, I performed amputation. On recovering consciousness, he asked,

'Is't a' ower, and d'ye think I'll no dee?'

'Yes,' said I, 'it's all over; and I think and hope you will do well.'

'God bless ye, doctor,' said the poor fellow. 'Ye're a guid freend;' at the same time holding out his left hand he took and pressed mine firmly, and, looking gratefully up into my face, the poor fellow continued: 'I wad like to gi'e ye a wee thing, jist to mind ye o' a' yer kindness, if ye'll tak' it. There's a bit horn in ma valise, which I made into a mull mysel' when we were in the Crimea. Ye'll ask ma comrade to gie't ye, an' ye'll keep it for ma sake?'

That little mull is now in my possession, mounted in silver, and I feel a pride in showing it and telling the little tale connected with it, whenever I have an opportunity.

All the mental and physical strain I had undergone, and all the danger I had passed through during the previous day, had not visibly affected me; but I had suffered acutely, and felt bitterly the loss of friends and comrades, and especially of young Macdonald, to whom I have already made allusion as having been killed in the assault of the Begum Koti. Now the confidence in and affection for me manifested by my wounded comrade and the kindly blessing of the humble soldier quite unmanned me, and I had to turn away to conceal my emotion.

George McK—— made a good and rapid recovery, and was sent home to be pensioned, and to gladden the heart of his 'puir auld mither,' who for years had been in a great measure dependent upon the little savings sent her by her soldier son.

During the last day's fighting at Lucknow, an officer of the regiment, Captain Burroughs, had been severely wounded, his leg having been broken very badly in two places below the knee and the skin lacerated. The general medical opinion in camp was that amputation of the limb was the only chance of saving his life. The surgeon of the regiment alone was of opinion that limb and life might both be saved, and refused to operate until his friend, having heard both sides of the question, should decide for himself. Accordingly he was told plainly that the almost universal opinion was that he must lose his leg or die, but that such was not the opinion of his own surgeon. 'Then,' said he, without hesitation, 'I accept *his* opinion, and will take my chance.' He recovered, and, though the wounded limb is a little shorter than the other, still, instead of being a miserable cripple, he can walk with perfect ease, and without even a perceptible halt.

I must say that he was very grateful to his friend, the surgeon of the regiment, at the time, and that, during all the long years since then, he has never wearied of expressing and showing gratitude for the service which was done him on that occasion. He was a captain at that time, commanded the regiment afterwards, and is now a General.

I will close this chapter by short extracts from my journal descriptive of two sad scenes at which I was present, probably the most painful that I was ever called upon to witness; for death came suddenly and unexpectedly to two friends in the very prime of their manhood, while they were absent from those they loved, and at a moment when fortune had just begun to smile on each.

I cannot refrain from alluding to these two cases, because the first proves the confidence in and affection for each other which long service and companionship engendered amongst officers, and also because both show how often a simple, childlike, unobtrusive faith may glow in the heart, govern and guide the whole life, and enable the Christian soldier at last to meet death, however and whenever it may come, not only fearlessly, but calmly and firm in hope.

In the interval between the capture of Lucknow and the resumption of hostilities in the following cold season, two regiments, which for several years had been constantly associated on active service, occupied temporary quarters in the same military cantonment. Two officers of these regiments, the subjects of the following sad reminiscences, had known each other long, had become intimate, and intimacy had ripened into friendship and affection. They belonged to different regiments; one was a surgeon, the other a lieutenant-colonel commanding, who had only lately, and at a comparatively early age, attained this position. Both were Highlanders of good old name, and had mutual friends at home; and perhaps these circumstances tended not a little to strengthen their attachment.

The field-officer was suddenly taken ill, and requested that his friend (the surgeon) might be sent for to assist his own medical attendant with advice and counsel. There was something about the illness which the medical officers failed to discover, and, though they knew that he was very ill, they could not trace the cause, and, though anxious, did not apprehend danger.

But on the third day the illness took a sudden and alarming turn; the pulse failed and fluttered, the voice grew faint and weak, the breathing quick and laboured, and it flashed across the sick man's mind that this was death; and then he read it quickly in the faces of those around his cot. He asked no questions, but merely desired that his friend might be called at once. On his arrival, the sick man bade all others leave the room, and then, holding out his hand, he took his friend's and drew him near, and, calmly looking into his face, said,

'Old friend, I know that death is near. No one has told me so, but I feel it, and have read it on the faces round me; but I think that *you* above all others might have come to tell and warn me.'

'I did not know; I never thought that there was any immediate danger. Not one of us thought so,' replied his friend, shocked at what he saw and heard.

'Well, never mind,' continued the sufferer, speaking more feebly than at first. 'I did not send for you to upbraid you or cause you pain, but to see you once more, to say good-bye, and to give you my last message of love for those at home. Tell them when you meet that I passed away in peace, and that my last thoughts were of them. Now go, old friend—you must not stay to see the very end. I know that another Friend is near, and I feel His presence, though I cannot see, for my eyes are growing dim. Good-bye.'

There was a sudden pause, and as I raised my head I saw that all was over.

With the second friend I had been associated only a short time. He was not a brother-officer, nor did he belong to the same arm of the service as myself. He was colonel of ——, had seen much service in India, and had been distinguished during the mutiny. He was a Scotch Episcopalian, but made no parade of religion, and seldom spoke on the subject. He was of such a retiring disposition that it was difficult to know him, but his gentle and modest address and manner, when you were admitted to his acquaintance, were striking and captivating.

Some time before I knew him, he had obtained leave of absence, and had left India with his family, a poor man, but on arrival in England found, unexpectedly, that he had become the possessor of an estate in Scotland by the death of a relative. There were some burdens on the estate, however, which he wished to clear off, therefore he returned to India, leaving his family at home, but with the intention of rejoining them at the end of two years. He had completed one year of the two in India when I met him, and his health, naturally delicate, had been so impaired during the hot season of that year that he thought of going home again, but the advent of another cold season so recruited him that he changed his mind, and decided to remain for the second year. He was, like all Anglo-Indians, a sportsman, so in the month of February, the coldest and healthiest of the season, he started alone for ten days' shooting in the jungle near the foot of the hills, but returned to cantonments before his leave had expired, feeling very unwell. Unfortunately, he did not apply to the surgeon of his corps until he was so ill as to be unable to leave his bed.

I was asked to visit him, and found him suffering from jungle fever of the most intense form, from which there appeared to be scarcely a possibility of his recovery.

I now copy from my journal the very words written therein many years ago, and a description of the scene just as I noted it at the time. It was too late, we could do nothing to save him; and he, seeing us anxious, asked if he was 'in danger and likely to die.' We told him plainly of our anxiety and fear, and he at once said,

'Thank you, I feel that there is danger. I *should* wish to live, if it be God's will, to see my dear ones again, but I have no fear of death, and if you wait with me to the end you shall see that I do not lose heart, though I have such a weak, frail body. My worldly affairs are all settled, but I wish to write a few lines to my wife, after that to see Dr. R——' (the chaplain), 'and partake of the sacrament.'

In conversation with the chaplain he said,

'I thank God for having given me pious parents, who taught me both by precept and example so to live that, when the end came, I should not fear to die. I have prayed from my youth upwards to be enabled to live a Christian life, and for years have been in constant communion with my God and Saviour, looking always to the probability of sudden death, and, now that it is near, I am ready.'

He then prepared to partake of the sacrament, but he was so weak, so nearly spent, that we were afraid to raise him up, so the bread was given to him as he lay in bed; but when the cup of wine was offered, he entreated us to raise him up for a moment that he might take it 'reverently and respectfully,' and as it touched his lip the 'silver cord was loosened,' and he passed away to be at rest for ever, leaving in his life and death a bright example to those who knew him.

At my first professional visit, he told me that one night in camp, when the air was still and calm, and the full moon shone in all its splendour in a cloudless sky, he was tempted to sit outside his tent to observe and admire the dim, weird light in the gloomy forest, the strange fantastic shadows of the great overhanging branches and the dense foliage above them which, in the uncertain light, were cast upon the earth; that, while so occupied, his thoughts wandered back over his past eventful life, with all its dangers and difficulties, but with its full share of happiness; then on to the immediate future, with its uncertainties and hopes, and then, 'in the multitude of his thoughts within him,' to the great future beyond this life, and that he became so absorbed in the contemplation of this last subject that he did not heed the lapse of time, did not think of the imprudence he was committing in sitting exposed to the night air in the jungle, did not feel the chill that was creeping over him till he began to shiver; that then, and not till then, he rose and sought his bed, trembling violently, and with aching head and limbs.

He was not sensible of it at the time, but it was while he sat out in the chill night air, absorbed in thought, that the deadly fever had seized upon him.

CHAPTER XX.

Encamped at Bareilly—Narrow Escape—General Troup—Nainé Tal—The Terai—Beauty of Hill Scenery—Cheenie—Almorah—View of Snowy Range—We enter Oude—Engagements of Posgaon and Russelpore—Rebel Cavalry attack Baggage Column—Noorunghabad—Attack on Mithoulie—Nepaul Frontier.

AFTER the battle of Bareilly, alluded to in Chapter XV, the army was encamped on the extensive plain beyond the ruins of the military cantonment, between two and three miles from the city. While encamped there, we had our first experience of a dust-storm, a very unusual occurrence in India in the month of May. The weather had been intensely hot for several days, during which not a breath of air stirred the oppressive, murky atmosphere, in which floated thin clouds of reddish dust, dense enough to obscure the sun.

This condition of the atmosphere continued for several days, and on the afternoon of the fourth day we became sensible of occasional little puffs of hot air, lasting for only a second or two. They gradually increased in frequency and strength, stirring up the dust from the ground in different directions at the same moment and whirling it into the air in little spiral columns, to which the term 'devils' is locally applied. These were followed by the appearance of a cloud low down on the western horizon, which gradually enlarged until spreading out it rapidly approached our encampment in the shape of a great black bank, curved like a bow, from which occasionally darted a flash of lightning, followed by a roll of thunder; and before which were driven flocks of crows and kites, cawing and screaming as if in fear. As these were swept past overhead, a furious storm of wind burst upon our camp, enveloping us in a cloud of dust so dense that we were shrouded almost in total darkness. This was followed by a terrible hail-storm, which raged for fully half an hour, and then ended in a downpour of rain. In a very few minutes the plain was flooded to the depth of quite six inches, and all the dry water-courses and nullahs were filled, and converted into rushing streams.

With the first blast of wind, tents were blown down in every direction, except those of the few whose servants, knowing what was coming, had closed all openings securely, and driven the pegs deeper into the ground. The large, double-poled tents, occupied by the troops, were the first to collapse; then followed the smaller ones of the staff-sergeants and officers, and last of all the mess-tents of the officers. That of the 93rd was pitched on the bank of a deep, dry nullah, which the cooks had selected as a convenient and safe spot for a kitchen, but which was suddenly converted by the heavy rain into a roaring torrent, so suddenly that the cooking utensils and their contents were swept away by the flood of water.

My own tent, owing to the energy of my old bearer, Sibburt, stood firm, so that I was at liberty to give my attention to those of my hospital and of my friends. The tent standing next to my own was occupied by a brother-officer, Lieutenant Grimstone, mentioned in a former chapter, convalescing from a severe attack of fever, and it was imperative that he should be saved from discomfort and a ducking for fear of a relapse.

As soon as there was light enough to enable me to see objects around me, I rushed out at the back-door of my tent, in very scant clothing and with naked feet, for the rain was still pouring down, and the water reached over my ankles; and, calling for the hospital servants and the dhooliebearers, succeeded with their assistance in securing my sick friend's tent and those of my hospital which had not already fallen.

The storm lasted about three quarters of an hour; but as soon as it had swept past the clear blue sky appeared again, the air became refreshingly cool, and the floods of water rapidly disappeared. It was the most severe dust-storm that I ever experienced in India, and it occurred, as I have said, at an unusually early period of the season.

As a rule these storms are preceded by several days of intense heat and clouds of dust floating in the air; their approach is heralded by lightning and thunder, and their subsidence marked by a few heavy drops of rain, seldom by such a deluge as I have just described, and very seldom by hail. The clouds of dust during the height of the storm are generally very dense, and shroud everything in a darkness that can almost be felt, like the darkness, probably, that fell on the Egyptians. They are always followed, however, by several days of bright sky and grateful coolness, and though disagreeable while they last, for they smother everything in dust, the advent of one is hailed with thankfulness, and accepted with gratitude as a little break in the long and almost intolerable monotony of the hot season.

On one occasion, I happened to be riding on the parade-ground in front of the barracks occupied by my regiment as a dust-storm was approaching. Suddenly from out of the black cloud of dust burst what appeared to me to be a ball of fire, which with a hissing noise shot past within a few feet of me, and flew close along the ground straight in the direction of the barracks. Not caring to expose myself on the open plain to another thunderbolt, which might come nearer than the last, I turned my horse and galloped home, and had scarcely entered my bungalow and closed the door, when a furious storm burst over the station, and blew like a hurricane for about fifteen minutes.

Just as the storm had passed over, a messenger, breathless with speed, came to tell me that one of our women, living in the married quarters, had been killed by the lightning which had preceded the storm. On arriving at the quarter, however, I found that the woman had only been thrown down and stunned, and was recovering.

Husband and wife told me that they were sitting side by side, the woman talking, as usual, and the man smoking his pipe and listening (as usual also, I presume), when something seemed to rush between them, striking them both on the side of the head, knocking the woman down senseless, and smashing to pieces the pipe which the man held in his teeth.

On examining the room, I found that the electric fluid had struck the metal handle of the door, twisting it completely off; that from thence it had passed obliquely across the apartment, struck and destroyed a watch hanging upon the wall—which was blackened round the spot—had been deflected from thence, passed between the man and woman, with the result I have stated, and escaped through the window, shattering the glass as it made its exit. On further comparing the position of the building, and the spot where I had seen the electric bolt, I perceived that both were exactly on a line with each other, so that it must have been the same electric flash which passed so close to myself that struck the house.

Towards the middle of May, 1858, Sir Colin,

and the greater part of the army, retraced their steps hurriedly to Shahjehanpore, where they attacked and defeated a large force of rebels which had assembled in that neighbourhood during the absence of the army at Bareilly.

Three Highland regiments, the 42nd, 78th, and 93rd, with artillery and native cavalry, were left in the Rohilcund district, under the command of General Walpole, with Colonel Colin Troup as brigadier.

We remained in temporary quarters in Bareilly during the hot and rainy seasons, sending from thence a number of our sick and weakly men to Nainé Tal, a sanitorium in the Himalayas, where within the last few years the destructive landslip occurred.

That was not the first landslip, however, that had taken place in that neighbourhood; for, on visiting the station in September, 1858, to recruit my own health, a landslip, consisting of a huge mass of mountain, which had occurred many years before, was pointed out to me. Being outside of the valley in which the station is situated, it had not been destructive to life or property.

After the great heat of the plains, the cool temperature of the mountain regions (always spoken of in India as 'the hills') was most refreshing and invigorating. The transition from plain to mountain, and from heat to cold was so rapid (effected in twenty-four hours), that one felt as if transported to another region of the world; everything was so different. From the still, damp, oppressive temperature of the plains, in which the least exertion was a labour, and even respiration difficult, one had passed into cool, crisp air, which circled quickly round the body, making the surface tingle and the pulse beat fast. Instead of a vast, uninteresting plain, bounded only by the distant horizon, one moved amidst grand and ever-changing scenery; some new beauty presenting itself at every turn. Instead of the everlasting mango groves, planted with stiff regularity, and of formal rows of trees, whose foliage drooped under the withering heat, the eye rested with pleasure on a wild and tangled luxuriance of forest vegetation, lighted up by the bright colours of flowering shrubs and gigantic creepers; and instead of stagnant pools and tanks, and of muddy streams flowing sluggishly and noiselessly along, the ear was saluted by the roar of mountain torrents rushing headlong through the deep and narrow ravines, or soothed by the trickle, drip, and murmur of little crystal springs and fountains hidden away among the lichen-covered rocks by the roadside, and shaded by a dense growth of ferns and mosses of many different species.

The vegetation in the Terai, a broad belt of marshy forest situated at the foot of the hills, and through which I passed at early morning, is tropical, and grows in wild and dense confusion, but brightened up by foliage of every hue, and flowers of rainbow tints, amongst which birds of showy plumage flitted and fluttered on restless wing. Many stately trees were there, some covered by thickly woven parasitic growths, and others locked in the embrace of gigantic creepers, which twined closely round the great trunks, and spread their tendrils out on every branch, even to the topmost. Indeed, numbers of these forest giants were lying prostrate on the ground, overborne beneath the weight and under the fatal pressure of their powerful enemy. Here and there too, in open spaces of the forest, broad sheets of water sparkled silvery in the sunshine, in and round which sported and waded water-fowl of varied or of snowy plumage.

But as I emerged from this forest of luxuriant vegetation, and ascended the steep and rugged mountain-path, I observed that different species of trees monopolized certain altitudes. Pines (the common fir) alone grew in one zone, rhododendrons and horse-chestnuts, the one ablaze with its bunches of crimson flowers, the other clothed in white, pink-tipped blossom, grew in another. Higher still, the noble oak (or ilex), thickly covered over with graceful drooping ferns and a species of mistletoe, clothed the mountain crests; and at a higher elevation still towered in graceful height the beautiful deodar.

The station of Nainé Tal is buried in a valley, at the bottom of which is a small but deep lake. At one extremity of this lake stands the town or bazaar, and at the other the barracks for European soldiers, and on the hill sides, which slope down to the margin of the lake, stand many private dwelling-houses nestling amongst trees, and surrounded by hedges of the bright scarlet geranium.

This description refers to a period thirty years ago, but I believe many changes, additions, and improvements have been made since the date of my visit.

From the valley itself there is no view of the outer mountain world, but from a lofty peak, some fifteen hundred feet above the level of the lake, a magnificent and extensive view can be obtained. To see this I commenced to climb 'Cheenie' (as the peak referred to is called, if I remember right) at an early hour, arriving at the summit just as the grey dawn was breaking, to behold a wonderful sight. In the far distance was a great dark mass of mountain, dimly seen, curving east and west far as the eye could reach, and sweeping round to the height whereon I stood, so as to enclose an immense circular space or basin, at the bottom of which lay a vast unbroken expanse of snow-white mist, so calm and unruffled in the uncertain light of dawn, that it presented the appearance of a broad lake. But as I stood gazing a change gradually came over the scene. The increasing light of coming sunshine brought out clear and well-defined the bold and rugged outline of the mountain chain, lit up the deep wooded valleys and narrow glens which intersected the rugged mass in every direction, and formed it into individual mountains heaped tumultuously together. As the sun rose above this great barrier, and shed his warm rays upon the bed of misty vapour, it began to rise and roll upwards, breaking into great masses, which ascended slowly along the valleys and glens, and crept up and up until they reached and settled on the highest ridges, shutting them out of sight, and changing the scene completely, enveloping the lofty mountain crests above in a dense veil of cloud, and exposing far down beneath me at a depth of three hundred feet, where but a few minutes before there had appeared to be a vast expanse of water, a beautiful undulating country, consisting of little rounded hills and smiling valleys, the former clothed in the richest verdure, and the latter marked by silvery threads of running water, dotted over with human habitations, and bright with the ripening harvest.

From Nainé Tal I rode to Almorah, some twenty miles farther into the Himalayan range. This, like Nainé Tal, was formerly a Goorkha town, but now is a military station, and always occupied by one of our own Goorkha regiments. From Almorah I had a good and distinct view of several of the great peaks or individual mountains of the snowy range. These were grand by daylight, but under the light of a full moon were indescribably magnificent.

I rejoined my regiment at the end of September, as it was to form part of a field force, to consist of the 60th Rifles, the 93rd Highlanders, and 66th Goorkhas, with a squadron of European and a regiment of Mooltanee cavalry, with horse and field artillery, under the command of Brigadier Colin Troup. This was one of several brigades which were to enter Oude simultaneously, but from different points, and to move on different lines of road, for the purpose of clearing the district of a number of rebel bands, and restoring peace and order.

We marched from Bareilly early in October, arrived at Shahjehanpore on the 17th of the month, where we found the other regiments of the force waiting for us, and from thence we entered Oude.

On the third day thereafter we had an engagement with the enemy at the village of Posgaon, in which the rebels were defeated with considerable loss. But while the brigade, broken up into small columns, was pressing after the retreating enemy, a body of rebel cavalry came down upon our line of baggage as it was defiling through the village of Posgaon. They had selected what they no doubt thought was the weakest part of the line to make their attack, far in advance of the rear-guard, and where they saw no red-coats. Either they did not see the line of dhoolies that was approaching, or, if they did, naturally supposed that they were empty, and, while engaged cutting at the defenceless camp-followers, must have been greatly surprised at the sudden appearance of a party of Feringhees, and to find themselves unexpectedly under the fire of a dozen rifles. These were twelve men of the 93rd, who were in hospital for slight ailments, and to whom, at my request, made only the night before, their rifles and ammunition had been issued, and who, turning out of their dhoolies, drove the enemy out from the line of baggage, keeping them in check until the arrival of the Mooltanee cavalry under Colonel Cureton, who dispersed and pursued the rebels. Two of the enemy, however, managed in some way (probably they were taken for our own sowars) to remain amongst our followers, and to ride quietly in the line talking to the camel-drivers, until they came near a 93rd man, who was walking along by himself. Without rousing any suspicion, they rode up to the soldier, as if they were friends, and, when his back was turned, one of them shot him from behind, and the other, dismounting, severed his head from the body. They both escaped.

Within a few days after the engagement at Posgaon, we again encountered the enemy at the village of Russelpore. They were in considerable strength, had thrown up entrenchments, and had a number of small field-guns. On this occasion the 93rd was in reserve, with the exception of the light company (Captain MacBean's), and as the regiment was advancing in column of companies (to the best of my recollection) several round shots passed in rapid succession right over the centre of the column. Had the guns been depressed but a very little, the shot would have torn through instead of passing over the column, and killed or maimed a number of the men.

We had no casualties in this engagement, but numbers of the enemy were killed by our artillery fire. They retired in confusion and in great haste, abandoning their guns as they hurried along the road and across country faster than we could follow.

From thence we moved to the large town of Noorunghabad, where we remained several days, and where the proclamation was read to the brigade with some ceremony, transferring the government of India from the Honourable East India Company to Her Majesty the Queen.

On November 8, we moved from thence, and on the following day made an attack on Fort Mithoulie. After a brisk cannonade on both sides, we made preparations to assault the place on the following morning, but during the night the enemy vacated it, and escaped; fortunately, perhaps, for us, for it was a very strong position, surrounded by a deep, almost impenetrable belt of bamboo, and by a deep, broad ditch.

From Mithoulie we fell back to Seetapore, where we remained a few days, and then again advanced towards the Nepaul frontier, and formed our camps; the head-quarters of the regiment at Tilliah, and the left wing at Baroulie; the former on the banks of a considerable river, which was fordable in several places. Our duty was to prevent the rebels returning by these fords from the Nepaul territory, whither they had been driven, into Oude again. The left wing had a similar duty to perform, and were encamped on the banks of another large stream in the vicinity of a shallow ford.

It was a wild country, consisting of immense grassy plains, alive with game, intersected by several large and many small rivers; dotted over with clumps of dense jungle, and with extensive lakes (or jheels) which swarmed with wild fowl, and in which lurked hundreds of the dangerous short-nosed alligators (or muggur, as it is locally called); while the long-nosed harmless species inhabited the rivers, on the mud banks of which I have seen them lying basking in the sun in dozens.

Very few villages were to be seen, and the few natives whom we met with were poor, emaciated-looking creatures, suffering from the malarious poison exhaled from the vast plains. I was told that these were almost completely under water during the rainy season, and were so little elevated above the surface of the rivers and lakes that water could be found anywhere at a depth of eighteen inches.

While encamped at Tilliah, those of us who possessed guns had excellent sport, and brought home 'good bags,' filled with a variety of game, such as florican (the small bustard), three different kinds of partridge (black, grey, and painted, the latter a beautiful bird, with plumage not unlike our own grouse), also peafowl, wild duck, teal, and snipes.

My companion and mentor on these occasions was Thelluson, of the Indian service, attached as interpreter to the 93rd; and as he had been long in India, and was a first-rate sportsman, I profited by his knowledge of the country and the people, and by his excellence as a shikaree. We generally left camp mounted on government elephants, lent to us by the commissariat officer. The one on which I always rode was an old female, stone blind, who, under the guidance of her mahout, went fearlessly anywhere, through jungle, across rivers, or into lakes, but as she walked along she always kept tapping the ground and feeling trees or other objects with her trunk. Occasionally we made excursions to the jheels, and went out paddling in canoes, made out of the trunks of trees, but I declined these parties after having been nearly upset by a muggur.

The large game which we met with were the Nhill-ghau and the antelope. The wild animals were the wolf, jackal, and fox, and on one occasion I came upon two large black otters playing with each other on the bank of a small stream. We saw no tigers or any traces of them, though the natives said that they were occasionally to be seen.

Wolves were numerous and very daring, coming close to, and even into, our camp, and one, more daring probably than his companions, carried off the little child of one of my servants from under a tent pitched in the midst of a number of others. My servant, with his wife and this little child of two years old, occupied a small tent pitched close to my own, the walls of which could not be pegged close down to the ground, so that the wolf was able to push his head under the tent, seize the child by the back of the neck, and walk off with it. Fortunately, as the animal with its prey was stealing out of the camp, the sentry saw and charged it, when it dropped the child and scampered off.

The little thing was brought to me, not much injured, and certainly not much frightened; but the wolf must have taken a secure hold, for there were four deep wounds in the neck made by the large canine teeth.

The head-quarter wing (that at Tilliah) never came in contact with the enemy again, but the left wing (that at Baroulie) was present at an affair between our Mooltanee cavalry and a body of rebel cavalry at a place called Biswah. It was a sharp affair while it lasted, and, though the enemy was defeated with heavy loss, there were a good many casualties on our side, and a very sad and distressing incident occurred.

There was a Ressaldar (native captain) in the Mooltanee cavalry, a gentleman and a man of considerable property, whose only son, as fine a young fellow as might be seen anywhere in any race of men, served under him as a private trooper. It is not uncommon to find native gentlemen serving in the ranks of irregular cavalry corps in India.

During the engagement, father and son charged together and fought side by side, the young man, quite regardless of his own person, devoting his attention to the safety and protection of his father by warding off the sword-cuts that were made at him in the *melée*. But, observing one of the enemy point a carbine at his father, he threw his body forward, received the bullet in his own heart, and dropped dead from the saddle.

It was a beautiful and touching example of filial love and devotion, but was a terrible blow to the old man, for, as I have said, the lad (he was only twenty-one) was an only son, handsome, brave, full of promise, and sole heir to his father's name and possessions.

We often met the old Ressaldar afterwards, always treated him with marked respect, and tried to show that we sympathised with him in his great loss and sorrow.

CHAPTER XXI.

Ordered to Subathoo—Bareilly—42nd Highlanders—Nawab of Rampore—Natch—Water Supply—Simla—Umballa—Ordered to Rawul Pindi—Lahore—79th Highlanders—Goldie-Scot—Intense Heat and Famine—Ordered to Peshawur—Climate and Scenery—Sir Sidney Cotton—Sir Hugh Rose—The Soldier's Soup—Attack on a Lady.

IN the spring of 1859, the mutiny having been completely quelled, the different field forces were gradually broken up, and regiments appointed to stations. The 93rd was detailed for Subathoo, a hill station in the Sirhind district, situated in the lower ranges of the Himalaya mountains, near Kussowlie, Dugshai, and Simla, but at a much lower altitude than either of these.

I presume we owed this little bit of good fortune to the fact that Sir Colin Campbell, the Commander-in-Chief, had been appointed colonel of the regiment, but probably also to our long service of eighteen months in the field, to the prominent part we had taken in the relief of the Residency and siege of Lucknow, to our losses in killed and wounded in these operations, and to our losses also from the effects of climate and disease during the campaign.

The regiment, however, was in excellent health and splendid training at the conclusion of the mutiny, and so hardened by constant exercise as to be fit for any service when we commenced our march for Subathoo at the end of February, 1859.

There was a long march, certainly, before us, the distance by road from the Nepaul frontier, where we were, to Subathoo, whither we were going, being four hundred and fifty-seven miles.

According to the route laid down for us, we were to march by the Seetapore, Shahjehanpore, Bareilly, Moradabad, and Umballa districts, to pass through villages, towns, and cities situated between the principal stations, in which a European regiment had never been seen, and whose inhabitants were inclined to doubt our power, and the fact of the reported arrival of many soldiers from England.

Besides, as the fame of the kilted soldiers (or Gagrah Wallahs, as they were styled), with their 'musical mussacks,' had spread over the whole of that part of India, it was considered a good opportunity to convince the incredulous of the truth of the arrival of many new regiments, and to let them see for themselves what one of these was like by sending the 93rd amongst them. Such was the common report and belief.

The people certainly took advantage of the opportunity, for they came out in crowds to look at the, to them, strange dress of the regiment, and to listen to the pipes, the music of which delights all natives of India; and, as we marched through the narrow lanes of their towns or cities, the men lined the way, the women peeped out of their windows, but they manifested no sign of surprise, and certainly none of fear, only gazed at and let us pass in silence.

I am not certain what qualification is necessary for a town to come under the designation of city in India. Whether it be the existence of a mosque, or temple, or celebrated saintly tomb, or the fact that a collection of dwellings is surrounded by an old defensible wall, occupied by a large population, and used as a place of residence by a native princeling, or nawab, or rajah; or whether it be that, in its past history, it had been the seat of independent native government, or celebrated for extensive manufactures, or for some special art.

I do not know if any or all of these are qualifications, but I think that several of the small towns through which we marched and which were spoken of as cities were scarcely entitled to the distinction.

Our route for the most part lay nearly parallel to the mountains, which, however, were too far distant to afford us more than occasional glimpses of the higher ranges; but *that* was sufficient to raise great expectations as to the pleasures of climate and scenery which were awaiting us on arrival at our future mountain home.

Though we made slow progress, and there was

something tedious and monotonous in our daily march of twelve or fifteen miles, we knew that each day brought us a little nearer to our destination; and we had the comfort of feeling that our minds and bodies were released from the state of tension in which soldiers live during a campaign; that we could lie down at night free from anxiety; would rise on the morrow refreshed by sleep; perform our day's march at our leisure, without that constant watchfulness necessary during a period of active hostilities; and that we might eat and drink in quiet and contentment. These were all pleasures to which we had long been unaccustomed.

Nothing exciting occurred during the march except a kindly and hospitable greeting from our old friends of the 42nd as we passed through Bareilly; and a ceremonious reception from the Nawab of Rampore, who, as we marched through his territory or principality, invited us to his house or palace, gave a splendid pyrotechnic display in our honour, entertained us at supper, and amused us with a natch. This last did not afford us much pleasure, but the dancing-girls were young and tolerably good-looking, except the leader, who was stout and *passée*, though still retaining the remains of beauty. All were gaily dressed in loose, flowing robes, the colours of which were tastefully selected, and harmoniously blended, though the effect was rather spoilt by too much tinsel. Their dancing was anything but graceful—indeed, was rather a series of slow movements of their bodies, accompanied by much gesticulation, to the music of several antiquated stringed instruments and of their own unmelodious voices. This was the only natch I ever was present at, and I never desired to see another. One was enough to satisfy curiosity.

On April 13, 1859, the regiment arrived at Subathoo, and remained there six months. During our stay there we had two short periods of excitement. One when ordered to hold ourselves in readiness to move down to the plains in consequence of the unsettled state of the Bengal (European) regiments of cavalry, the men of which were 'on strike,' as I believe they themselves spoke of their conduct, but in reality and in a military point of view it came under another designation. We were not required to move down to the plains, however, as the strike came to an end. The second little excitement was a similar 'strike' amongst the men of the 1st Bengal Fusiliers (a regiment with as glorious a previous history as any in the army), which was stationed at Dugshai, a hill station about ten miles from Subathoo.

In both cases the men obtained their object, which was to be sent home to be discharged, and the recognition of the fact that, having enlisted to serve the Honourable East India Company, they had been transferred to Her Majesty's regular army without their own consent having been first obtained.

Subathoo is by some not considered a desirable

station for an European regiment, and I do not know why it was selected for this purpose, unless it may have been that at the time when we conquered the whole of that mountain district it was a Nepaulese military and civil station. What is the bazaar, at present occupied chiefly by Cashmere merchants, was formerly a Goorkah town, and a square tower situated above the town, almost a ruin now, was in former days a Goorkah fort.

The position, though five thousand feet above the level of the sea, stands on a mountain spur in a basin surrounded by much higher hills, and though it has the disadvantage of a high range of temperature during the hot, it has the advantage of a more equable climate during the cold, season. The rainfall also is much less, as the clouds are attracted by the surrounding higher mountain ridges, and the drenching fogs prevalent at the more elevated stations of Simla, Dugshai, and Kussowlie are unknown at Subathoo.

There is one great defect, however, and that is the difficulty of procuring a plentiful supply of water. There are rivers in the valleys below, and there are springs on the sides of the Subathoo spur, but there is no water within the station or near the barracks, so that it has to be brought up from some distance and at great expense every day in leather bags by mules. This might be remedied, and may have been by this time, for I know that it was a matter officially brought to notice more than once. True, there are several wells just above the bazaar, or old town, which may have afforded a sufficient supply for a small Goorkah garrison, and for a limited civil population, but not for the many necessities of a European regiment.

This insufficient water supply is remediable, and is the only objection to Subathoo that I am aware of, and I have been often there since 1859; but even with this objection it is a paradise compared with the plains. Possibly the position was selected by the Nepaulese government as a suitable site for a military station and a town as being a central point on the road between the more remote hill towns and the plains.

The regiment remained at Subathoo only six months, and during this time many of us paid occasional visits to Simla, the hot-weather residence of hard-worked Indian civil and military officials, and the great centre of fashion and gaiety, and, I fear, extravagance. There we were always sure of a kind welcome from our colonel, Lord Clyde (Sir Colin had been elevated to the peerage), and, those of us who knew him, a kindly greeting from Sir W. Mansfield.

At a ball given by Lord Clyde, at which a number of us were present, his lordship came up to me as I entered the ball-room, and congratulated me upon having been made a C.B., informing me at the same time that he had recommended Goldie-Scot of the 79th and myself, and that he had just received a telegram informing him of the arrival of the mail bringing the *Gazette* in which the names of medical officers recommended for this distinction were included. Naturally both Goldie-Scot and I were gratified at the information, but as naturally our disappointment was great when the *Gazette* arrived, but without our names.

In November, 1859, the regiment moved from Subathoo to Umballa, there to be encamped during the cold season for rifle practice. But in December of the same year we received orders to proceed to Rawul Pindi, in the Peshawur district, four hundred miles distant from Umballa, and on the way thither to act as escort to the Governor-General, Lord Canning, on His Excellency's viceregal progress through the Punjaub.

The Viceroy and suite left Umballa in January, 1860, and arrived at Lahore early in February. Here we found our old comrades of the 79th, and I had again the pleasure of meeting my dear old friend, Goldie-Scot, the surgeon of the regiment, the most popular regimental surgeon that I ever knew.

We remained in camp at Lahore for some days, until our services as escort were no longer required, and then received orders to proceed to our future station, which we reached in March, 1860; but, as there was not sufficient barrack accommodation at Rawul Pindi for the whole regiment, a large detachment was sent to Jhellum.

The first hot season that the regiment passed in Pindi was, without exception, the hottest I ever experienced in India. No rain fell in the Punjaub that year—1860—for six months, consequently the heat was intense, and the crops failed. We were visited by famine, and afterwards by pestilence in the form of low-fever amongst the village population throughout the district, and, in the following year, in the form of cholera amongst both natives and Europeans, especially amongst the troops quartered in Meean Meer, the military cantonment of Lahore. At Pindi we were mercifully spared from the appearance of the pestilence.

The regiment remained at Rawul Pindi twenty months, and in November, 1861, moved on to Peshawur, the *ultima thule* of our eastern empire in that direction (in those days, at least), and the Golgotha of India, as I have often heard it styled; but whether deserving of this character generally is doubtful, though in our experience it certainly was, as I shall explain in the next chapter.

Peshawur is a beautiful and extensive valley, containing upwards of two thousand square miles, surrounded by lofty mountains, and traversed by three considerable rivers, which pour their united waters into the Indus at Attock. The surrounding scenery is magnificent. Facing the cantonment are the mountains of Cabul, bold and rugged, and their higher ridges capped with snow far into the hot season; on the south and east are the lower ranges of the Kohat and Cherat hills, and on the north a vast extent of mountain region.

The cold season in the valley is long and bracing, the hot weather generally seasonable—that is, hot and dry; but the rainy and two first months of the cold season are unhealthy, sometimes very unhealthy, and few persons in those unusually unhealthy seasons escape an attack of Peshawur fever or of ague, the effects of which cling to them for years; and though they may shake off ague, and be exempt from it for a long time, they are liable to a recurrence of it on the least exposure to malarious influence, or even to a common chill. But, for my own part, I enjoyed robust health in Peshawur, and were it not for the sufferings of the regiment, and the painful memories attached to our short service in the valley, I should give it the character of being the best and most charming of all the stations in the plains of the Bengal Presidency.

Our general of division at that time was Sir Sidney Cotton, as gallant an officer and as good a soldier as ever lived, and one who had passed a long and eventful life almost entirely on foreign service. He was extremely strict on all points of discipline. The men thought he was too fond of drill and too exacting on parade, and he certainly *did* know how to move troops. Off duty he was a kind and courteous friend, and in his own house a hospitable English gentleman.

Our brigadier was General (afterwards Sir O'Grady) Haly, of whom I shall have more to say by-and-by.

At the time of our arrival in Peshawur, Colonel R. Lockhart Ross was in command of the regiment, but in the spring of 1862 he went home on leave, when the command devolved on Major

Middleton. I was still the surgeon; my four assistants, Sinclair, Menzies, Pollard, and Bell, who had served with me in the Crimea and during the Indian Mutiny, had been promoted by this time, and left India—all good men and true.

The cold season of 1861-62 passed quickly and pleasantly, the principal excitement being a visit from the Commander-in-Chief, Sir Hugh Rose (now Lord Strathnairn), who, during his short visit, kept us in a state of constant commotion, activity, and hospitality.

On arrival, His Excellency issued a programme detailing days and hours for his intended proceedings, but seemed to derive pleasure in deviating from it and taking people by surprise. He had named day and hour for the inspection of the hospital of the 93rd, but walked in with all his staff on a different day, at a much earlier hour than had appeared in orders, and found me in plain clothes, surrounded by the women and children of the regiment, whom I was vaccinating. On my attempting to apologise, his Excellency remarked, 'Never mind; I have heard of you, and have purposely taken you by surprise, as I wished to see you at work.' It was the most searching inspection that I ever was subjected to. Sir Hugh visited every corner of the hospital, spoke to every patient, saw the articles of diet, inquired about the cooking, asked innumerable questions, and required a reason for everything. From the hospital he went to the barrack-rooms, also unexpectedly, while the men were at their dinners.

In going round the different messes, his attention was attracted by several large bowls, which he thought contained a very rich soup, and being anxious to know what it was like, but unwilling, apparently, to trust to his own palate, he requested the Inspector-General of Hospitals to taste it and give his opinion. My old friend Dr. L——, who had a very great appreciation of good things, approached the table, as I thought, rather reluctantly; but, taking the offered spoon, stirred the contents of one of the bowls carefully, tasted it once, then a second time, and, while making a wry face, pronounced it excellent soup. On this, Sir Hugh turned to the man nearest him, and asked if the soup was always as good, but the reply, 'It's no soup ava, it's the sauce for the pudding,' caused a deal of merriment.

There is more excitement in Peshawur than in any other station in India, for there is constantly some little disturbance going on in the cantonment, or city, or neighbourhood. The wild, turbulent tribes who dwell in the surrounding mountain fastnesses are never at rest. They are either quarrelling or fighting with each other or amongst themselves, and, if not so occupied, they come down into the valley singly or in couples, commit thefts in or near the station and city, and even occasionally commit murder if they meet unwary individuals wandering too far beyond the limits of safety, particularly if they are riding good horses and decline to part with them.

While we were quartered there, scarcely a night passed that some theft great or small was not committed—a horse stolen from the stable, arms carried off from the barrack-room, or any and every trifle that thieves could lay their hands on taken from officers' bungalows; and all these thefts committed in spite of the two vigilant, armed chowkedars employed for every house, who kept up a constant fusilade all night. But whether this use or waste of powder was meant to scare away the robbers, or draw their attention to any particular spot where there was something to steal, is, I fear, doubtful.

Individual thieves often prowled about the barracks, and, being armed with knives, did not scruple to use them if opportunity occurred or necessity arose. One of our married men was stabbed in the side by a thief of this sort, and though the soldier, who was a large and powerful man, grappled instantly with his enemy, he was unable to secure or even to hold him, for the rascal was naked, and covered over with oil.

The last excitement we had during the cold season was the desertion of three of our men with their arms and ammunition. Only one of them returned, who reported that they had been attacked by the natives, his two companions killed, he himself only escaping by speed of foot, and by swimming the Cabul river.

Their object in deserting was never satisfactorily explained, though the survivor stated among his comrades that their intention was to try to reach England, which they imagined could not be very far beyond the Cabul mountains; but it was hardly possible to believe that their knowledge of geography was so limited.

For some years before we were stationed in Peshawur, and for several years after we had left it, murders of European officers were not uncommon, and I will just mention three.

A lady of my acquaintance, wife of a military officer at the time I met her, had, before her marriage, spent some time in Peshawur with her father, who was also in the service. One afternoon, escorted by an officer, an intimate friend of the family, she went out for a ride. They had not ridden far, and were returning slowly homewards, when they were unexpectedly surrounded by a band of robbers, who demanded their horses. On being refused, they attacked and killed the officer, spared the lady, but desired her to dismount and find her way home on foot. She was fortunate to be allowed to escape at all, for these wild, fierce, and fanatical hill-men do not usually show mercy, once their blood is up, to the Feringhee, man or woman.

The second murder was committed some time after we had left the valley, and was as follows:

An officer, a friend of my own (Captain MacDonald), commanded at one of the small outlying posts which encircle the station. He was out riding in the immediate vicinity of his fort, when he was attacked and killed without warning, and without any provocation having been given by him. He had been only a short time in command, and could not have made himself obnoxious in any way to the hill men, who doubtless murdered him because he was a European, and to satisfy their fanatical hatred of the white man.

The third was a much more daring murder than the other two; for it was committed in the very heart of the station, and on a bright moonlight evening, when people were astir. Mr. Leoenthall, a missionary, who had spent years in Peshawur and on the frontier, who knew the hill tribes intimately, and was a thorough master of their language in all its dialects, who spent a quiet, unostentatious life in efforts to do good, and in the performance of acts of kindness and mercy, was shot while walking in his own garden by one of his own servants.

This was a cruel murder; for independently of his being a man of peace, whose heart was full of Christian love and goodwill, he was frail and weak, and almost incapable from physical infirmity of offering resistance. It was said to have been an accident, and that his servant shot him under the belief that he was a thief prowling about the house. But this could hardly have been the case, for Mr. Leoenthall's person was so peculiar that even in the bright moonlight it must have been impossible to have failed to know him.

There are several beautiful rides and drives round Peshawur, the more especially that a good macadamized road runs along the front of the cantonment, and another (but not a macadamized road) in the rear of the cantonments and city. From the former, a splendid view of the noble Cabul mountains can be obtained, and from it also can be seen the fort of Jumrood and the entrance to the celebrated Khyber Pass. The other road runs through extensive peach gardens, which cover many acres of ground, and in which, during the spring, hundreds of trees display a wealth of rich blossom, and in the autumn yield an abundant harvest of good fruit, so abundant, indeed, that in those days a large basket of peaches could be purchased for a rupee.

There are two luxuries in Peshawur which are not to be found in any other military station in the plains, viz., running water and green sward.

CHAPTER XXII.

A Sad Chapter—Earthquakes—Cholera—Archie White's Kind Assistance—Increase of the Pestilence—Middleton—MacDonald—Hope and Drysdale—Flying before the Pestilence—A Surgeon's Responsibility—Our Chaplain—General O'Grady Haly—Leave the Peshawur Valley—Encamp at Campbellpore—March for Sealkote—Thanksgiving.

AS I sit down to write this chapter of my reminiscences of a period of great suffering in my old regiment, and of intense labour and anxiety to myself, mournful recollections of old comrades come crowding fresh upon my memory, and I seem to live the last twenty years over again—recollections of comrades with whom I had often shared in the dangers of the battlefield, but who, having survived these, were at last stricken down suddenly by disease during the period of which I write, and of others who lived through that terrible period, who encouraged me in my labour and sympathised with me in my anxiety, but have since passed away also.

All of them were men whom I knew intimately, friends to whom I was deeply attached, and whose confidence I had gained from long companionship, and from the fact that we had often been helpful to each other in all the vicissitudes of a soldier's life. They have only gone before; passed from this life to another, having finished their duty here; but they are not forgotten, for those few of the old circle who are still left—and there *are* a few—cherish their memory faithfully.

All went well with us during the cold season of 1861–2. We enjoyed good health, and had many pleasures and amusements. The weather was delightful; so cold occasionally that ice formed to the thickness of nearly half-an-inch upon stagnant water and along the edges of our little streamlets. We had convivial and dancing parties, and garrison theatricals, in which Fenwick and Gordon Alexander, of the 93rd, took prominent parts. We had a little shooting and hunting; for at that time the regiment kept a pack of hounds. George Greig had formed the pack originally, and acted as a most efficient master and huntsman, then and for several years afterwards.

Occasionally we heard of a robbery, as I have explained in the last chapter, and three times during the season we were startled by smart shocks of earthquake, by no means an uncommon thing in the Peshawur valley, and along the foot of the hills.

At Christmas there was a very severe shock, preceded and accompanied by a loud, rumbling noise, like the passage of artillery along a hard road, and by strong vibrations of the earth from south-west to north-east. A second severe shock occurred on Good Friday, 1862, while the troops were at church, which shook the building so violently that clergyman and congregation made a rapid exodus.

The same shock threw down one of the masonry partitions in our hospital. Fortunately the *débris* fell into an empty ward. Had it fallen into the occupied one on the other side, many of the sick must have been killed or injured. A third shock occurred later in the season, which threw down a number of native dwellings in the city; and by it one angle of my own house was rent and shattered. I happened at the time to be at Cherat, in the Affreedie hills, and felt the mountain heave and tremble violently for some seconds.

A remarkable stillness and quiet follow the shock of an earthquake. There is no motion in the air, not a twig stirs or leaflet quivers; birds seek shelter and are silent; even man is awed for a moment. It would appear, in fact, as if Nature, animate and inanimate, was subdued by the dread of some unseen and supernatural power.

In the spring came a change in our lives. Towards the end of April disquieting rumours reached us of the prevalence of cholera amongst the Wazeree tribes occupying one of the broad valleys in the mountain range bordering the British district of Bunnoo. Then, after a little while, came *fresh* rumours of the appearance of the disease in Bunnoo itself; and again, after an interval of several days, we heard that the pestilence was coming nearer to ourselves; that it had extended to the neighbouring district of Kohat, that it was spreading rapidly there, and far and wide amongst the villages of the Kuttuck and Affreedie hills, which form the southeast boundary of the Peshawur valley.

At last, early in June, we knew of its appearance in the city of Peshawur, and, from thence, early in July, it spread to the military cantonment, the first cases occurring in the artillery and cavalry barracks, and within a few days after, these two corps were sent out to camp, each going in a different direction.

On July 7 it appeared in the 93rd barracks; the first to be attacked being an old soldier, who had suffered from the disease once before while with another regiment. This case was soon followed by others, some slight and some severe, the latter all ending fatally. This outbreak lasted only ten days, from July 7 to 17, and in these few days we had thirty-seven cases of cholera. Then the disease suddenly disappeared, and we were in hopes that it had passed away completely; but in ten days it reappeared, and lasted fifteen days, during which we had forty-one cases, slight and severe, a number of which died. Then it disappeared again, and we were free from it for thirty days; but on September 9 it broke out again for the third time amongst us, and, though the numbers taken ill were not so many as during the two preceding outbreaks, the disease was of a more severe character, and the deaths more numerous in proportion. After the first outbreak, the two companies in which it had appeared were sent up to and encamped at Cherat, a spot in the Affreedie hills about twenty miles distant from Peshawur and three thousand feet above the valley. After the *second* outbreak, all the companies in the headquarter barracks were moved out and encamped on the plain in front of the cantonment; and after the *third*, the hospital, in which it had broken out, was vacated (except so much of it as was required for cholera cases), and all men suffering from ordinary illness were placed in tents out on the open plain.

Without doubt, on the very first appearance of the disease we should have accepted the warning, and removed the whole of the European portion of the troops to some distance from the cantonments; but it was not considered prudent to denude Peshawur entirely of British soldiers; consequently, while artillery and cavalry were removed, the infantry were retained.

But on the reappearance of the disease for the third time in the 93rd, and also in consequence of the alarming and progressing increase of Peshawur fever amongst us, it was at last decided to send the regiment into camp, retaining one company, in which the disease had not appeared, to represent the European portion of the garrison and to protect the station.

During the first and second outbreaks in the regiment, the men alone suffered, but during the third, men, women, and children all alike fell victims, only the officers escaped. *They* were to have their turn, however, afterwards. Why they escaped during the three outbreaks that occurred in cantonments I do not know. Perhaps, because they lived in comfortable dwellings surrounded by trees, and therefore protected from the choleraic atmosphere, while the barracks had no protection, but were completely open to the valley. In proportion to their numbers, the women and children suffered more severely than the men, for out of thirty-one of the former admitted to hospital thirteen died; and out of twenty-nine children fifteen died.

During the first and second outbreaks I had two assistants, Bouchier of the 93rd, and Archer of the 98th (temporarily attached to the 93rd); and nobly these two shared the work with me. During the third outbreak I was alone. Bouchier had been sent to Cherat, and Archer restored to his own regiment, as the long interval between the second and third had led us all to suppose that the epidemic was at an end.

Alone, I found the duty more than I could accomplish, though labouring day and night. I was therefore compelled to ask for aid, and to request that two of the medical officers of the regiment (just appointed, and who were in the country somewhere) should be ordered to join. Meanwhile I was alone with one hundred and fifty cases of fever, and a number of men, women, and children ill with cholera.

A kind friend of his own accord came to my assistance. While I was at work one day Dr. Archibald White, of the Bengal Medical Service, walked into the tent where I was, and, resting his arm upon my shoulder, said,

'I have come to help you, old fellow, for if this goes on you'll die; only give me your orders, and I'll obey them.' And he *did* take my orders, obeyed them, and helped me loyally until other assistance arrived.

Dr. White was my senior in the service by years; but, like a noble-hearted fellow as he was, waived his rank, and acted as if he had been my junior in every respect. I speak of him as the noble-hearted fellow that he *was*, for my friend has passed away—another of those gone before, having finished his duty here—and in his last years he was a great but patient sufferer.

It was an anxious time to all, and to myself especially. I had to witness many a sight of suffering and sorrow, as I watched every case myself, and was present at every death-bed, for I felt that a great responsibility rested upon me; but everyone was not only willing, but eager to help.

It was terrible to see husbands, great, strong, rough men, who had looked on death so often, who had become inured to sights of horror during war, and who usually did not show outward signs of affection, when their wives were taken ill, become, as it were, changed beings altogether. They came to hospital, and nursed and tended their wives gently and devotedly, showing that, though the exterior was rough and rude, the heart was tender and the feelings refined. And the wives? They forgot all else, left their children to the care of other kindly souls amongst the women, and came to watch and tend their husbands, and comfort them by their presence.

One wife especially, though far advanced in pregnancy, and in delicate health besides, forgetting her own almost helpless condition, grew strong for the occasion, spent two days and nights in weary, hopeless watching by her husband, and could not be induced to leave him till she closed his eyes after death. Then she had to take to bed herself to give birth to a new life. But there was *one* most distressing amongst the many distressing cases. An old soldier was taken ill, and his wife came to hospital and begged to be allowed to attend upon him, but she was herself almost immediately taken ill also, and was removed to the female hospital; *then* both lay dying at the same time, each calling for the other. They had four children, the eldest eight, the youngest an infant at the breast; and when Martha, the little girl, the child of eight, was told that both father and mother were dead, she bravely dried her tears, took her infant brother in her arms, and nursed, fed, and cared for him, refusing all assistance for a time. Poor fatherless, motherless little things, it made one's heart ache to look at them, and to think of what might await them in the future. Martha lived to marry a sergeant in the regiment and to have children of her own.

There was amongst the children a boy of some four years of age, whose short span of life, after his first year, had been a succession of infantile diseases, each following fast upon the other, so that it might be said he never had an hour's health. In consequence of these repeated illnesses, his growth had been arrested, and he had not increased in size or weight during his three years of suffering. His frame was thin and weakly, and the skin hung in loose folds about his attenuated limbs and body. Constant pain and sickness had retarded not only his physical, but his mental development. Besides being so small, he had never attempted either to walk or speak. Still there was something like premature intelligence about him, for as he lay quietly in his cot, or was carried about in his mother's arms, his small, pale, wrinkled, puckered face, and his thin, bloodless lips, always tightly compressed, as if in an endeavour to suppress pain, gave him the appearance of a little weird-looking old man; and, to increase this likeness, from under his prominent brows shone large bright eyes, which looked wistfully out from the deep caverns in which they were set, as if he took in all that was passing round him, and understood all that was said.

One would have thought, or hoped at least, that cholera might have spared such a poor little creature, or expected that, if it did seize upon him, he would have succumbed at once. But no; the disease *did* lay hold of him, and a very bad attack it was. Wonderful to say, he recovered. It was heartrending, as I stood by, to witness the sufferings of the poor little thing writhing in the agony of cramp, crying piteously, while he clung to his mother, and looking imploringly at myself (whom he knew well, as I had always attended him in his previous illnesses) for the help which I was powerless to afford. But it was just as heartrending to see the anguish of the poor mother as she hung over him in his cot at one moment, or carried him in her arms at another, trying to soothe him with loving words, or giving him water to allay his thirst, or chafing his aching limbs, for the little creature was endeared to her not only because he was her only child, but because he was such a poor frail thing, and had been such a source of anxiety and trouble to her.

To the surprise of all, and especially of myself, he recovered, as I have said, and the attack of cholera seemed altogether to change his nature, physical and moral. He began to thrive after it, and eventually grew to be a strong, active, and intelligent boy.

On the evening of October 15, the head-quarters of the regiment marched out of the station, and encamped at a distance of six miles beyond it. Early on the following morning (at three o'clock) I left the cantonments at the head of a long procession of carts and dhoolies, containing one hundred and fifty sick, and soon after sunrise reached the camp, which was situated on an extensive sandy plain, without tree or blade of grass, by no means a safe spot on which to encamp a sickly regiment, but there was not sufficient carriage to move us further.

I was in hopes that even this change might be of benefit; but, on the evening of the 17th, the pestilence again broke out (for the fourth time) amongst us; and between that evening and November 3, we had one hundred cases of cholera: fifty-seven of these were severe cases, the others mild; and, besides these, we had upwards of one hundred cases of fever.

During one night the pestilence swept across our camp, following a narrow, straight line. Every man along that line was smitten either by cholera or fever, not a single person along that line escaped; and *except* along that line there was not another case of illness in the camp.

Early on the morning of June 21, I met Major Middleton, the commanding officer, near the hospital, and we went together into the cholera tents, from whence he went to parade, apparently quite well. But within half an hour I was called to him, and, on entering his tent, found that he had been stricken down by cholera, and was hopelessly ill. While with him in his tent, the second in command (Brevet-Lieutenant-Colonel MacDonald) entered, not knowing what had happened. He was greatly shocked at what he saw; but within twenty-four hours he was stricken down himself. Then another (Dr. Hope) was taken ill, then another (Ensign Drysdale), and then another (Ensign Loyd). All these were attacked with cholera, and several other officers were attacked with fever at the same time.

We were obliged to remain in that camp four days, because transport and carriage to move the regiment were not available; but on the afternoon of the 21st we fled before the pestilence, carrying all our sick and dying with us, and encamped some eight or ten miles from our last camp. During the twenty-four hours we remained there, the command devolved upon four different officers in that short time. Middleton, MacDonald, Hope, and Drysdale all died, and for several days many deaths occurred amongst the men.

We fled again, and to higher ground, nearer the foot of the hills. Here we remained several days, and then fled again still higher, and sought shelter in a thick belt of trees. There the severity of the pestilence seemed to be arrested; for from that day until the day on which we passed out of the Peshawur valley only a few cases of cholera occurred, and a milder form of fever became prevalent.

Poor Middleton had acted nobly throughout the period of the prevalence of the epidemic. He had been a constant visitor at hospital, and up to the very day of his death had made a point of seeing every case of cholera. I often had to remonstrate with him, and beg him not to remain long amongst the sick; but he paid no heed to my request, believing that it was his duty to encourage the men by his presence. As I have said, on the very last morning of his life, he had visited the cholera tents, and remained so long that I had to insist upon his leaving, which he did, to go to parade.

I have heard it said that he had great dread of cholera, but it was impossible to credit this, for he showed no sign of fear; yet, if it was the case, his moral courage must have been great. He moved about amongst the sick and dying constantly, at all hours, day and night, cheering everyone by his presence, and setting a good example, though an example was hardly necessary, for every officer was willing and anxious to be helpful. We buried him with military honours. Every man who could be was present; and, though there may have been some risk in this, still, as all desired to pay a last tribute of respect to his memory, I made no objection. The funeral took place early on the morning after his death. MacDonald was present in command, but before evening was ill himself.

Middleton was a first-rate soldier, and had he lived but a few months longer he would have succeeded to the lieutenant-colonelcy of the regiment, and also to a fair fortune. As he lay dying, the mail from England brought a letter informing him that, by the death of a relation, he had come in for a good annual income. While we stood by the grave, one officer (Greig) and several men fell to the ground insensible, struck down by fever. I was prepared for this, and had stretchers and bearers at hand, so that they were carried off to the hospital at once.

I trust I shall not be considered egotistical if I say something of myself. The labour and anxiety which had devolved upon me during the four months of the prevalence of the pestilence had told severely on my health. My nerves felt stretched like bow-strings. I could take no rest, and to sleep was impossible. So constant were the calls on me in camp that at last I had to ride from tent to tent to see my patients, and one night, while attempting to walk to see two officers (Hyslop and Drysdale, taken ill in the same tent), I stumbled, and would have fallen had not Burroughs and MacBean supported me on either side. All, officers and men, were gentle and attentive to me. I felt, as I moved about the camp, as if every eye was bent upon me. There certainly were always several near and ready to help should I personally require assistance, and I was made aware that all were thinking of, and feeling for, me by non-commissioned officers and men often stopping me and kindly inquiring if I was 'well.'

Only those who have been placed in such a position of responsibility as I was placed in at that time can know how great and harassing it is. To live for days and nights amongst the sick and dying, to hear on all sides the muttered raving of the delirious, the low moaning of the dying, and to feel that to you alone all are looking for help, is a trial enough to shake the nerves of the strongest. To see death strike comrades down in the full-flush of health and strength on the battle-field has nothing revolting in it, but to see them, smitten suddenly by pestilence, die by inches of disease, racked with pain, tortured by a burning thirst, maddened by a nervous restlessness, or prostrated by intense debility, and sinking slowly into unconsciousness is terrible, and more terrible when you feel your utter powerlessness to help. Yet it often happens that the army surgeon is placed in such a position.

Of the two assistants with me, Hope died. Poor fellow, he had been with the regiment only a few days. Dr. Baxter, the other (now retired into civil life) was very helpful to me.

Our chaplain, the Rev. Hugh Drennan, was throughout untiring in his attention and devotion to the sick and dying, and was a great comfort to myself. He had a slight attack of cholera. It would have been wonderful if he had escaped, so constant was his attention to the sick. I was indebted to every officer for assistance and encouragement, but more especially to Major Burroughs (commanding), Major MacBean, and Quartermaster Joyner.

And the men, poor fellows! How they worked for each other, and what a help they were to me; how willingly they came to hospital to nurse their comrades; how gently and tenderly they did it!

Not a man held back—not one showed the least fear to face the pestilence, or the least desire to avoid the dreadful duty, and yet every man must have felt that he himself might be the next victim, the next to require the attendance of a comrade. But it is the character of the soldier (I have found it so) to be always ready to attend to his comrade in sickness, no matter what risk he may run or what danger he may encounter in doing so.

Sir Sidney Cotton paid us a visit in camp, and, when things were at the very worst, General Haly came and pitched his tent amongst us, and remained with us to share the danger as long as there was any danger. It was a brave thing to do, and, I think, required more courage than to fight a battle; but, as he remarked to me, his 'presence might encourage the men, and would enable him to see at once how he could best help us.' He had succeeded Sir Sidney Cotton in the command of the division.

On October 30, while encamped on the wooded plateau, we received orders to leave the Peshawur Valley, to march by the Khunnekheyl Pass, cross the Indus at the Nelaub ferry (both famous in the history of Alexander the Great's invasion of India), and to encamp at Campbellpore; there to remain until, cholera having disappeared from amongst us, the whole regiment should be brought together again preparatory to commencing our march to Sealkote, whither we were to proceed.

Accordingly, on November 1, we commenced

our march, and moved short distances along the foot of the hills for four days. Cholera and fever still followed us, however, and deaths from the former occurred each day. But on the 4th, having cleared the Khunnekheyl Pass and got beyond the limits of the Peshawur Valley, cholera entirely disappeared.

On the 8th we crossed the river, and on the 10th encamped at Campbellpore. On the 11th, the married men and their families (who had been sent out of Peshawur after the regiment went into camp) joined us at Campbellpore. They were in a miserable condition, and, on the day of arrival, it was necessary to admit fifty-three women and children to hospital.

We remained at Campbellpore until December 4, when we moved to Huttee, near Attock. Here the whole regiment was again united, and on the 7th of the month we commenced our march for Sealkote, which we reached on December 30. The men were in a very weakly state, all suffering more or less from ague, and our train of sick and convalescent numbered one hundred and seventy-nine.

When we were certain that the pestilence had disappeared, we had a thanksgiving service. It was held in the open air, and a very solemn and impressive meeting it was. Our good chaplain, the Rev. Hugh Drennan, read and expounded to us the 107th Psalm, and all joined with him in reverently giving thanks to Him ' whose mercy endureth for ever.'

A VERITABLE GOLGOTHA.

The non-commissioned officers and men manifested their gratitude by subscribing fifty pounds to be sent home to Scotland as a thank-offering, to be devoted to some charity.

To give some idea of the sickness and mortality in the regiment during our year in Peshawur, I add the following details. The total average strength of the regiment, officers, men, women, and children, was one thousand two hundred and fourteen.

```
Severe cases of Cholera .. 130 ...... Deaths ......... 89
Mild     do.    do.    .. 137 ...... Do.  .........  4
                          ---                        ---
                          267                         93
Severe cases of Fever ... 801 —I have no record of the deaths
Mild    do.    do.    ... 650   amongst these cases of fever, but
Other diseases ........ 939     many of the sufferers were inca-
                          ---   pacitated for further service in
                                India, and many more were long
            Total ..... 2657    in recovering health.
```

These figures will give the reader some idea of what the 93rd suffered in the Peshawur Valley during the year 1862, and of the responsibility and labour which occasionally devolve upon the army surgeon.

I acknowledge that this is a mournful chapter, but it is nevertheless a true statement, a faithful record of events; and there are several persons living who can bear witness to the facts, and who, like myself, have painful recollections of our service in the Peshawur Valley, a veritable Golgotha as it proved to us.

I personally came out of Peshawur uninjured by the climatic influence of the valley, but the labour and anxiety which I underwent during those four months of epidemic visitation caused great nervous depression, accompanied by painful and irregular action of the heart, from which I did not recover for years.

CHAPTER XXIII.

The Punjaub—Aspect of the Country—Settling down in Quarters—Hunting the Jackal—George Greig—Rajah of Jummoo—Ordered back to Peshawur—The Umbeylah Campaign—Baggage Attacked in the Pass—Colonel Hope, 71st—The Travelling Artist—Old Peter—The Hill-men—Labroo—Derbund—Return to Sealkote.

THE Punjaub (land of five rivers) is divided into ten large districts, for the purposes of civil administration, and each of these is subdivided into three or four smaller districts. The former are presided over by commissioners, and the latter by deputies.

Sealkote, one of the sub-divisions of the Umritsir district, is in the Rechna Doab, a large tongue of land enclosed by the rivers Chenab and Ravee, and the city and cantonment of Sealkote are situated in the north-east corner of this Doab, on a long low ridge of land in a wide plain of sedimentary deposit. The cantonments, standing at an elevation of 1,129 feet above sea level, are about twenty miles off the Grand Trunk road, six to eight from the Chenab, seven or eight from the Jummoo Hills, which are the lowest range of the Himalayas, between twelve and twenty from the Ravee, and forty from Lahore and Meean Meer, the head-quarters of the military district.

I do not know why the site was selected for a military cantonment. It may have been in consequence of its proximity to Lahore, and possibly with a view to the abandonment of Meean Meer, which had not proved healthy; or it may have been that it was deemed advisable to establish a military station near the large city of Sealkote, and on the borders of the independent territory of Jummoo and Cashmere; or it may have been simply because the district was considered healthy. Whatever may have been the reason, a large cantonment was built, with barracks and hospitals for European artillery, cavalry, and infantry, and for native cavalry, and a large military prison was also erected.

I believe the original intention was that the station should have been much larger, but why that intention was not carried out I do not know. Probably expense had something to do with it, and perhaps the money which was expected to have been sufficient to complete the station, according to the original plan, was expended in building the present substantial brick barracks, hospitals, prison, and two churches, one of these a large and handsome gothic structure.

The district is a wide open plain, without hill or valley. Several small unimportant rivers flow through it, and here and there, at wide intervals,

CLIMATE OF THE PUNJAUB.

there are small jheels, or shallow lakelets, formed merely by the rainfall, and of no use except as the haunts of wild-fowl during the cold season. The cultivators of the soil depend almost entirely upon deep wells, fitted with the Persian wheel, for the irrigation of their lands. Wheat, barley, rice, and sugar-cane are extensively cultivated, also cotton and indigo, but these last not to any great extent. Vegetables of all kinds are grown, and even the potato will produce abundantly under ordinary care.

During the months of February and March, and even the early part of April, the natives are employed day and night in the work of irrigation, and the noise and creaking of the Persian wheel are heard incessantly. It is a dreary, monotonous noise. The labour of the ryots at this season is great, but it is followed by a rich reward, for in April, when the wheat is ripe, the district is one great plain, covered with a golden harvest.

The temperature ranges high during the short hot season, and proportionately low in the long cold weather. The rainfall is considerable during the rainy months, but surface-water is rapidly drained off by the small rivers I have alluded to (the only use they appear to be of), into the jheels or lakelets that exist, so that the soil throughout the district is perfectly free from damp.

Taking everything into consideration, there is probably no station in the plains where the climate is so equable or so well-suited to the

European constitution. No better selection of a quarter could have been made for a regiment which had served and suffered in the Peshawur Valley as the 93rd had.

We were soon settled in our new quarters; officers' and sergeants' messes were equipped with necessary furnishings; library, reading, and recreation-rooms established for the men; schools re-opened both for men and children; and all were looking forward to much enjoyment during the remaining months of the cold season. Those who still suffered from ague and the effects of the Peshawur climate were hoping to recover health and strength before the advent of the next hot season; and we commenced, as we had done at all our other stations, to plant trees around our barracks and hospital, not only because they are ornamental and beautiful to look at, but also because they act as a protection against sun and wind.

Several officers joined soon after our arrival, and amongst them Colonel Stisted (who had been absent for two years, in command of the convalescent dépôt at Darjeeling), also Major Dawson and Captains Fenwick and Losack, old friends, and the following new ones, Lieutenants Campbell and Gazelee, and Dr. Jaezdowski.

In January and February, the whole plain was covered with the young wheat-crop and with numerous patches of densely growing sugar-cane. In these we never failed to find jackals (for the country had not been hunted over for several years), and, our pack being strong and in excellent condition, we had many good runs. We never went out without finding one or two jackals, at least we never had a blank day.

The meets were well-attended, and the following officers of the regiment were seldom absent: George Greig (our master) on the Rummun, and always to the front, Nightingale on the Tosser, Williams on Billy, R. Gordon on Donald, Haynes on the black Arab, Burroughs on Hakeem, Losack on the General, J. Campbell on the grey Cabool, and Munro on the Khan. From other regiments there were several regular attendants; and there were two ladies who often graced the field by their presence, both good riders, but one of them the best lady rider I ever saw. Their names, of course, I cannot allow myself to mention, but, should they read this, they will perceive that they have not been forgotten.

There was no large game in the district, but geese and wild-duck of many varieties abounded on the rivers and jheels, and were brought-in in great numbers by officers and men. Many of the soldiers were keen sportsmen, some having good double-barrelled guns of their own, and others keeping greyhounds and indulging in coursing. I always remarked that the sportsmen of the regiment were the most sober and the most healthy. Occasionally Greig, or Campbell, or Nightingale, or our quarter-master-sergeant (Fraser), who was an old gamekeeper, or at least an old *game-killer*, shot a black buck in the

Jummoo territory; but this, I suspect, was without permission, for the rajah was himself a sportsman, and did not encourage others.

Once, and once only, he gave a pig-sticking party, and was present himself, but it was not a success; through some mismanagement, I suppose. Very possibly the rajah did not wish it to be a success, for fear that he might be asked to give another, or that we might come again without an invitation. He was always jealous of Europeans visiting in either Jummoo or Cashmere.

Our cold season passed all too quickly, and then came the hot weather, the time when all who can fly from the plains and take refuge in the cool regions of the hills.

Several of our officers started for Cashmere, that valley of delight, and those of us who could not get leave, or whose means were exhausted, remained at home to prepare for, and to endure, the heat as best we could.

We had a very hot season, and were twice visited by flights of locusts. They came in myriads, darkening the air, and making a noise in their flight like a rushing wind. They settled upon every green thing, and the rapidity with which they stripped a tree or shrub of its leaves, and devoured every blade of grass was astonishing, and the noise they made while eating was distinctly audible. What a feast they furnished for the crows which flew round and amongst them in hundreds, but made no apparent impression on their number.

During July and August, we had seasonable rains, and cool and pleasant weather in September and October. But our rest and enjoyment were soon to come to an end; for in November, 1863, we received orders to march back to Peshawur as quickly as possible, to augment a force which had already been assembled, and had commenced a campaign against several of the hill tribes on our north-east frontier. Amongst other hostile acts, they had given a refuge within their fastnesses to a body of rebel fanatics, whose expulsion and destruction, or at least dispersion, our government required and insisted on.

It was not a pleasant prospect to return to the neighbourhood of Peshawur, but the desire of the soldier for active service is strong, and especially of the young soldier, of whom we had a number in our ranks, who had not seen service, who longed for some experience of war, and to be decorated with a medal like their comrades, many of whom wore several.

We could not be considered a healthy regiment when we commenced our march back to Peshawur, as a great many of the men were still liable to attacks of ague. But there is nothing so certain to improve health in India as tent-life and a campaign during the cold season. I personally, therefore, was glad for the sake of the regiment that we were to take part in the coming war. A little war, as we expected it would be, in which we should begin with the long march, to be followed by the bivouac and the fight.

On our arrival at the scene of operations, the men had already much improved in health, and their appearance was quite fit to be compared with that of any regiment of the little army.

In October, a force of five thousand men (European and native) had been directed to enter the Umbeylah country, for the purpose, as already stated, of punishing certain troublesome and hostile hill-tribes, and of enforcing our demand for the expulsion of the rebel fanatics who had been allowed to form a little colony within the hills. But, after a sharp and unsuccessful engagement with the Boneyrs and other tribes in one of the passes through the hills, another attempt was made to enter the country by the Umbeylah Pass. Here the little army again met with a check, and lost severely in killed and wounded; amongst the latter was Sir Neville Chamberlain, the general in command of the expedition. His wound proved to be of so severe a character that he was obliged to resign the command, in which he was succeeded by Sir John Garvock. At the same time it was considered necessary to augment the field-force to ten thousand men; and it was in consequence of this proposed augmentation that the 93rd was ordered up from Sealkote.

On arrival at the entrance to the Umbeylah Pass early in December, 1863, the regiment was ordered to enter the pass and join the headquarters of the force collected and encamped at the other extremity of it, where it enters the

TRYING DISCOMFORTS.

Umbeylah Valley. We started at daylight, and, by the afternoon of the same day, took up our allotted position in the camp.

As we were climbing up the rocky, narrow pass, which was in many places just wide enough for one man or animal at a time, our baggage-train was attacked about the middle or weakest point of the line; and, though the enemy was driven off, we lost a number of the field blankets of our men; a serious loss at the beginning of a campaign, and a great inconvenience to the men during several days and nights of intense cold and heavy rain. At one moment my own little field-kit was in the hands of the enemy, but was recovered by my native servants, and brought into camp next day. I lost nothing but my horse's clothing; a serious loss to the old Khan, for he had to stand out in the cold and rain without any covering during the rest of the month.

In consequence of this attack on our baggage, our first twenty-four hours in camp were spent in great discomfort; for our clothes were wet through, and in these, with only a great-coat as a covering, we lay down upon the damp ground at night and slept, or tried to sleep.

Somehow on active service men do not think much about the discomfort of wet clothes and a damp couch, and seldom suffer at the time. The effects are felt afterwards, years afterwards perhaps, when age is coming on, or when other ailments begin to afflict the body.

On arrival in camp, being the senior medical

officer present, I was removed from my regiment and appointed principal medical officer of the field-force, and continued to hold the appointment until the conclusion of the campaign, when I returned to my regiment.

Our position in the Umbeylah Pass was a very peculiar one. The whole force was packed closely round a little hill, along the crest of another adjoining little eminence, and was protected from attack in front and on either flank by deep ravines. Those on the flanks were deep and narrow, that in front deep, wide, and gradually widening out as it opened on the Umbeylah plain. On all sides except the rear the position was overlooked by considerably higher ground; on the right front especially the high ground was so close that we were obliged to occupy it by a strong picket during the day, and by a still stronger at night.

The position on the heights thus held by us was called the 'crag picket,' I presume because it was on the edge of a very abrupt crag, and approached from our side by a steep, narrow, rocky path.

This crag picket was, I believe, the key of our position, and is a memorable spot in the history of the campaign, as we were once fairly driven out of it by the enemy, who, however, did not hold it long. Within a couple of hours after they had taken it, they in turn were driven out (not without a hard fight, however) by the 71st in gallant style and at the point of the bayonet.

I do not remember, and have no note on the subject, if our loss was great when the enemy drove us out of the crag picket; but the medical officer on duty with the party, Dr. Pile, was killed, and killed in a very cruel manner, within sight of the whole force.

At the re-taking of the position by the 71st, Colonel Hope of that regiment, who led the attack, was severely wounded.

Amongst the headquarter staff, I renewed my acquaintance with several old friends. Major Jenkins, principal commissariat officer, I had known at Rawul Pindi; Colonel Wright, Assistant Adjutant-General, I had served with in Peshawur; Colonel Allgood, Assistant Quartermaster-General, I had met at Lucknow, when he was with Sir Colin's staff; and Colonel (now Sir ——— Wylde) I had seen when badly wounded at the siege of Lucknow. The commissioners, Major James and Colonel (now General) Reynell Taylor, C.B. (a gallant frontier officer), I had met in Peshawur during 1862.

My old friend, Dr. Simpson, of the 71st, was with his regiment in camp. He was in very bad health, and died about two years afterwards. He had never recovered from the effects of fever in the Crimea.

I had taken up my quarters in camp with the staff, and one day, while standing beside my little *tente d'abri*, a gentleman in plain clothes accosted me. He was followed by several natives carrying photographic apparatus. He very politely asked ' if I was the adjutant-general.'

'No,' I said, in reply; 'I am the principal medical officer.'

'Oh!' said he, a little less politely than at first, 'only a doctor?'

'Yes,' I continued, 'that is all, and pray may I ask who does me the honour to address me?'

'I am Captain —— of the —— Native Infantry.'

It was certainly complimentary to be taken for the adjutant-general by an officer of a native infantry regiment, but not very flattering to be sneeringly spoken of as 'only a doctor' by a travelling amateur-artist.

While we remained inactive in camp, shots were exchanged every and all day between our pickets and those of the enemy. There was one single individual of the enemy who had ensconced himself behind some rocks on the other side of the ravine to our left front, just above the camp of the 93rd, and who amused himself from daylight until long after sunset by potting at any of us that passed or stood for a minute within the range of his matchlock. He was particularly troublesome in the evening while we were sitting round a fire smoking our pipes, and trying to make ourselves comfortable. He would then send his bullets right in amongst us, into our fire, scattering the embers about, and sending up a cloud of sparks; and it always ended by our having to trample out the fire and turn-in. Fortunately no one was killed or wounded; but we got tired of being potted at so constantly, and determined to drive him from his covert, if possible.

Accordingly, several of our good shots took up positions at different points, and waited for an opportunity to fire at him. But he had selected such a well-protected and safe spot, which concealed him so completely, that none of us ever caught a glimpse of his person, and only knew when he was about to fire by seeing his matchlock suddenly protruded, followed by a puff of white smoke and a report. Our marksmen returned the fire immediately, but without effect, for 'old Peter,' as the men had named him, always showed his contempt for us and our shooting by waving aloft a rag, hoisted above his place of concealment on the end of his matchlock.

The hill-men in that part of India are fanatical, and when in a frenzy of fanaticism are reckless and indifferent to life. At all times, however, they 'love a row,' delight in war merely for the excitement it affords, and when not under the influence of fanaticism are merry and jocular in the midst of danger.

A singular example of this occurred during the campaign. The 20th Punjaub Infantry (I think it was the 20th) was on outlying picket duty, and opposite to it was a large body of the enemy on similar duty. Both were lying behind sungahs, or stone walls, hurriedly thrown up as shelter, and were firing at each other at one moment in regular volleys, and at another in single dropping shots. During a short lull, one of the men of the 20th struck up a song, and, when he had finished the first few notes, one of the enemy took up the air and sang in reply, and then they went on singing alternate verses, both sides joining in a sort of wild chorus. It was then agreed that they should cease firing at each other for a while, so as to prolong the musical entertainment.

While the men were engaged in their duet, the officer commanding the 20th called out to inquire who was the merry, musical fellow in the enemy's ranks. The man answered for himself and gave his name, and, if I remember rightly, said that he had a brother in the 20th. On being asked why he had come out to fight, answered 'for the fun of the thing.'

When tired of singing, the enemy called out that they had had enough enjoyment, and were going to resume hostilities. Immediately they discharged a volley, which our people were quick in returning; and then both sides blazed away at each other for some time. I believe, however, that there was little or no result from this *feu d'enfer* except the noise, for all were well under cover behind their sungahs.

I have not told this story quite as fully as might be, because I write it from memory; but the facts are correct, I think, for not long since at a dinner-party in London I sat beside Sir Charles Brownlow, who commanded the 20th on the occasion, and who, on my reminding him of the circumstances, repeated the story to me much more at length than I have written it.

RENEWAL OF ATTACK. 299

When the whole force was collected in camp, the general made his final arrangements. These were to hold the camp with a portion of his force, and go out with the rest to attack the enemy. The troops to remain in camp were the 71st and 93rd, and the 1st and 5th Punjaub Infantry, with some artillery, all under the command of Colonel (now General) Vaughan, C.B.

The column with which the general proposed to go out and attack the enemy consisted of the 7th Royal Fusiliers and 101st Fusiliers, the Guides, the 3rd Sikhs, the 23rd and 32nd Pioneers, native infantry, two batteries of mountain guns, and the 11th Bengal Cavalry. These details I give from memory, and therefore may not be quite accurate.

Early on the morning of December 15, the column of attack filed out of camp, and, forming on the heights on the right of our camp, fell suddenly upon the enemy in and around the village of Labroo, drove them down into the plain, and followed in pursuit.

Next day, while the general renewed his attack at the Umbeylah village, the enemy made a counter attack upon the camp, coming in a daring manner close up to it. They were repulsed, however, with some loss by the 1st Punjaub Native Infantry, led on by Colonel Keyes, who jumped over their sungah, and drove them down hill in confusion. At the same time, the general completely routed the enemy in the valley, so that they made overtures of peace, one of the conditions being that no opposition would be made to our sending a column further into their fastnesses, to attack the rebel fanatics and destroy their stronghold. This having been accomplished, the campaign came to an end, and we retired to our own territory.

But, as there were suspicions felt as to the good faith of another tribe, which was known to be hostile to one of our allies (or rather protegées), the Rajah of Umb, whose little principality bordered on our own district of Hazara, a column was despatched, on December 23, to Derbund to overawe the suspected tribe, and support the friendly rajah. With this column went the 93rd.

Derbund is on the left bank of the Indus, just where the great river—pure and green as an emerald—rushes through a succession of rocky chasms and glens in the lower hills on its course to the plains. There we remained for a month, and, having no enemy to deal with, amused ourselves shooting in the low hills round our camp, in which small game was abundant. We often met small parties of hill-men, and of the inhabitants of the Derbund district. They are a fine race; of fair height, strongly-built, with fine aquiline features, and fair complexions. Their dress is picturesque, consisting of dark-blue cotton tunics and wide trousers, with black turbans (or paghris) and waistbands (or cumberbunds), relieved by broad borders of crimson silk. They were never without arms; sword, shield, and matchlock. Indeed, in that land of constant disturbance and uncertainty of life, no man ever goes abroad without his weapons, and whether on the mountain-path leading from one village to another, or in the field guiding his oxen in the plough, is always prepared either for offence or defence.

On February 1, 1864, we received orders to return to Sealkote, where we arrived on the 27th of the month.

CHAPTER XXIV.

Back at Sealkote—Dalhousie—Difficult of Access—Travelling by Dhoolie Dâk—Scenery—The Snowy Range—The Ravee—View from Buckrota—Climate—Trees—Flowering Shrubs—Population—Meeting the Leopard—Ten Thousand Feet above the Sea—Broad Valley—The Golden-headed Eagle—Fitzroy Macpherson.

AFTER our return from the Umbeylah campaign, the regiment remained nearly three years in Sealkote.

During the year 1865 I was granted six months' leave of absence, from May 1 to the end of October. From the date of my entering the service until then I had never obtained long leave, and from the date of my arrival in India, in 1857, with the exception of seven months in Subathoo, I had remained in the plains, so that I thought I had fairly earned a little relaxation.

I spent my six months' leave at Dalhousie, at that time a comparatively new station, in the Himalayas. It is, or at least was at that time, difficult of access, and the journey had to be made in dhoolies, a slow but fairly comfortable mode of travelling. The native bearers carry you at the rate of three miles an hour during the day, but not quite so fast at night, when they require torch-bearers to light and guide them on the uneven and often broken country roads.

The distance from Sealkote to Dalhousie (one hundred and fifty miles) was accomplished by dhoolie dâk, as it is called, in three days and two nights. Travellers generally commence the journey to the hills at night, as the heat in the month of May, in the plains, is too great to admit of travelling by day; indeed, until they arrive at the foot of the hills, they travel by night only, halting during the day at government (or dâk) bungalows, which are erected at distances of from ten to twenty miles from each other, along all roads upon which there is any traffic. The last part of the journey, the ascent of the hills, is performed by day, for the temperature is then agreeable, and opportunity afforded of enjoying the scenery, ever changing and beautiful, and becoming grander at every step.

Dalhousie, as the name implies, was so called after the great Earl and Governor-general, and was selected by his order with a view to being made use of as a sanitorium for European troops. It lies within the territory of the Rajah of Chumba, and consists of three principal hills, the highest of which is at an elevation of seven thousand five hundred feet above the plains.

These hills have the euphonious names of Buckrota, Putrain, and Terah. Besides these, there are several lesser hills, Bucklogh to the south, five thousand feet above the plains; and three, still smaller and lower, to the north, called Sanana Tala, Baloon, and Kuttullagh, generally spoken of, however, as the Baloon hills. Each individual hill, great and small, has its own peculiar name in the Himalayan range.

In 1865 there were no troops at Dalhousie, but during my stay there I was ordered to report as to the suitability of the locality for the formation of a military station, and a convalescent dépôt for European troops, and was subsequently appointed member of a committee presided over by General O'Grady Haly, to decide whether Bucklogh (the little hill south of Dalhousie) was suitable for a Goorkha regiment, and Baloon, on the north side, for a convalescent European dépôt. Our report was favourable, and accordingly, since that date, a Goorkha regiment has been located in Bucklogh, and barracks and hospital for European troops erected at Baloon.

The scenery about Dalhousie is magnificent. To the north lie extensive fertile valleys, well-cultivated, producing wheat and Indian corn and a variety of vegetables (amongst these the potato), and fruits of several kinds. Beyond these valleys rise range upon range of mountain, until in the distance, extending from west to east, far as the eye can see, is the snowy range, the great barrier between north and south, the grandest work of the great Creator. To the south also (of the Dalhousie hills) are low mountain ridges and projecting spurs enclosing many valleys, some broad and open, therefore the homes of man, and under cultivation; others deep and narrow, their precipitous, rugged sides clothed with forest-trees and tangled undergrowth. Through one of these latter flows the Ravee on its course to the Punjaub plains, which, during certain conditions of the atmosphere (generally after rain), are visible from the summit of Buckrota, stretching far away to the distant horizon, with three of the five great rivers, Sutlej, Ravee, and Chenab, winding over the vast expanse, and shining like silvery threads under the bright noonday sun.

The climate is cold, and very variable up to the end of May. Boisterous winds prevail during this month, with heavy hail-storms and biting showers of sleet. In the rainy season there are frequent severe thunderstorms with tremendous downpours of rain, followed by the densest fogs I ever saw in any part of the hills, more particularly on the south side overlooking the plains. In the broad, deep valley beneath the house in which I lived, the fog often settled down so thick and heavy that, under the bright moonlight, it presented the appearance of an unbroken expanse of snow, in strange contrast with the dark hills around it.

The sides of the hills near their summits are covered with the beautiful ever-green ilex, a magnificent tree, from whose gnarled trunks spread out immense branches, which in the rainy season are covered with a graceful drapery of ferns and a species of mistletoe; in the deep valleys, amongst the higher ranges, are extensive forests of the beautiful deodar, some of the trees measuring eighteen and twenty feet in circumference, and reaching to a height of from one hundred and forty to one hundred and sixty feet.

The horse-chestnut and rhododendron clothe the sides of the lower hills, and in the valleys grow the walnut, peach, apricot, apple, and pear-trees. Flowering shrubs and plants are in wonderful variety, and brilliant with flowers and blossoms of every hue, especially during the rains.

The population in the immediate vicinity of Dalhousie is small, but they are physically a fine, handsome race. Though they rarely touch any animal food, but live entirely on milk supplied them by their very diminutive cattle, and upon Indian corn and vegetables, they are robust and enduring. I was surprised, at the commencement of the rainy season, to see men and women going about working in the fields with mantles made of broad leaves sewn together so as to overlap like the scales of a fish or plates of armour. These mantles were perfectly waterproof, and had the advantages of being inexpensive and easily made, and of being light and cool during the hot, steamy rains. It was a striking verification of the original fig-leaf garments of our first parents.

The leopard and bear are occasionally seen and killed in the valleys round the Dalhousie hills.

Once during my stay there a leopard came prowling about the house at night and carried off a favourite dog belonging to one of the servants. On the following day two brother-officers (who were also on leave at Dalhousie) and myself, with a large following of natives, beat the jungle in the valleys beneath and around the house, but without success. A day or two afterwards, however, as one of the three, Joyner, was walking alone along a mountain-path with nothing but a stick in his hand, a splendid leopard (the thief, no doubt) stepped suddenly out of the bush and stood in the path within a few feet of him, looking straight at him with wide-open eyes. My friend never moved, but kept his eyes steadily fixed upon those of the animal, which, after a second or two, began to blink, until they at last closed under the steady gaze of the human eye, and the beautiful, lithe creature turned, and, apparently without fear or haste, disappeared in the jungle. It was never seen again, though several times we tried to tempt it at night by tying a kid to a tree as a bait, while we lay concealed ready with our rifles to take a shot at it. Even this, however, failed to bring it out.

On two occasions we (the same three) went bear-hunting, and, though we came upon the fresh tracks of one—apparently a large one—and traced them to a cave, we could not induce Bruin to show himself. But, a few days afterwards, one of my brother-officers came up to my house in haste, and asked me to arm myself and accompany him in pursuit of a bear that he had seen and wounded. Away we went, and were soon on the ground with our beaters, but, to our confusion, we met a native leading a large bear along by a rope. The animal went very quietly, but was bleeding from a wound in the side.

True enough, it was the bear which had been fired at and wounded, but it was a *tame* one, belonging to a native of that class who train them to dance, play grotesque tricks, and lead them about the country to exhibit their accomplishments to the inhabitants of villages and native towns. The animal had escaped during the night, and wandered into the jungle in search of berries.

In the valleys and in the thick scrub covering the sides of the lesser hills, chicôre and junglefowl are abundant, and in the valleys amongst the higher hills the beautiful Himalayan pheasant, the monal, and argus are found, and I often went in quest of them.

On one occasion, while out pheasant-shooting, I witnessed as sublime a sight as human eye ever looked upon—a thunderstorm close to, but below me. I was at an elevation of about two thousand feet above Dalhousie, or ten thousand feet above the sea—so high that the crisp, rarified air made the pulse beat fast and quickened respiration, causing a sensation of constriction of the throat and chest. I looked down into a broad, deep valley, the bottom of which was probably (as far as one could judge) five thousand feet below the height on which I stood, all objects in which were indistinct, owing partly to distance and partly to a dense haze that hung over and obscured them. A thunderstorm was gathering in the distance, and I watched it as it rolled up swiftly into the valley, and concealed everything completely from view. I stood on frozen snow, but in bright sunshine, while below me the depth was shrouded in the dark thunder-cloud, and, as it rolled along, the vivid lightning, flashing out, brightened up the dense cloud for an instant, and struck straight down into the valley, each flash followed by a peal of thunder that made the mountain tremble, and, echoed back from hill and crag, caused one continuous deafening roar.

This lasted for half an hour, and when the storm had expended itself, and the clouds drifted away, the atmosphere was so pure and clear that all objects in the valley indistinctly seen before appeared to be quite near. Every knoll crowned with trees, every little hill with village on its summit or nestling at its base, was brought out in clear relief; little cascades and waterfalls sparkled in the sunshine as they leaped over lofty crags, or plunged in tortuous course down deep fissures on the mountain sides, and innumerable little streams rushed and fretted along their rocky channels.

I had never seen a thunderstorm so immediately beneath me before, nor have I seen one since. I never looked upon a fairer scene than the broad deep valley bathed in bright sunshine after storm.

The golden-headed eagle and the large bald-headed vulture make their home in the Dalhousie and upper ranges. The former is a magnificent bird, and, when soaring and circling round on outstretched wings that never seem to move, gives an idea of majestic strength. I shot one which measured nine feet six inches from tip to tip of wing, and another which measured nine feet three inches. In both cases I broke the pinion of one wing with No. 5 shot, as the birds were flying past and close overhead. When they fell, we had to approach them carefully, and as they stood erect, looking so grand and defiant, I felt regret at having wounded them.

One of my constant companions in all walks and shooting expeditions during my six months' residence at Dalhousie, Fitzroy Macpherson, was as kind and gentle a fellow as ever lived; but he, too, is one of the number of my old friends 'who have gone before,' leaving with me a kindly recollection of his good qualities.

CHAPTER XXV.

I Rejoin my Regiment—Changes in my Absence—Charming Cold Season—General Haly—Dr. Beatson—Amusements—Hospital—Regimental Arrangements—The Apothecary—Ordered to Jhansi—Our Route—Delhi—Agra—Gwalior—Putteala's Piper—Arrival at Jhansi—Scenery—Ruined Castles—Lakes—Deserted City—Unexpected Promotion—Take Leave of my old Regiment.

AT the end of October, 1865, I rejoined my regiment, and, after six months of professional idleness, was glad to return to duty.

The following changes had taken place during my absence. An old friend, Major Brown, had joined head-quarters from the dépôt; Colonel Stisted had been promoted to Major-General, and was succeeded by Major Dawson as second Lieutenant-Colonel of the regiment, and George Greig had retired from the service. The promotion of Colonel Stisted gave Colonel Burroughs the position of senior Lieutenant-Colonel.

We had a charming cold season, 1865-66, and set ourselves to make the most of it, the last probably we should spend in Sealkote. The quiet of our lives was broken only twice during the season. First by the inspection of the troops in the station by Major-General O'Grady Haly, and second by that of the hospitals by Dr. George Beatson of Her Majesty's Service. These visits, however, were of short duration, and did not greatly interrupt our amusements.

Many of the officers, and the sportsmen in the ranks, were constantly employed with their guns and dogs during the season, for by this time we had made ourselves familiar with the geography of the district, and had found out all the haunts of the wild-duck, teal, and even snipe. The hounds still met, but no longer as our own. In the absence of Greig, who had retired, we had no one to act as master or huntsman, so we had parted with the pack to the 7th Hussars, and thereafter attended the meets as guests.

Different amusements and recreations were provided for the men, such as quoits, cricket, and football; and a gymnasium was established where single-stick and boxing were taught and practised. A dancing-club also was set a-going, but a curious difference of opinion between the Highlanders and Lowlanders nearly wrecked it at the first. The former preferred their own exciting reel, strathspey, and country dance, while the latter desired to cultivate the more modern quadrille, valse, and polka. The club, with the commanding officer's permission, occasionally gave evening-parties, to which all the officers were invited, and also the ladies of the regiment and of the station. I attended one or two of these with my wife, but found them rather a hindrance. If one has to be early astir and early at work every day in the week, as

OUR HOSPITAL.

the surgeon of a regiment in India has, late hours do not suit him. We had a theatre also, under the supervision of Gordon Alexander, himself a good actor; and though this was a great source of pleasure to the men, and they had frequent performances, it always led to certain little irregularities.

A great source of amusement and recreation was the reading-room and library. It was supported by the voluntary contributions of the men, and superintended by our chaplain. There were as many as four hundred subscribers at one time, the amount of subscription being small. In this comfortable and reasonable retreat the men passed many hours of the day and evening. Besides a considerable selection of books, periodicals and newspapers were supplied; and, for those who preferred games to reading, there were chess and backgammon-boards, and bagatelle and billiards. The room was large and comfortable, well warmed and lighted, and there was another room attached to it where coffee was supplied at very low cost.

This reading-room was not only a great addition to the comfort and enjoyment of the men, but a wise institution, for it was a means of preventing, or at least lessening, intemperance and crime in the regiment. It was first established in Peshawur by Colonel Ross, C.B.

Our hospital was so large that we were able to accommodate men, women, and children in the male hospital alone, as it consisted of two large wings, connected by a covered verandah to a centre building, which contained offices, stores, &c. By this arrangement we were able to make use of the female hospital, a detached building, as an infant-school, and to accommodate the school-mistress, good old Mrs. McLaren, who served the regiment as school-mistress for twenty years, and her husband. So ample was the space in the large hospital that, in the wing where men were placed, we were able to convert a ward into a sitting, reading, and recreation-room for convalescent patients, and to use the spacious inner verandahs as dining-rooms.

We took some little trouble to make the recreation-room attractive as well as comfortable. Cots were arranged as couches, arm-chairs placed in convenient positions, and tables with suitable covers stood round the room. Newspapers and periodicals were kindly supplied from the officers' mess. Pictures were hung round the walls, and bouquets of fresh flowers brightened up not only this room, but those in which the sick lay. Besides planting trees and cutting walks in the hospital enclosure, we had laid out vegetable and flower gardens, and were thus able to supplement the ordinary diets of the patients with a variety of vegetables, and to supply fresh flowers daily. These are little matters, perhaps not of great interest to the reader, but it is a pleasure to myself to recall them to memory and write of them.

General Haly, at his inspection of the hospital, was much pleased with all he saw, and especially with the flowers in the sick wards. My friend, Major Hudson, the assistant-adjutant-general, asked 'if all the display was on account of the general's visit,' and was rather surprised to hear from the commanding officer that such were the usual arrangements in our hospital.

I have seen the interior economy of many regiments, and have served with and been attached to several, but never knew any regiment in which more care was bestowed on the cleanliness of barrack-rooms and furniture than in the 93rd.

There was a regular cleaning-up every Friday afternoon, and on Saturday the commanding officer, attended by the adjutant, quarter-master, and surgeon, visited every barrack-room, kitchen, and out-office, and the married quarters. This was part of the system introduced by the late Sir Duncan McGregor when he commanded the regiment. There never was what is, or was, called 'Health Inspection' in the regiment during the period of my service with it. I was so constantly about the barracks, was so much amongst the men, and knew them so intimately that no special inspection by the surgeon, beyond that made with the commanding officer, was necessary. There was not a man, woman, or child in the regiment that I did not know by name, and with whose character and peculiarities I was not perfectly acquainted. I was never absent from hospital. Punctually at six o'clock a.m., in the hot season, and at eight o'clock a.m., in the cold, I made my appearance there. As a rule, I saw every man reported sick, and none were admitted, except sudden or accidental cases, without my knowledge. I myself invariably attended sick officers and their families, and the women and children.

My wife visited regularly the female hospital,

and frequently the women and children in their quarters. These visits were not only a pleasure to herself, but were expected and appreciated, I am glad to say, by the women. In anticipation of them they always made some little preparation in their own and children's dress, and in the arrangement of their rooms.

The regimental female hospital in India was a great boon. I say was, for I do not know whether any changes may have been made under the new hospital-system. It was a refuge where all women and children of the regiment received medical attendance and suitable nourishment in time of illness. There they found comfort far superior to that afforded by their own quarters, and had the kind attendance of a European nurse, one of themselves who had been trained and instructed by myself, and who was advised and assisted in my absence by the resident apothecary (Mr. Hogan). Of him, I must add that he was the most trustworthy, the best educated, and, professionally, the best informed of his class that I ever met in India. All in the regiment had the greatest respect for him. Poor fellow! he died in the service of the regiment, and, I think, from the result of an injury received in the performance of his duty.

The hot season of 1866 I spent in Sealkote. It was a long and severe one, but we all enjoyed excellent health. In October we received orders to be prepared to proceed to Jhansi in Bundelcund, central India, six hundred and sixteen miles, or fifty-seven marches distant from Sealkote, and in the Gwalior military district.

Our stay at Sealkote, though a long one, had been pleasant, as all the members of the community were anxious to be on intimate and kindly terms with each other. Friendships then formed I still retain, and hope to do so to the end, with my good old friends General Norgate and Colonel Montagu.

On November 1, 1866, the regiment commenced its march, and, at the same time, I accompanied my wife and children to Mooltan, put them on board the river steamer there, *en route* for Kurrachi, where they were to embark in a sailing ship for England, *viâ* the Cape of Good Hope. Having seen them on board the little steamer, I followed and overtook the regiment beyond Lahore.

Our route, as laid down, passed through Lahore, Umritsir, Umballa, Delhi, Agra, and Gwalior, a most interesting march, during which we should have opportunity and time to see three of the most interesting spots in India (Delhi, Agra, and the Fort of Gwalior), as at each of these places we should halt for several days, for the purpose of changing our baggage animals and bullock-carts.

We were acquainted with the route as far as Umballa, but beyond that everything would be new to us; for hitherto our service had been confined to Oude, Rohilcund, and the northern districts of the Punjaub.

We passed through the territory of Putteala (near Umballa), and halted for one day near the residence of the Maharajah. His Highness, on being made aware of our presence, sent his vakeel to invite us to an afternoon entertainment, and to request that we would bring the band with us. Accordingly, several of us went, and the band attended as requested. The Maharajah, a very young man, received us with the politeness which Oriental princes understand so well, and conversed with us in English. He paid little, if any, attention to the music of the band, but when the twelve pipers struck up a reel and strathspey, his countenance brightened up and his eyes sparkled. He listened with evident pleasure, and, when they ceased to play, exclaimed,

'Beautiful! *That* is the music for me. Can I get such a band? Can I buy it?'

He was informed that it might be possible to purchase the discharge of one of the pipers, and engage him to instruct his own men. He was pleased at the suggestion, and, one of the pipers (John McK——) agreeing to the very liberal terms offered by His Highness, application was made for his discharge by purchase, and, this having been sanctioned, McK—— took up his new appointment.

Some time afterwards, on the occasion of the great durbar, held by His Excellency Lord Mayo, at Umballa, a number of the native princes attended, each bringing a certain number of their military retainers.

Amongst these princes was His Highness of Putteala, accompanied by a considerable body of troops. His camp was close to my house, and one afternoon I was surprised to receive a visit from McK——, whom I hardly recognised. He was magnificently arrayed in a scarlet tunic

covered with gold lace, blue-cloth trousers, with
general officer's lace down the seams, a splendid
blue and gold turban, or paghri, on his head,
and a broad heavy sash to correspond round his
waist. Such was the dress of the head musician
of His Highness of Putteala. He looked uncom-
monly well, and, I think, was well pleased with
his own appearance. He told me that he had
instructed fourteen pipers, and asked me to come
and hear them play. Of course I went, heard
them play singly and together, and was really
surprised at their proficiency. Their pipes had
been supplied by Glen in Edinburgh. The men
were dressed in green cloth tunics and 93rd tar-
tan trews. McK—— told me that the Maharajah had at first intended to dress his pipers in
full Highland costume, but that he (McK——)
'couldn't stand seeing a native dressed up in a
kilt,' insisted on trews, and carried his point.
He also told me that his highness treated him
with a liberality far beyond his agreement, gave
him a good house, several cows, furnished him
with a horse and buggy, and whenever his services were required with his own pipes either to
amuse 'or soothe his royal highness to sleep'
(these are McK——'s own words), a handsome
present in money was given to him.

McK—— remained five years in the Maharajah's service, and on leaving India for home
took with him a considerable sum of money which
he had saved, and which was sufficient to set him
up in some business.

The country between Sealkote and Umballa is

a perfectly flat plain, almost entirely under cultivation. Between Umballa and Kurnal (once our frontier station, but abandoned because thought to have been unhealthy), and between the latter and Delhi, there are extensive tracts of jungle, in which game of many varieties abound, and which afforded us a good deal of sport.

The present city of Delhi was founded by Shah Jehan in 1631, and succeeded Agra as the capital of the Mogul empire in 1658. It stands on the right bank of a branch of the Jumna, and is enclosed by the river on one side, and by a high and irregular wall on the other three sides. In the district, and in the immediate vicinity of the city, long low ridges of grey sandstone crop up and run in different directions, and those near the city were made use of during the siege in 1857 as a means of defence and offence.

We remained encamped at Delhi several days, and employed the time in inspecting the city, its defences, objects of interest, and the positions outside on and behind the sandstone ridge occupied by our small army during the siege operations. Of course, the most interesting spot to *us*, and the one first sought for, was the Cashmere gate and the breach beside it, through which our gallant fellows had stormed the city. Nothing had been done to repair the breach, which we found just in the same state as it was on the day of the assault.

From thence we proceeded to the Jumma Musjid, a beautiful building, or rather pile of buildings, the basement consisting of a broad flight of steps of red sandstone, and the lofty and graceful domes of white marble. We were permitted to enter the sacred building, and to look at two remarkable objects—one the footprint of the Prophet on a piece of clay slate or sandstone. The impression certainly bore some resemblance to that of a human foot, but not of a well-formed one. The other object was a hair of the Prophet's beard, a coarse red bristle, but 'by the beard of the Prophet,' if an unbeliever may say so, it was impossible to accept the sacred relic as a human hair, or to believe that it could have grown upon the chin of man.

From the mosque we walked to the fort, within which are the Dewan-i-kas, the Dewan-i-am, and the Mooti (or Pearl) Mosque. The Dewan-i-kas is a beautiful pile of buildings, situated close to and overhanging the river. We were not impressed, however, so much by the appearance of the buildings, now despoiled in a great measure of their original magnificence, as by the historical recollections attached to them. We visited the Dewan-i-am also, and the little Pearl Mosque close to it. This mosque is built entirely of white marble, and, though small, is of exquisite beauty.

These sights occupied our first day. On the second we rode out to the ruins of ancient Delhi and to the Kotab Minar. The ruins of the old city are of great extent, and indicate the magnitude and magnificence to which it must have attained; but to us, who then looked upon a scene of desolation, it was sad to think that the spot which had once been the home of busy man, reared and beautified by his skill and energy, was now tenanted by the lowest of the wild beasts (the jackal), and fast falling into decay.

The Kotab Minar, a beautiful column, was erected by Kutb-u-Din to celebrate his conquest of the Hindoos. It is upwards of two hundred and fifty feet in height and forty-eight in diameter at the base, is built of red sandstone, beautifully chiselled, and ornamented with white marble tracery. A spiral staircase leads from the base to the top, which formerly was surmounted by a dome or canopy, supported on graceful pillars. This dome, with its supporting pillars, was thrown down (by lightning, I believe), and now stands on the ground near the base of the column.

Close to the Kotab, amongst some extensive ruins of Hindoo temples, stands *the* large, wrought iron pillar, deeply embedded in the ground.

Between Delhi and Agra the country is well-cultivated, especially along the line of the Grand Canal, and in the vicinity of its irrigating branches. There are also large tracts covered with jungle filled with game, of which we shot immense quantities; indeed at this time, and during the rest of the march, antelope, geese, wild-duck, partridges, hares, and pea-fowl, &c., constituted to a great extent the food of both officers and men.

On Christmas Day, before our arrival at Agra, Captain (now Colonel) Ewen MacPherson, the present very popular commanding officer of the regiment, joined us, having just returned to India from leave of absence in England.

THE TAJ MAHAL.

On arrival at Agra, we were encamped beyond the city, and not far from the Taj Mahal, which we visited immediately after encamping, and each day during our halt. This beautiful structure, as everyone knows, was erected by Shah Jehan as the mausoleum of his queen. It does not strike one as very imposing when seen for the first time from a distance, but on near approach one is astonished at its size and exquisite beauty; the oftener it is visited the grander and more beautiful it appears. It stands in a conspicuous position in the midst of extensive gardens, planted chiefly with sombre evergreens, on a terrace overhanging the Jumna, and consists of a lofty dome of pure white marble, erected within a large square, paved court, at each corner of which is a graceful minar, also of white marble. Within, it is richly decorated with the most elaborate mosaics, and light is admitted to the central apartment through double screens of white marble trellis-work of exquisite beauty. Immediately under the centre of the dome is a screen of similar exquisite workmanship, enclosing the tomb of the queen. No words can express the wonderful beauty of the central apartment, seen under the subdued light that enters through the half-closed surrounding openings. Altogether, as a structure and work of art, I believe it is acknowledged that the Taj Mahal is unequalled, certainly not surpassed, by anything in the world.

Our chaplain (Mr. Drennan), always kind and thoughtful, took all the children of the regiment to spend a day in the gardens of the mausoleum, and while there the assembled little ones sang together several hymns under the dome; their voices, echoing throughout the spacious apartment and lofty dome overhead, had a sublime effect, and caused a singular vibration of the marble trellis-work.

It is said that twenty thousand men were occupied during twenty-two years in the erection of the Taj Mahal, and that to complete the mausoleum and the different buildings attached to it cost upwards of three millions sterling.

The historical recollections attached to the fort at Agra are interesting, but I will only refer to those which are fresh in the memory of the present generation. On the breaking out of the mutiny in 1857, Agra was garrisoned by a European regiment, a troop of European artillery, and two regiments of native infantry. The two latter (portions of which had mutinied and gone off to Delhi with a large amount of treasure) were disarmed and disbanded. These disbanded Sepoys, joined by mutineers from other quarters, made several efforts to gain possession of the fort; but the European troops and European civil community, who had retired within its defences, held it securely. They thus ensured their own safety, and by their presence prevented the city from becoming another great focus of rebellion.

The fort is enclosed by a high, defensible wall of red sandstone, and contains within its area the Dewan-i-am, which is built of marble, and has a beautiful white marble balcony overlooking the river; also extensive ruins of a Hindoo palace, and a handsome mosque, the interior of which is lined with a peculiar grey marble that reminds one of an ice-chamber.

From Agra we proceeded on our way to Gwalior, and on arrival there were encamped on the plain beneath the sandstone hill on which stands the celebrated fort of Gwalior. In former days, with a sufficient and vigilant garrison, this fort would have been impregnable to an enemy supplied with the old class of artillery, as it is placed on the flat summit of a hill which rises abruptly from the plain, and to a considerable height above it, and can only be approached at two points. It is commanded, however, by adjacent hills, from which, with modern artillery, it could be destroyed in a short time.

The Maharajah Scindiah of Gwalior maintains a considerable army, and is very fond of military display. His highness, it will be remembered, remained loyal to us during the mutiny, but his troops revolted and broke away from his control. This force (the Gwalior contingent, as it was called) was defeated and dispersed by Lord Clyde on December 6, 1857, at Cawnpore, with the loss of all its guns and field equipment.

From Gwalior we marched through Dholepore, and thence on to Jhansi, which we reached on January 18, 1867, our march, including the necessary halts, having occupied seventy-nine days.

Bundelcund, so called from having been in the possession of the Bundela race, is one of the central provinces. It consists of plain and mountain; the former to the north-east, along the right bank of the Jumna, and the latter stretching southwards, through a rough, hilly district, towards the Vindhya mountains.

Jhansi is memorable in recent history as the scene of horrible atrocities committed during the mutiny by order of a cruel Ranee; and also as the scene of one of Sir H. Rose's battles fought in the neighbourhood of the Betwah, and for the subsequent storming and capture of the fort. The city of Jhansi is situated in the hilly portion of the district, and the military cantonment is about two or three miles distant from the city, both being close to the river Betwah.

The scenery in the neighbourhood is very pretty, enlivened by low chains of hills, composed in a great measure of pure quartz, on the highest points of which stand ruined castles and towers, their structure and position reminding one of the old grey ruins so numerous in the Western Highlands, and of the old Border Peiles of Scotland. Their number affords evidence of the state of constant disturbance and hostility in which the inhabitants must have spent their lives before the advent of the British Raj.

There are several small lakes in the immediate neighbourhood, and many small streams in which trout, or at least some species of trout, are found. Extensive forests clothe the banks of the Betwah, as it flows through a deep, wild, rocky channel on its course to join the Jumna. The district abounds in game, and in the forest jungle about Sepree and Saughur the tiger is often shot.

During the short time I remained at Jhansi, and while the cool weather lasted, I made frequent short excursions in the neighbourhood of the station in search of ravine deer and small game. On one of these occasions I came to a large town or city situated along one side of a small lake, on the other side of which, on elevated ground, and approached by a narrow bridge, stood a battlemented building, the house of a native rajah or prince.

Everything was in good order, the streets well paved and clean, the houses standing and in good repair, with wide open doors. I looked, but looked in vain, for a human being, or for any sign of life. Perfect silence reigned around and within. It was a deserted city, and on inquiry subsequently I found that the inhabitants had fled, driven from their homes by the terror of a pestilence.

About the beginning of April, I obtained leave of absence for four months, which I intended to spend in the Himalayas, visiting the source of the Ganges, &c. I had made all my arrangements for a start, even to the paying of my dhoolie dâk, and was spending the last Sunday evening with my friend the Chaplain.

While we were at dinner, English letters were brought in. Amongst them was one addressed to me. I saw it was in the handwriting of my friend, Sir Galbraith Logan, then Director-General of the Army Medical Department; but, as a former letter from him had been somewhat discouraging, I laid this one aside, saying that it would keep till after dinner. My friend Drennan and I then resumed our dinner, and ate in silence, but he suddenly broke a rather long pause in conversation by remarking, 'I should like to know what news your letter contains.' So I opened it and read what was a great surprise to both of us, and especially to myself—I read that I had been promoted.

This came upon me unexpectedly. Only a few months before I had been so distinctly given to understand that there was no prospect of promotion for me, that I had given up all thoughts of such a thing, and was perfectly contented and happy to remain with my regiment.

Well, promotion had come; and what did it mean? Perfect change of duties and responsibilities, a higher position, larger pay and allowances, every certainty of further promotion, with better retirement at the end of my service. But it also meant separation from a regiment with which I had served for thirteen years, and to which I was deeply attached; separation from friends and comrades with whom I had been in constant fellowship in many stirring scenes of war, in terrible periods of pestilence, and in quiet times of peace, with their varied scenes of social pleasure and occupation; and, now that I was to leave them, I could not but feel regret at the prospect. But promotion was acceptable, as I was not rich in this world's goods; in fact, a poor man, with many depending on me for present and future provision, and it afforded me the means to meet these responsibilities.

Next day the English papers arrived. My

name was in the *Gazette*, and officers, non-commissioned officers, and many of the men, and even of the women came to congratulate me, and at the same time, in their kindness, to express regret at losing 'the Doctor.'

Then, the day of my departure having been fixed, I was invited to dine at mess, that all might take leave of me at the same time; but, when the moment came, I felt it a trial to be received as a *guest* by comrades who had for so many years looked upon and treated me as a friend, one of themselves, a member of the regiment.

During dinner the thought of the impending separation depressed me, and memory, reverting to the past, recalled old familiar faces that were absent, many of which I should never see again. On looking round the room, I was startled to see that only *three* were present (Burroughs, Dawson, and Joyner) of all those with whom I had commenced my service with the regiment, and who had been with me at the battle of the Alma. Until that evening, I had not quite realized the great changes that had taken place in a period which, in the retrospect, appeared so short. Fifty-three officers had disappeared from the regiment since I joined as surgeon. Of these, seven had been killed in battle and three by accident; ten had died of disease; and thirty-three had exchanged or retired, fifteen of whom have since passed away.

After dinner, my old comrade and friend, Colonel Burroughs, proposed my health, saying, as he did so, many kind things to, and of, me, which were generously responded to by all; then my health was drunk with Highland honours, followed by 'Lochaber no more,'—the Highlander's farewell—played by the Pipe-major as he stood behind my chair.

In reply, I expressed a fervent hope that I had done my duty by one and all; acknowledged the great kindness I had received, the gratitude that had been shown to me for whatever I might have been enabled to do for those committed to my care, and concluded by saying that, in taking leave of them, it was a comfort and a pleasure to me to feel that during my long and varied service with the regiment, I had never had a personal disagreement with a brother-officer; never been reminded that I had failed in or neglected aught that came within the sphere of duty; and that in the future I should look back upon the thirteen years passed with them and in the service of the 93rd as the most useful and happiest of my life.'

Here terminate my reminiscences of that period of my service which was passed as surgeon of the 93rd Sutherland Highlanders,—the portion of my life which I now think of with the greatest pleasure and thankfulness, and which I would gladly live over again, were it possible to do so, and to be surrounded by the same old friends and comrades.

THE END.

www.ingramcontent.com/pod-product-compliance
Lightning Source LLC
Chambersburg PA
CBHW020807100426
42814CB00014B/365/J